LANCHESTER LIBRARY

3 8001 00529 6292

Yes? No! Maybe....

Yes? No! Maybe . . . Seductive Ambiguity in Dance is a book about performing
and watching dance. Using a unique combination of historical, academic
and autobiographical voices, it covers 50 years of British dance, from
Margot Fonteyn in the 1950s to innovative contemporary practitioners
such as Wendy Houstoun, Nigel Charnock, Lloyd Newson, Javier de
Frutos and Fin Walker.

Emilyn Claid's thought-provoking investigation of performing presence is illuminated by episodes from her own history as founder member
of X6 Dance Space, the experimental dance collective, and as one of the
UK's most radical and exciting practitioners.

Using the 1970s revolution of new dance as a hinge, the author looks
back to ballet and forward to British independent dance, which is new
dance's legacy. This book explores the shifting dynamic between performer and spectator through feminist, psychoanalytic, post-structuralist
and queer theoretical perspectives. In the process, the concepts of seduction, androgyny and ambiguity are re-figured as embodied strategies with
which to enliven performer–spectator relations.

Emilyn Claid is Director of Choreography at Dartington College of
Arts, Devon. She was a founder member of X6 Dance Space (1976–80)
and in the 1980s was Artistic Director of Extemporary Dance Theatre.
As an independent dance artist in the 1990s, she choreographed for
dance companies such as Phoenix and CandoCo and performed her own
shows including *Witch One* (1992), *Virginia Minx at Play* (1993) and *Laid
Out Lovely* (1994). Emilyn is Director of PAL Dance Labs (Performing
Arts Labs) and m&de@dartington (music and dance exchange).

Yes? No! Maybe...

Seductive ambiguity in dance

Emilyn Claid

Routledge
Taylor & Francis Group

LONDON AND NEW YORK

First published 2006
by Routledge
2 Park Square, Milton Park, Abingdon, Oxon OX14 4RN

Simultaneously published in the USA and Canada
by Routledge
270 Madison Ave, New York, NY 10016

Routledge is an imprint of the Taylor & Francis Group, an informa business

© 2006 Emilyn Claid

Typeset in Baskerville by
Florence Production Ltd, Stoodleigh, Devon

Printed and bound in Great Britain by
TJ International Ltd, Padstow, Cornwall

All rights reserved. No part of this book may be reprinted
or reproduced or utilized in any form or by any electronic,
mechanical, or other means, now known or hereafter invented,
including photocopying and recording, or in any information
storage or retrieval system, without permission in writing
from the publishers.

British Library Cataloguing in Publication Data
A catalogue record for this book is available from the British Library

Library of Congress Cataloging in Publication Data
A catalog record for this book has been requested

ISBN10: 0–415–37156–2 (hbk)
ISBN10: 0–415–37247–X (pbk)
ISBN10: 0–203–969502 (ebk)

ISBN13: 978–0–415–37156–8 (hbk)
ISBN13: 978–0–415–37247–3 (pbk)
ISBN13: 978–0–203–969502 (ebk)

Coventry University Library

Contents

Figures

Acknowledgements

I am most grateful to the artists who appear throughout the book, particularly those independent dance artists with whom I have worked and had such vibrant discussions over the years: Jacky Lansley, Fergus Early, Mary Prestidge, Maedée Duprès, Rosemary Butcher, Lloyd Newson, Kirstie Simson, Annelies Stoffle, Chantale Donaldson, Mary Fulkerson, Sue Smith, Kuldip Singh-Barmi, Helen Baggett, David Toole, Charlotte Derbyshire, Celeste Dandeker, Jon French, Eva Karczag, Jonathan Burrows, Siobhan Davies, Greta Mendez, Vena Ramphal, Mavin Khoo, Diane Torr, Miranda Tufnell, Katie Duck, Russell Maliphant, Matthew Hawkins, Javier de Frutos, Michael Clark, Brenton Surgenor, Nigel Charnock, Liz Aggiss, Sue MacLennan, Carol Brown, Wendy Houstoun, Jenny Tattershall, Fin Walker, and David Waring and Stine Nielson. Their performances continue to inspire me. Their comments have enriched and shaped the arguments in the book. Thanks also to American artists David Gordon, Karole Armitage, Mark Morris, Yvonne Rainer, Bill T. Jones and South African artist Vincent Sekwati Mantsoe. I am indebted to them for allowing me the privilege, as a spectator, to interpret their work.

Alongside the artists, I thank the photographers whose work is reproduced in the book. They have played a significant role in documenting British dance. In particular, I acknowledge Geoff White who documented the work at X6 Dance Space in the 1970s, providing a unique record of that time. My thanks also go to Chisenhale Dance Space in London and the National Resource Centre for Dance at the University of Surrey for archive material on X6 Dance Space and Extemporary Dance Theatre respectively. And I acknowledge my father, George Kent Harrison who, inconspicuously, photographed my dancing childhood, providing me with a vivid account of my life in the 1950s and 1960s.

Thanks to academic colleagues: Susan Melrose, Christopher Bannerman, Susan Kozel, Janet Lansdale, Christie Adair, Ramsay Burt, Valerie Briginshaw, Susan Foster, Sue-Ellen Case, Richard Cave, Sherrill Dodds, Phillip Zarrilli, David Williams, John Hall, Janet O'Shea and Alexander Carter. Their insight, knowledge and advice at various stages of writing – from Ph.D. to publication – have helped me to appreciate wider contexts for the ideas. I am grateful also to the anonymous Routledge readers. Their reports offered honest, rigorous critical feedback while simultaneously recommending publication.

My students have continued to sharpen the edges of debate at the University of Surrey, Dartington College of Arts, E15 Acting School, Central School of Speech and Drama, and Middlesex University. Forthright, with nothing to lose, students tell me what they think. I am grateful for their toughness.

There have been extraordinary people in my life who fill the gaps of the writing: my first inspiring ballet teachers, Audrey Kraft and Letty Littlewood; Sue Hoyle, X6 colleague and partner, who worked with me at Extemporary Dance Theatre; Cecilia McFarlane and Maggie Semple, the outreach team at Extemporary; Sylvia Hallet, friend, musician and composer for so many shows; Betsy Gregory, dance colleague through all the changes; Josephine Leask, who listened to my life story; Becky Scott, a queer androgyne to be reckoned with; Carolyn Partrick for a room looking over a London garden; Margaret Thomas for her memories of my mother; my brother Malcolm who reminded me that I never wanted to dance; Stefan Szczelkun, father of my son Lech; my cousins Judi and Chas Cochand who give me their house in the New Forest as a writing retreat every summer in return for looking after their dogs. I thank them all for their love and encouragement.

This book could not have happened without the diligent support of two editors. The first is my sister Lucy who took a shrewd glance at the indulgences of an early manuscript. 'Cut the crap', she said. 'Don't give it all away.' She made me laugh with anecdotes about her experiences at the Royal Ballet School as she set about correcting my grammar and wresting order out of chaos. Two years later, Ian Bramley has guided the text through the final editing stages before delivering the manuscript to the publishers. I very much respect his knowledge, and I am grateful for his precise comments, his ability to spot the 'woolly' bits, his understanding of issues and his thorough attention to detail.

My thanks to Chi for her unwavering belief in us.

And finally, thank you to Lech, my son. As a child, Lech introduced me to the seduction of real becoming illusion. Walking on the beach, he stopped to pick up shells. If there was a creature inside, he was not interested, saying, 'Too real.' But if it was shiny and empty, he picked it up and put it to his ear and said, 'I can hear the wind, I can hear the sea.'

Project funded by Arts & Humanities Research Council (Fellowship in the Creative and Performing Arts), University of Surrey and Dartington College of Arts.

Introduction

1 SETTING THE SCENE

I stand still and look at you looking at me, holding
the space with our eyes. We attend inwards. The
constant throbbing is our heartbeats. We sense
the breathing lines, never ending, constantly
moving, between us, running through our bodies.
I am caught, suspended, particles of dust on a
current of air. I look out, across to you, waiting,
expanding the moment just before we begin. You
look back and my flesh is alive, rushing, tensing,
shivering. Breathe out, slow down. Arms hang loose,
hands drop, fingers long, weight to feet. I hush the
adrenaline surging through my blood. I look out,
scan through you, observe the details. Time
stretches. I sense the tension before the game, the
steely quality of anticipation, an out of body-ness.
You look at me and my skin becomes vulnerable,
becomes warm from your gaze, and is fed by your
desiring to know. We feel the pleasure of the
thousand tiny shifting flickers of our bodies, faces,
knowing we are looked at, waiting. Here it is, that
sharp point, the sparked fuse, out there between
us, when my attention to stillness becomes active
through your eyes.

This moment, just as a performance begins, is a fraction of time that
expands and suspends, allowing performers and spectators to experience

the fully alive action of performing and watching. That is what this book is about – performing and watching. For there, in the meeting between the two, between the looking out and the looking in, is the ambiguous and seductive tension of performing presence – the moment of engagement – that enlivens performer–spectator relations. Performing presence is not fixed to either body but is sparked by both. It is something intangible, where receiving and giving is mixed up, thrown back and forth, and moves in the gap between performer and spectator, enacted by one and the other. Performing presence refuses to be fixed. It is always becoming something else, somewhere else and may be simply imagined. The urge to frame it in practice and theory has become the spine of this book.

The writing spans across the past 50 years of British dance and the development of British independent dance culture. It also spans my life's experience and I use the lived events over this period of time to physicalize the narrative. The text conjures up a spectrum of performers from ballerina Margot Fonteyn in the 1950s to the physical theatre performer Nigel Charnock in 2003. The 1970s British phenomenon of new dance provides a core focus, offering a crucial framework of structures, forms and politics that instigated independent dance culture and supported its practitioners. Situating itself in this context, the book is concerned for the most part with British artists. The vibrancy of this Western dance culture lies in its unique and contradictory layering of genres. These include American post-modern minimalism, British ballet, South Asian and African dance forms, and European theatre expressionism. British dance may be a microdot on the global map of performance, but the ideas, debates, investigations, strategies, analyses and illustrations of this book ripple outwards to reach an extensive range of performance practices across a wide arena.

Aside from the Introduction and Conclusion, the writing is divided into three main parts: 'Yes?', 'No!' and 'Maybe . . .'. The first of these sections begins in the 1950s and examines the Western aesthetic of beauty and the transcendent dazzling perfection of ballet dancers. Here, the real flesh-and-blood body of the dancer is surpassed by her/his externally illusive image that draws the spectator to watch, to desire. This is the 'Yes' story of my childhood, typical of the stories of many young ballet hopefuls. But the 'Yes' of obedience and submission to the conventions of Western dance training is snagged by the possibility that perhaps not all is perfect here. The willingness to obey holds a tentative questioning. The question mark that follows 'Yes' indicates a rebellion that is lurking. The 'Yes?' has a 'No!' within.

As the narrative moves forward in time so, it unravels the transcendent myth of ballet, peeling away the layers of illusion to allow dancing bodies to come down to earth. The journey pauses to focus on the 1970s and the British new dance experiment. An anchor was dropped as we plummeted, twisted, turned sideways and inward, consciously bringing ourselves to ground. The linear directed time of the past collapsed; we were now in an undirected present. This was an extraordinary, challenging and radical time in the British dance scene, one that was to have resounding repercussions in the independent dance culture that was to follow. Dancers became performer–choreographers, subjects of their own work. Energized by feminism, we said 'No!' to past conventions. But it was an emphatic 'No!' where the exclamation mark carried a positive and joyous 'Yes!' within as we subverted our roles as objects of desire controlled by the spectator's gaze.

The successful rejection of convention also created challenges, particularly for female dancers. Our new subject positions that gave attention to body–mind wholeness provoked a contradictory play of in/visibility within the framework of performer–spectator relations. Our thinking bodies turned inward to oppose the convention of external out-to-the-audience expression. Rejecting seduction and illusion, women ran into the danger of becoming non-desired objects on the stage – performing an act of disappearance. Peggy Phelan (1993: 6) emphasizes that '[t]here is real power in remaining unmarked' and that visibility can be a 'trap'. But in dance I suggest there were problems for performer–spectator relations as women re-claimed their bodies as unmarked subjects. Furthermore, while white artists were rejecting conventional European aesthetics of identity, black British dance artists were seeking an identifiable presence within that same culture. 'No!' investigates this paradox between subjectivity and in/visibility.

The narrative resumes with a shift in direction turning to investigate the presence of male dancing bodies that, in the 1990s, usurped women's position as objects of desire in dance performance. Male dancers displace fixed subjects and objects through a seductive play of femininity and masculinity on their bodies. Drawing on the tactics of queer theory and performance, the text describes contexts of watching and performing men and women that evoke a multiplicity of meanings – the 'Maybe . . .' of dancing. Here, performers re-claim the 'Yes' with the knowledge of the 'No'. Acknowledging that there is no single truth does not mean there are no truths. Instead, there are many. Writing about a range of independent dance performers illustrates how the seduction of ambiguity returns to play on the bodies of performers and the eyes of spectators.

'Yes?', 'No!' and 'Maybe ...' are mutually interchangeable terms, emphasizing the complex crossings between identity and ambiguity that are necessary to the engagement of performer–spectator relations.

The *Concise Oxford Dictionary* (1995: 39) defines ambiguity as a term of 'double meaning either deliberate or caused by inexactness of expression'. Ambiguous is described as being 'difficult to classify'. Thesauri list the term along with the uncertainty, vagueness, indefiniteness and the doubt that might be considered to exist when there is no fixed and decisive meaning. Western post-structuralist/postmodern/post-feminist/ academic/queer/independent dance culture thrives on a multiplicity of meanings in performance. Spectators are engaged by a practice of 'not knowing' but desiring to know – a play between a multiplicity of perceptions and interpretations rather than a fixed single truth about a performer. However, the ambiguous 'not knowing' that engages spectators has nothing to do with vagueness or inexactness. Rather, it is the spectator's knowledge of possible identifiable points that make the play of not knowing possible. And it is the performer's attention to precisely defined action that evokes the ambiguity of meaning for the spectator.

The ambiguity does not lie in the identifiable interpretations themselves but in the practice of playing between them. In a sense, ambiguity becomes a verb – 'to ambigu-ize'. An apt parallel is Jacques Derrida's play of *différance* in language whereby identifying a single meaning becomes impossible (Derrida 1978).[1] The meaning of every term only comes into play through its placement in relation to other terms, opening up each and every language term to a displacement of a single truth. For Derrida, the way to open up a fixed truth is to 'make it possible to get beyond (or beneath) two kinds, not just to three, but to the "innumerable", that is, to the indefinitely new, because differential, possibilities that are opened up once you acknowledge the contingency of "two"' (Caputo 1997: 105). The ambiguities that I am concerned with erupt within and between performing, watching and writing; movements of playing between fixed points that do exist but are not the end game, opening to the multiplicity of other possible things between points. Ambiguity becomes a physical action playing with meanings in a space/place that defies a single definition. To be engaged by ambiguity as an act of watching dance suggests that while the dancer's body has a history of stories and identities that have been played, for the spectator it becomes a body that is empty and ready to receive new stories. 'Each tale is thus the receptacle of another' (Derrida 1995a: 117). How ambiguity surfaces on the body of the performer – when s/he is a living author, a fully desiring body and an expressive identity – is a persistent and contra-flowing vein that courses through the following pages.

Seduction in Western culture has signified a variety of elements relevant to sexual desire without being the sexual act itself. It has included flirtation, temptation, artifice, superficiality, allure, capture, wickedness and manipulative wiles undertaken by both men and women. Seduction has also suggested a narrative, a subject who seduces and an object who is seduced, a linear story familiar to most sexual scenarios, with a goal of conquest. Letting go of these interpretations of seduction – but not forgetting the act of desiring – seductiveness is re-figured here as a play of desires and meanings between performers and spectators. Seduction, like ambiguity, becomes an embodied practice. 'Seduction . . . an ironic, alternative form, one that breaks the referentiality of sex and provides a space, not of desire, but of play and defiance' (Baudrillard 1991: 21). Seduction becomes ambiguous – ambiguity becomes seductive.

My initial motivation for writing this book came from examining the question of subjectivity in my own work as a performer and choreographer. I had been part of the 1970s dance experiment in London when we, as feminists, began to address the crisis of form in dance practice. Looking back, I felt a need to investigate and understand the paradox of in/visibility in both theory and practice that began to emerge as we became subjects of our own work. I needed to figure out our strategies for re-claiming engaging relations between performers and spectators.

The research began in 1995 with a Ph.D. thesis (Claid 1998). I turned to French feminist and post-structuralist theories to investigate and find parallels for what was happening for women in 1970s new dance performance. The investigation focused on a re-figuration of androgyny, seduction and eroticism in a queer context of performance. These themes were relevant to me at that time, both as a performer and choreographer, as they offered theoretical strategies to re-engage performer–spectator relations. The writing investigated how seductiveness in dance performance could be re-figured on/in a performer's body through an oscillation between embodied attributes of masculinity and femininity, power and pleasure, as an ambiguity of gender identity. Echoes of that particular manifestation of performing presence haunt this book, particularly through the theme of androgyny, which is interpreted from three contrasting perspectives: classical, feminist and queer.

Re-reading the Ph.D. in preparation for writing the book, I realized the most obvious motive for writing had been overstepped. The spectator's watching practice embraces ambiguity of meaning, but the performer's dancing practice is often in contrast to that of the spectator and, subsequently, the writer. In fact, it is frequently the performer's focused attention to the full inhabiting of the performed material that instigates the ambiguous surface of meanings. In other words, what the performer does is not what the spectator sees. The underlying dichotomy between performing and watching was only hinted at in the Ph.D. manuscript. Writing now, as someone who embodies both the 'I' and the 'eye', has been a challenging task. Raising questions about performer–spectator relations of engagement has required a physical unravelling of the different embodiments of performer, spectator, academic and writer to give validity, historical context, and lived reality to theoretical investigation.

Hence, as you read this book, you will find a cacophony of voices as I have separated the different strands of embodiment. There is a spectator's voice that describes performances. I write these descriptions in the present tense to emphasize the immediacy of the act of watching, regardless of whether the performance took place in 1957 or 2003. The use of I/eye in the present tense hopefully draws attention to the subjective and personal view of myself watching. Partnering this voice is one that describes my own work as a performer. Again in the present tense, I re-place myself in the space of the performance to describe the action.

There is the academic voice that interprets and applies philosophical, written theories that exist alongside the practices. I have included these to illustrate how dance and written languages can inform one another, and how written theories and philosophies can exist in parallel to embodied forms. Plato rides alongside the classical androgyny of male ballet dancers; Theresa DeLauretis' feminist critique of psychoanalysis picks at ballet girls' smiles; George Bataille-esque eroticism attracts the pain and pleasure of ballet; Foucault frames new dance as a discourse; Carolyn Heilbrun's feminist androgyny finds embodiment in 1970s women; Julia Kristeva puts a spanner in essential feminist agendas; Jacques Derrida teases out performer–spectator relations of presence; Deleuze and Guattari validate post-modern minimalist dance.

There is an autobiographical voice. Linking the narrative, sometimes gingerly, sometimes forthrightly, this voice shapes a structure by drawing a chronological time line from the 1950s to the new millennium. Separated from the main text in typeface and layout, the autobiographic fiction is also written in the present tense as I relive memories from my past. The memories are here to give expression to the love, loss and dreams that underlie, bubble up and thread through the narrative.

There is a contemplative voice that discusses the historical events. This is my thinking that has emerged out of performing and watching and is realized through writing. Some of this thinking might appear provocative. For instance, many feminist artists (performers and spectators) will disagree with me that our rejection of the role of object of desire in the 1970s was problematic and led to a disappearing act for women in dance. But here I am stepping outside the intimate, academic, knowledgeable visual art audience that supported new dance in the 1980s to appreciate how the work might have been seen by mainstream dance audiences and, inherent to that context, by funding bodies.

Provocative again, the contemplative voice dedicates a section of the book to describe black dance in the 1970s. This might appear as a separatist strategy. However, it is to make a point. 'Black' in the 1970s and 1980s was used as an umbrella term embracing a range of artists from different cultures: African, African–Caribbean and South Asian. In the 1970s, feminist dance did not necessarily embrace all women, and certainly not all black women. As black and white dance artists, we worked in parallel with each other but not together; we had different agendas. African, African–Caribbean and South Asian dance artists were striving for identifiable voices and recognition within the same dance heritage that white artists were attempting to reject.

Similarly, I write about masculinity and femininity, men and women dancing, separately, which might seem to be dated gender politics and not relevant to dancing bodies. But masculinity and femininity, rooted in gender desire and sexuality, become signifiers, symbols for a range of attributes for dance: power and pleasure, linearity and fragmentation, vertical and horizontal, fixed and fluid as performative devices that interweave on male and female anatomical bodies. As symbols, the terms evoke the differences and contradictions that can spark the ambiguity of a dancer's presence. Desire is the living breathing physical driving force, behind, in front and beside performers and spectators, the passion for life that urges us to the performance arena.

The contemplative voice acts as a guise, a container into which I pour thoughts about strategies of reality and illusion; the agency of pain; post-modern minimalist dancing; dance improvisation as *jouissance* dancing; the practice of sadomasochism; queer and lesbian androgyny – all of which might seem to stray from an objective academic view of British dance. Well, that is also the point – to put seductive ambiguity into practice, to remember the roots of British contemporary dance, but also to make connections, to reveal the routes in which it can be interpreted.

Finally, there is an experiential voice that discusses my professional experiences as director, choreographer and teacher. This voice is not academic, autobiographical or performative. It is descriptive and discursive. I use it to describe choreographic works that I have directed.

Towards the end of the book, it takes over from the autobiographical voice to discuss Extemporary Dance Theatre and dance training.

The spectatorial, autobiographical, academic, contemplative and experiential voices link through the pages. Woven in are the voices of other artists, professional colleagues who are currently performing. All the voices link with one another throughout the book without hierarchy. The writing constantly switches from one role to another, doing and watching, living and analysing experience, sidestepping, turning backwards and forwards from past to future. In this way, I hope to demonstrate the dynamic contradictions of being absent and present in the writing, interweaving body and language, internal and external focus, and the depth and the breadth of ideas and expressions that keep the relations between reader and writer alive and intelligent. In so doing, I lay down some of the clues for seductive ambiguous play in performance.

Inevitably, this book is subjective: it is my experiences, my body and mind and imagination that fill the fathomless gaps between you and me. I am a white middle-class woman living in the UK writing within the context of Western theatre dance and influenced by feminist, postmodern, queer and post-structuralist ways of thinking. I do not attempt to embrace a historical overview, claim a privileged position or presume generalities. I have a particular view of performance, one that emerges from autobiographical and experiential narratives. Furthermore, British dance provides a microscopic fragment in the global performance puzzle. By zooming in and blowing up this micro view, it becomes full. Its fractals reveal complex narratives emerging from being a performer and witness to five decades of dance practice. The widened lens reveals differing genres, styles, art frameworks, political structures, dance institutions, creative methodologies, theoretical perspectives, contexts of performer–spectator relations and different artists' voices, dance training and personal experiences. Enlarging the lens still further reveals the many expressions of gender; language articulations and expressive desires that inspire each and every performing body. By writing subjectively and then theoretically about my experiences, I hope that the reader will take up the parallel threads and pathways, and connect them to a myriad of other views that make up different worlds.

How many times have I returned to this introduction? Many, many times. It is not an introduction, it is an ending. Each time I return to it, I step a little further away from the content in order to answer the question, 'What is this book about?'. Now I see that, for the most part, I focus on the role of performer–choreographers. Highlighting a role that is endemic to the British independent dance scene, I push forward performers who are authors of their own seductive and ambiguous images.

When I refer to choreography where the choreographer stands outside the work, it is because, for the most part, the work has been devised, and is therefore owned, by the performers. I do not focus on the music, stage design, costumes, lighting, even though these might be integral to the performance. Dancing presence is the core, the nugget, the point of friction around which this merry-go-round of watching and writing revolves.

2 X6: A HINGE IN TIME

The shadow of the 1970s that infiltrates this narrative is informed by the events of X6 Dance Space. X6 combined the practices of five artists: Jacky Lansley, Fergus Early, Maedée Duprès, Mary Prestidge and me. We came together out of necessity. We had a question to ask: how had the systems from which we had arrived, or were escaping, ruled our lives? Other questions emerged and were argued, challenged and continuously shifted through the art practices at X6. The outcomes of our creative quests were individually different but, for a time, we had a shared philosophy within a shared social and cultural context. We came together as supportive comrades, encouraging our different voices before stepping out and dispersing into diverse and individual futures. Here, respectful of my colleagues, I became a witness (and partaker) of the work that has retrospectively become known to many as new dance.

X6 took place in a breath of five years: 1976–80. There was a before and there was an after. For me, looking back, X6 cannot be defined as a fixed root, the cause or the origin of anything, yet its time signifies a crucial shift in British dance culture. X6 was part of a network of 1970s experimental environments including the London Musicians' Collective, initiated in 1976, and the London Film Co-op, founded in 1966. X6 provoked ideas in practice that influenced the development of teaching, performing, choreography, writing and management in the independent dance culture in Britain throughout the final third of the twentieth century.

X6 Dance Space has been given a slot in the dance history books of twentieth-century dance. Writers, including Christy Adair and Stephanie Jordan, have written lucidly and respectfully of X6, its political stance and its public products.

X6 occupied a pivotal position. It became the London centre special-ising in alternative practice in dance.

(Jordan 1992: 62)

It was within the New Dance community that X6 had the most profound effect.

(Jordan 1992: 82)

X6 brought dance firmly in touch with the women's movement, the most significant social movement of the 1970s and 1980s.

(Jordan 1992: 87)

X6 raised the consciousness of British independent dancers that they were developing a tradition of their own: there was now a move-ment with its own label.

(Jordan 1992: 87)

New Dance in England developed from the early classes, perform-ances and writing of X6.

(Adair 1992: 182)

Indeed, the contribution of X6 to the UK dance scene is now a focus of academic dance history. X6 is recognized as a 1970s radical movement, a hotbed of feminist politics and experimental performance. This was a time when the machinery of Western dance jarred and shivered. But the X6 key for change was not fixed to its political statements or perform-ance products, nor was it located in the unifying notion of a new dance style. The primary key for change, the one that cannot be absorbed or overlooked, is that X6 was run as a collective without an artistic director. The force behind the shifts that X6 heralded was the subversive tactics of collective collaboration that, as an art practice, contradicted estab-lished and previously classified systems of production.

Collective working at X6 was, in turn, challenged by 1970s feminism. Feminist agendas encouraged us to bring the whole person as a political, social, cultural and essential body to the performance arena. Collective working, however, encouraged the networking of group process rather than the individual voice. Here, seeds were sown for the paradox between subjectivity and invisibility, which will be unpacked and investigated in the following pages.

X6 provides the pivotal locus for this book, the hinge to a door that opens backwards to a view of the past and forwards to a construction of the future. Poised in this doorway, within the architectural designs of

Western dance, I explore the shifts in performer–spectator relations. With my present knowledge of that era's innovations in performance processes, language and expression, I look over my shoulder to the world of ballet and forwards to the evolution of independent dance theatre. I begin by looking back, remembering what happened to instigate the new dance scene in the second half of the twentieth century.

Yes?

Figure 1 Emilyn Claid (1965). Drury Lane Theatre, London.

Photographer: author's father, George Kent Harrison.

I Yes?

Fantasies of perfection: setting the scene for change

3 THE UPWARD LINE

Pinned. Up. The year is 1959 and I am standing
with bare feet on the cold kitchen lino floor. I am
wearing a pair of knickers attached to a white
satin bodice that is tightly fitted and boned at the
sides. Mother kneels; all around her are long strips
of white netting gathered into frills. She attaches
the frills to my knickers with pins. Round and
round, one layer of frills after another. Down low
the frills are narrow, about an inch wide. Coming up
to my hips the gathered frills get gradually wider.
The top frills sit stiffly, horizontal to the floor, the
lower layers supporting them. I stand for hours,
knees itching, trying not to breathe, I wait while she
fiddles. I never wanted to dance. Then the reward –
costume jewellery, white and pink dropped pearls,
satin flowers, glittering sequins, delicate pink ribbon
in loops and bows arranged in a formal design –
sewn to a piece of white netting. Mother pins it to
the bodice. And so another tutu is constructed.

In the 1950s, it was all about the myth of beauty – Western culture's
awesome obsession with symmetry, balance, transcendent line, central
perspective, spiritual perfection, whiteness, lightness, and all things bright
and beautiful. The art form of ballet perpetuated the myth in its training,
language, choreography and aesthetic. Many young girls, across class and
culture, were hooked into attempting to realize that myth on their bodies

and I was no exception. As a ballet dancer in training, I embraced a sensation of longing for something higher and outside of myself.

I need to remember the sensation in order to write about it. I lie on the floor and concentrate, kinaesthetically, on the physicality of transcendence. In re-imagining the physical memory, I notice, with a slight shudder, the shadowy markings of an upward lift in my limbs, held in the nerves and sinews of my body. The memory of transcendence returns with a gesture.

My right arm unfolds forward and up in front of my body. My eyes follow the line of my wrist to the upturned palm, past outstretched fingers and beyond. I automatically connect with the tension that rises through my body. My legs and feet lift from the ground seemingly with a mind of their own.

Before the gesture can unfold comes the desire, for unattainable perfection that pervades every muscle in my body. Each day as I learn the technique, between the ages of seven and 17, I am told that the prize is always just a little further, a little higher, that there is a perfection of line that can be mine and become me. I am the gesture; it and I are attached at the core, a core as fragile as it is unreal. As the gesture arrives on the surface of my body from a desire to transcend my flesh-and-blood body, I believe that the true performer is one who yearns for something more.

Ah yes, back then, before the 1960s, the Rolling Stones, Marianne Faithfull, Bob Dylan, San Francisco and all those flowers; before I knew of feminism and Foucault; before the questions of inside and outside; before issues of liberation, gender, race and class. Back then, before I had a voice and many, many years before I had an academic voice. Like many other aspiring ballerinas – with their preadolescent bodies and minds just emerging or perhaps trapped in magical thinking – I believed in transcendence.

This persistent Western aesthetic of beauty has its philosophical beginnings with Plato, in roughly 400 BC in Athens, Greece. Plato expounds on his philosophy of beauty. He interprets the spoken words of his contemporary philosopher and the revered master, Socrates.

Plato's quest is to define the essential form of beauty as a universal concept of beauty that is higher than that found in all natural and mortal things. Yet it is through nature and mortality and their representations in art that humankind is reminded of the concept of the higher beauty. This higher beauty cannot be seen with the eyes but grasped only with the mind: it is a beauty that follows the line of rationality and reason. Plato tells us that we have always known of this glorious concept of beauty but have forgotten it:

> Every soul of man has in the way of nature beheld true being; this was the condition of her passing into the form of man. But all souls do not easily recall the things of the other world . . . they may have lost the memory of the holy things which once they saw.
>
> (Cited in Hofstadter and Kuhns 1964: 57)

Through the beauties of the natural world humankind is 'transported with the recollection of the true beauty; he would like to fly away, but he cannot; he is like a bird fluttering and looking upwards and careless of the world below' (cited in Hofstadter and Kuhns 1964: 57).

For Plato, it is the artist's role to imitate the beautiful through representation in music, dance and poetry. The properties within the arts that characterize this higher concept are those of mathematical proportion, balance between parts, simplicity of geometric form, the straight line and the circle. 'The qualities of measure (metron) and proportion (symmetron) invariably . . . constitute beauty and excellence' (cited in Hofstadter and Kuhns 1964: 43).

Ballet, as a physical art that adheres to this aesthetic, depends on the choosing and construction of bodies that will conform to the symbol of idealized beauty of Western culture – that of the vertical line. In 1925, Volinsky writes about classical dance:

> The Greeks clearly set the vertical in opposition to the bent and crooked . . . To see straight, to speak straight – all this is at once pictorially sensible and heroic. Only in ballet do we possess all aspects of the vertical in its exact mathematically formed, universally perceptible expression . . . everything . . . is the direct heritage passed down to us by the sublime, proud, and pure antiquity.
>
> (Cited in Copeland and Cohen 1983: 256–7)

Ballet training focuses on defying gravity – disciplining muscles, bones, tendons and joints to push outwards and upwards from the ground. The ballet body is never present to itself but always seeking perfection outside itself. In the process of training the ballet body, any signifying connections to human-ness are magically sidestepped. The physical, linear, proportioned form of the dancer's body evokes the concept of perfection. The static positions, set vocabulary and mathematical virtuosity of the language embellish the beauty myth. In 1996, Susan Foster's feminist critique supports my childhood memories: 'The years of bodily disciplining have re-figured fleshly curves and masses as lines and circles. Geometric perfection displays itself at both core and surface . . . Via this geometry her movements turn mess into symbol' (Foster 1996: 14). And transforming confused and messy bodies into distinct, clear, rational ideals is essential to classical aesthetics of beauty.

Young bodies are constructed to fit this aesthetic – to be taut, muscular and straight, with legs that unfold to a great length, spines that arch upwards and backwards away from the central axis of the pelvis. I lengthened an already long neck and forced my feet to further extend the length of my legs into a needlepoint. Up, up and away: chin up, tits up, eyes lifted, bum clenched, knees pulled up, stomach lifted, hair scraped back – fight, fight, fight against the falling expanse of the flesh. The upward-ness is structured as a hierarchy that pervades the technique, language, training structures and each ballet company's organization. Jenny Tattershall who spent nine years in The Royal Ballet tells me:

> No one goes into The Royal Ballet company without wanting to go up, particularly those who have gone through the [Lower] School. Every year at the school your mind is set on the company, then when you get in the company you just want to progress upwards. Everyone is reaching for perfection in the basic ballet steps and that follows through. You are striving to be a principal, but that is about having the perfect line, being able to do 32 triple *fouettes*.[1]
>
> (Tattershall 2003)

In the 1960s, the Royal Ballet School (RBS) selected each body for its perfect symmetry and potential linearity. Legs and wrists were measured to estimate adult height. Parents were measured. These auditioning bodies were destined to being shaped into the ideal where sexual features could be made invisible, to appear anatomically gender-less, to be stripped of any identifiably sexual signs: roundness of hips and breasts, dangling dicks and fleshy behinds. The possibility of this transformation was essential for entrance into the RBS Lower School, and essential to perpetuate ballet's signifying status – aspiring to a higher truth and beauty, the Enlightenment concept of aesthetic beauty.[2]

Not only do Plato's philosophies expound the unobtainable transcendent but the idea of perfect beauty is also associated with goodness and morality in the arts. There is good and bad art, high and low art. High art inspires in man the concept of pure beauty, which in turn can only be appreciated by educated men who understand the spiritual form of perfection. For Plato, low art evokes the physical passions, moves its audience emotionally. It is corrupt and vulgar.

In this Western philosophical framework, pleasure appeals to an inferior part of the soul and therefore to an inferior class of being. In other words, low art appeals to more immediate impulses and to those who have no inclination to strive towards the higher knowledge of beauty. This morality, embedded in the technique, infiltrates into the hierarchical structure of ballet companies: 'Enjoying the benefits of a comfortable lifestyle in the ballet company, without progressing upwards, is an attitude definitely frowned upon' (Tattershall 2003).

The abstract imagery of the upward vertical line moving from the 'lowly and bad' pleasures of the body to the 'high and good' conceptual pleasures of the mind is a concern that travels through the centuries of Western philosophy and culture. Followed through in the philosophy of Hegel, Schiller, Descartes, Baumgarten and Kant, the vertical line elucidates the notion of an absolute knowledge obtainable only by the educated and encourages the hierarchical binary oppositions of mind/body, thought/feeling, white/black and beauty/ugliness (Beardsley 1975).

The high art of ballet upholds this classical tradition, the language and aesthetic signifying not only beauty but also goodness, supposedly triggering the innate memories of spiritual beauty that humankind has lost. For ballet audiences, this illusive, transcendent image of goodness and perfection, surfacing through the real flesh-and-blood bodies of the dancers, draws them into the seductive relations of engagement.

4 WATCHING BALLET: ILLUSION BECOMING REAL

The spectators for ballet are as responsible as the performers for conjuring a performing presence that is seductive and alluring. Seduction is perhaps a provocative term to apply to ballet at the dawn of the twenty-first century. However, the terms 'seduction' and 'ballet' are historically and inseparably linked. They recall dance traditions, from East to West, anywhere where performers have been positioned as both objects of and creators of desire. As an illusion of transcendent perfection, the ballerina's presence personifies the act of theatrical seduction. Her body has been sexualized, eroticized and phallocized. Theorists have rationalized, analysed and criticized her, framing her in the context of psychoanalysis, philosophy, postmodernism, post-colonialism and feminism. Others have queered her, hung, drawn and quartered her. Yet, through it all, she continues to seduce her audiences. Thinking and writing about seduction in ballet forms the first platform, the initial strategy from which to re-figure performer–spectator relations.

As a child, I sit in the gods at Covent Garden to watch Margot Fonteyn in the title role of *Ondine* (Frederick Ashton 1958). Fonteyn appears in a grotto, stage right, which separates the water world from the human world. She pauses under the archway hovering in fifth position on pointe, arms above her head. Coming down off pointe, she becomes aware of her human arms, and caresses them. She watches each arm with its mermaid-like undulating movement, acknowledging how her water nymph persona has taken on a human form. Cautiously, she moves out of the grotto, stepping carefully with pointed feet onto the stage. Tentatively she explores her surroundings. Walking and looking about, she encounters her shadow for the first time. She begins to dance. Fonteyn's long black hair is loose; her shimmery, see-through nightdress-type costume emphasizes her childlike abandon. Fonteyn dances with her shadow, moving this way and that, watching its shifts of shape. Flitting here and there she appears joyous, playful, a sprite.

Through the illusive image of herself, Ondine (Fonteyn) recognizes her own alive-ness. Her innocent play with her shadow accentuates ballet's seduction. This simple dance illustrates the complex relations of engagement between performers and spectators. At the heart of ballet and inherent in its form is the play between the real and the illusion for performer and spectator. By 'real' I am referring to the reality of the flesh-and-blood body, the physical living, doing, seeing, feeling and thinking body engaged in the work of daily physical tasks at the moment of the lived time and space of the performance, a breathing corporeality with an experiential history. By illusion, I am referring to the constructed artifice or performed surface that the real body creates through the rigorous practice of balletic skills and linear techniques with which and through which the dancer performs.

The ballerina, then, is a real body performing an illusion. The more skill her real body demonstrates in becoming surface illusion, the more engaging her performance becomes. The oscillating relationship between her real body and performed surface creates intrigue and wonder. The intrigue triggers a seductive play regarding what is present and what is absent, between knowing and not knowing, depth and surface. As a spectator, I am drawn to imagine, interpret and identify with her real body. Through my perception, I search her performance for her body that has become absent – an illusion. In searching, the further the ballerina's body becomes an external illusion, the further the real female body slips away. The surface appearance becomes all the more seductive for holding the body secret: reality and illusion maintain the seductive allure.

The illusion itself is a multi-layered construction. Prior to performance her pre-selected body takes on a boyish shape: she becomes muscular, physically powerful and sinewy, and she has lost her layer of female body fat. This construction is now a new real body ready to speak the balletic language of linear transcendence. On stage the illusion comes into play. This tough little body suddenly appears tall, long-legged and regally elegant. In the classical and romantic ballets, this body is re-constructed, yet again, through soft expressive gestures of arms and hands, high extensions of the legs, framed by the lights and the proscenium perspective of conventional theatres. The costuming draws her body into the clutches of fetishistic femininity; an illusive sylph of the patriarchal imagination. The completion of this illusion is dependent on the pointe shoes, the hallmark of ballet, the signifier, signified and sign of transcendence and elusiveness. Dancing in pointe shoes the ballerina is caught in a dance between fetish and freedom. A pretty pink in colour with satin ribbons and hidden bows, pointe shoes bind the muscular strength of the female body, restrict her movement, simultaneously representing her power and fragility. Completing the accentuated line, the pointe shoe stabs the air relentlessly, an articulate pointed weapon, capable of causing damage. The flesh and blood, anatomical body is dressed with multiple layers of constructed illusion: the boyish geometric body construction, the language of transcendence and the costume of fetishistic feminine. This is a multi-layered image far removed from the soft, curved, gravity-weighted body usually associated with female bodies. Yet she is a woman.

The illusions allow the meaning and identifiable presence of the real female body to remain hidden. But it does not always disappear. When Lynn Seymour takes the stage in *The Two Pigeons* (Frederick Ashton 1961), *Romeo and Juliet* (Kenneth MacMillan 1965) or *Anastasia* (Kenneth MacMillan 1971), the fullness of the real seeps through the empty illusion. A personalized 'real' can still be recognized. Her passion expands beyond the restrictions of pointe shoes and verticals, her not-so-thin body seeps through the barriers of the perfect line. Her seductive illusion is not a perfect simulation; it is not a completely empty body, a code of signals with no original as Baudrillard (1991) would have us believe.[1] Although ballet training attempts to transform bodies to appear ever more transcendent, simultaneously this training is a tool for the expression of the dancer. There is a real body doing and the surface illusion appears full of traces or shadows of that real. The spectator sees this and knows this, which in turn encourages the act of desiring to identify between the real body and illusion, presence and absence. In other words, the oscillating relations between the real body and the illusion are what draw the spectator to watch.

5 PERFORMING BALLET: REAL BECOMING ILLUSION

But what the spectator sees is not what the performer does. If the key to understanding the dynamics of seductive presence is in the play between real and illusive identity occurring at the site of the performing body, then, ostensibly, a strategic manoeuvre for the performer would be to create that illusive surface so that the spectator's art can come into play. But how does an expressive body, wholly engaged in the physical act of performing, create an illusive surface? In my experience of ballet, the answer lies not in performing illusively, but in the rigorous physical practice of an identifiable technique. This is a practice transferred onto the body via an external system and embodied as 'natural', as one's own construction and articulated intelligence. For myself, as a performer, I created the illusion, representing beauty external to my body, through real hard physical painful work. This work was often not at all beautiful or perfect.

I wait backstage in the wings. I see the line of light, how it laps at the side of the stage; one small step to take between the dark and the light. I stand in preparation, turned out from hips; knees and thighs pulled up, shoulders and head balanced

symmetrically, weight evenly distributed through
the centre of my feet. My right leg prepares by
unfolding out in front of my body, foot stretched
and pointed, right hip parallel with left hip, spine
straight, shoulders centred above hips, neck
relaxed, arms moving forward delicately curved,
hands spaced apart by the width of my head.
I count myself in. After precisely four phrases of
eight counts, my left leg bends in preparation and
I push off using stomach, buttocks, back, pelvis,
thigh, calf and foot. I take my weight forward onto
my right leg in one co-ordinated step into that
white light, onto the brightly lit ramp, lifting my left
leg high behind me in a *penche arabesque*, my right
arm reaching forward, the left lifting behind, a long
diagonal line from the front arm to the back foot.
I work with mathematical precision to keep my hips
square over right leg, shoulders parallel and
relaxed, stomach lifted, chest lifted, back arched,
knee and thigh pulled up, both legs turned
outwards. My left leg lifts behind, using muscular
strength in back and buttocks and under my thigh,
the left foot is stretched and pointed upwards,
toes higher than heel. From the depth of the
penché, I step back through fourth position *plié*,
my body sweeping down.

I watch the timing of the girl in front, noticing
how her leg, lifted high in *arabesque*, goes slightly
to the side of her body allowing me room to step
directly in line behind her. I notice how ungainly her
body looks from this angle, leg angled outwards,
back twisted, shoulders uneven, hands twisted, foot
like a hook with a cramp. The lower frills of her tutu
that cover her backside, which I can see when she
lifts her leg, resemble the stunted feathers of a
plucked chicken. But I know the trick of perfect
linear illusion her body creates when watched from
the other side of the footlights.[1]

I am describing the experience of dancing in *La Bayadère* (Marius Petipa
1877) a romanticized portrayal of the temple dancers in India. In this

ballet we slowly made our way down a ramp, a vast number of identical white bodies that decorated empty space with formal shapes, weaving lines across the stage. Together our bodies created a choreographic symmetry of delicate white skeletal patterns wafting and shimmering like a moonlit mist. The illusion we created for our audience was that of the ghostly shades of Hades.

A ghostly play of illusion for the spectator, yes – but for the performer, no. As a member of the *corps* in *La Bayadère*, the reality had nothing to do with embodying or expressing a 'ghostly shade'. It did, however, have everything to do with exact timing, staying in line, taking the identical sized steps, arms and legs replicating exactly the same height as the girls in front and on either side of me. This ballet sequence required an enormous output of energy and strength, intense physical and mental concentration, a kinaesthetic awareness of body centring and co-ordination, aching limbs, shortness of breath, sweat and pain. In creating this illusion, our bodies were involved in a precise, exhausting, demanding and fully concentrated action.

For the performer's real body, the ethereal illusion of 'not being there' is a working of physical precision to perfect the external image – a task requiring intelligence and memory, perception and judgement, focus and stamina. This is a total being there in order to not be there.

> You get a certain feeling being in the *corps* when there are 24 of you. I remember doing *Giselle*. It was a really solid group of dancers, who all knew each other. We did some fantastic shows. I have never felt a buzz like it, where you can just feel the entrance of the Willis, all 24 of us moving at exactly the same time: there is nothing like it. To stay in line behind someone who is three inches taller than yourself – it can be awkward, but it's about looking exactly the same. It is completely selfless, you are not dancing for yourself, you are dancing within a visual spectacle.
>
> (Tattershall 2003)

The ballerina creates illusion with her real body. This illusion is a complex layering of constructed body, physical skill and balletic imagery. As an illusion of perfection the ballerina engages the spectator. But the oscillating tension is between what is there and what is not there. For a performer who engages the spectator does so because a shadow of the real seeps through the illusion. The performer works her real body very hard to create the surface image that will keep that body secret and keep the spectator wanting more. Simultaneously she uses her surface image as the tools with which to express herself. The contradictory sparks on the performer's body between expression and technique feed the spectator's desire to know her.

6 CLASSICAL ANDROGYNY

The ballerina's presence is not the only one to engage the audience. Since the early 1900s, with the appearance of Nijinski, male bodies in ballet also evoke seductive relations between performers and spectators. This is the seduction of androgyny. Nijinski's muscular masculine yet feminized body signified a spiritual, airborne beauty that contributed to his mythical and legendary status.[1]

I watch Anthony Dowell in his performance of Oberon in the final *pas de deux* with Titania in *The Dream* (Frederick Ashton 1964). He emerges from a forest glen, a scenographic backdrop. He steps into *arabesque* poising there on half pointe, before running silently and swiftly across the stage, arms trailing behind him. Stopping stage right, he unfolds his right arm and gesticulates off stage to where Bottom has just exited. He turns to observe his fairyland, pivoting smoothly on half pointe in fifth position to face Titania (danced by Antoinette Sibley). The *pas de deux* begins. Dowell is dressed in a forest green all-in-one leotard, which fades into flesh colour on his torso. There are leaves and flowers decorating his arms, shoulders and scattered over his chest. He wears a crown of flowers. Dowell's first pose into *arabesque* says it all. As he steps, his front arm floats softly upwards to symmetrically balance the height to his back leg. His movements are simple, there is no showiness. This is cool constrained passion, truly English – and desire-less. While the worldly creatures in *The Dream* are mundane, clumsy and desire-full, the creatures in Dowell's fairyland are perfectly transcendent. His is a geometrically proportioned body, muscular yet delicate, colt-like, with high insteps, pert backside and arched back.

Androgyny, like beauty, upholds the traditions of classical Greek aesthetics. It materializes through its signification as a harmonized union of masculine and feminine qualities in and on one body. Performers such as Nijinski, Anthony Dowell, Rudolf Nureyev and Mikhail Baryshnikov brought masculine muscular anatomy and feminine dance fluidity into harmony on their bodies, providing the images with which androgyny plays. The following writing unpacks a little of the history of androgyny, as its force, as an expression of beauty, persists in its influence of culture, art and performance.

The Western love of the androgynous male body emerges from the homoerotic world of Athenian culture, around 400 BC.[2] A well-known reference to androgyny appears in the text of Plato's *Symposium*. Waterfield (1994) describes the symposium as the meeting-place or conference for Athenian (male) elite society. This particular symposium was concerned with a popular topic of the time – the meaning of love and beauty. Aristophanes, a guest speaker, expounds on the story of the androgyne, a mythical being that was both male and female. As Aristophanes' story goes, Zeus became jealous of the androgyne's beautiful perfection and split the unified being in half. The result was that each half desired and searched for its other half. In this way, sexual desire was conceived as an earthly pursuit.

Foucault describes the Athenian world that frames Plato's *Symposium* as being one that encouraged love between men, where the Greeks 'practised, accepted, and valued relations between men and boys' (Foucault 1985: 187). Halprin describes how the elite group of adult males controlled the political and social life of classical Athens (Halprin 1990). Older men, mostly married, were attracted to young boys aged between 12 and 18, between puberty and the growing of a beard, when young boys looked both feminine and masculine. These young men were expected to submit to the older men, to cast their eyes down and to show no desire either actively or passively. In other words, unmarried, young, feminine-looking male bodies were worshipped and idolized by the older elite male class. These boyish bodies were androgynous, masculine and feminine in one body – the ideal of perfect beauty. Adhering to Athenian philosophy these young men would be inspired to become greater and better men in adult life. They symbolized Greek philosophers' ascending struggle away from the physical and sexual in search of purest beauty. To reiterate: sexual desire was considered to be the lowest rung on the ladder in the classical Greek search for pure beauty.

> And the true order of going, or being led by another, to the things of love, is to begin from the beauties of earth and mount upwards for the sake of that other beauty, using these as steps only, and from one going on to two, and from two to all fair forms, and from fair forms to fair practices, and from fair practices to fair notions, until from fair notions he arrives at the notion of absolute beauty, and at last knows what the essence of beauty is.
>
> (Socrates cited in Hofstadter and Kuhns 1964: 762)

Echoes of this classical search for androgynous beauty resound loud and clear in the context of ballet with its historical conventions of male patronage and wealth. Performer–spectator relations have been constructed whereby young male performing bodies are worshipped, as are the ballerinas. Anthony Dowell, with his geometric uplifted line, high jumps, soft landings, athletic grace, English reserve, fluid, feminine gestures and muscular strength, engages male and female spectators' sense of wonder and yearning for perfection.

7 CRACKING THE MYTH

Western ideals of androgyny and beauty are mythical concepts. The ancient myths represent an attempt to understand the enormities of existence in human terms. Within a logocentric culture, one dominated by language, myth has held the privileged position of providing the metaphorical tools for the resolution of conflict. For Lévi-Strauss (1963: 229) mythical thought creates the models for resolving contradiction. Fraleigh's phenomenological approach suggests that the origin of myth be found in the human body (1987: 145). Myth encourages the idea of completion and perfection, providing a paradigm for human endeavour. Holding such a position has enabled myth to shape both history and culture (Coupe 1997).

The particular paradigm that androgyny attempts to embrace, through the transcendent union of masculine and feminine qualities on one body, offers Western culture a resolution to the ancient philosophical enquiry into the conflict between physical passions and spiritual purity.

Roland Barthes (1973) deconstructs the mythological paradigm. His deconstruction primarily exposes bourgeois ideology. He draws attention to myth as a cultural construction, in language, rather than as a natural phenomenon. Barthes' deconstruction of myth brings androgyny face to face with the embodied reality of men dancing, positioned in a social, political and cultural context from which the myth draws sustenance.

For Barthes, myth is a 'type of speech' and therefore a textual concern (1973: 117). As such, myth can be analysed by semiology – as signifier, signified and sign. However, as Barthes points out, myth is a 'metalanguage', a 'second-order semiological system' (1973: 124). In other words, the signifier for the mythical system is already a complete sign within the first semiological language chain. Applied to androgynous figures in ballet, this first sign is composed of the signifying image, that of the Western male body dancing (a real body with a name, history, age, class and culture), together with its signified meaning, that of a harmonized union on one body of (masculine) physiology and the feminine qualities of dancing.

When myth gets hold of this full sign of the first semiological language chain, it becomes the new signifier, the raw material for a greater system, and the metalanguage of myth. The new signifier is 'at the same time meaning and form, full on one side and empty on the other' (Barthes 1973: 126). On the one hand, as a sign in the first semiological system, the image is full of meaning signifying the union between masculine body and feminine dancing. On the other hand, that image is an empty form ready for myth to fill it with a new set of signifiers. In this instance, the signification is that of the androgynous ideal, one that transcends sexuality, mortality and procreation of the real body. The feminized male dancer becomes an empty form, and onto its surface appearance is thrown the illusion of androgyny – evoking, for the spectator, mythical aspirations towards a spiritual and higher state.

In this way, the mythical status of androgyny holds the sexuality and sexual identity of the real male dancing body as a 'secret'. However, this is where the mythological system reveals its own disruption. Barthes points out that the meaning of the sign in the first semiological system – in this instance provided by the male body dancing – is still present once the body becomes an empty form for myth – in fact, myth depends on the first meaning for its ideal realization.

> One believes that the meaning is going to die, but it is death with reprieve; the meaning loses its value, but keeps its life, from which the form of the myth will draw its nourishment . . . It is this constant game of hide-and-seek between meaning and form that defines myth.
> (Barthes 1973: 127–8)

This is particularly so in dance, an art form performed at the site of the real live body. The mythical meaning of androgyny constantly feeds and is dependent on the real male body. Even though the myth aspires to transcendent ideals, it can only do so through its dependency on what it denies – the physical real of the flesh-and-blood body. Anthony Dowell's real male body dancing the (feminine) language of ballet becomes the androgynous sign that spectators fill with mythical signification. The oscillating relations between his real male body and his androgynous illusion provide the spectator with a seductive play of presence. Spectators of ballet are drawn by their play of ambiguity between physical desire and spiritual perfection at the site/sight of Dowell's body.

In short, the young man becomes doubly seductive. The masculine body embodying feminine qualities of dance language becomes an androgynous illusion. Here, in performer–spectator relations, the male dancing body plays a game of hide-and-seek, between real and illusion, full sign (male body dancing) on one hand and empty signifier (androgyne) on the other. Then, as empty form, this androgynous body signifies mythically as spiritual beauty, appealing to the classical aesthetic conditioning of Western culture. At this level, the flesh and blood identity of the male body becomes a secret, seductive as a shadow but one that nevertheless feeds the mythical properties of transcendence. Thus, as with the ballerina, real and illusion provoke a play as presence on the male dancing body.

I have begun this book by dredging up the seductive power inherent to Western aesthetics between flesh-and-blood bodies and spiritual beauty and perfection. It is against this hierarchical dualistic backdrop of flesh and spirit that feminism, gay politics and race politics would run riot in the challenge for subjectivity and visibility. But the stage is not quite set to speak of feminism. I am going to rub salt in the wound, drive the wedge deep, expose the blood and blisters that have been the history of all of us young girls who were seduced by ballet in the 1960s. I am going to get right inside the young girl's anguish and desire for transcendent beauty.

imitated

8 THE OEDIPAL NARRATIVE

My fragile and petite mother says, 'It's wonderful to be tall as long as you are thin, but if you are tall and fat you will be called a big girl and that's not attractive.'

On Monday mornings, along with all the other girls, I hand in my weight card, duly signed by my mother. This card is initialled by the school secretary and handed back. Throughout seven years of stage school training this little ritual is upheld. Sunday, that family day, becomes one of conflicting desires. Relaxing, eating and sleeping are

infected with the demand to be thin and the
moment of truth, standing naked on the
old-fashioned upright weighing scales. The longing
for comfort food on cold rainy Sundays is marred
by the efforts to retain the same weight as the
previous week or even the previous year. The
inevitable first meal of my inevitable first diet
comes in the form of one grilled ham steak (four in
a pack, from the supermarket) with one slice of
pineapple laid on top. The Monday morning weight
card – signifier for feminine beauty – signals the
route to secret eating.

What follows is a particularly personal narrative of the effects of growing
up as a ballet girl in which I look at how the ideals of perfection failed
my body – but I am by no means alone. The spotlight falls on ballet
but this is not the only form that prides itself with its representations of
idealistic beauty. Ballet dancers parade on the same metaphoric catwalk
as do models, pop stars, jazz dance performers, beauty queens and the
icons of advertising and the media. All are challenged on a daily basis
by the contradictions between their real bodies and performed illusions.
Upholding the glamour of Western beauty often has tragic consequences
on the bodies of its protégés in their efforts to sustain the purity of the
transcendent dream. Behind the seduction of illusive appearances, in the
extra daily grind of institutional physical practice, the oscillating relations
of real and illusion often become unhinged. The issues raised by the challenge to perform and maintain the illusive seduction as a real body led
to the radical deconstruction of ballet in the 1960s and 1970s.

Throughout Britain, the training path most commonly undertaken by
young people wanting to perform is that of the stage school. Dotted
throughout the country, these performing arts institutions offer a wide
variety of performing arts: ballet, tap, modern, jazz and national dance
(i.e. dances from different cultures), singing, speech and drama, to name
a few. Training in these styles is driven by competition, packaged with
specific correct/incorrect mirror images that inevitably throw back and
perpetuate the desire for a beauty in perfection. I spent my childhood at
one of these stage schools. I trained through a yearly cycle of learning
12 dances each year: 7 solos, 3 duets and 2 group dances in different
styles. These dances were performed at various festivals and competitions across London and the South East of England. Medals were given
to the winners and, best of all, there were silver cups to be won. I became

Figure 2
Awaiting adjudication in the All England Sunshine Competitions (1965). Drury Lane Theatre, London.
Back row, Jacky Lansley (third from the left); Emilyn Claid (fourth from the left, in Portuguese costume).
Front row, the adjudicators, including: Grandison Clarke (second from the left) and Beryl Grey (fourth from the left).

Photographer: George Kent Harrison.

addicted to the moment of winning, a totally consuming pleasure and an adrenaline high. Fear of failure was always present as a force of persuasion to continue training. The addiction to success was a clinging parasite camouflaged as a jewel: there was always another, better medal to be won. In striving to win, I was striving for a reward far more complex to identify and ultimately impossible to win – love. The successful dancer became synonymous with being the loved girl. Training, dancing and performing were all about desire. But I could never be the best; she was always out of reach. I fell for this narrative hook, line and sinker. I went blindly, but willingly, pulled along towards enticing dreams of possessing the ultimate prize – just around the next corner the glitter of love and success would be mine.

As I re-conjure an embodiment of longing, I can only do so with the theories that bring it down to earth. I cannot go back to the past without taking its future with me. That future was the theoretical tools of feminism and psychoanalysis, theories of the male gaze and the Oedipal narrative (Mulvey 1975).[1] The desire to be loved, as the object of desire, has an unabashed parallel to the role of the female body in the Oedipal narrative. I acknowledge fundamental psychoanalytical concepts as deeply conditioned on my performing body through patriarchal traditions – in particular the concept of desire in its relationship to loss.

Originating in the relationship of separation between mother and child, loss provides the backbone for the Oedipal process. Loss, and desire for the lost one, become a perpetual and interdependent chain of events for spectators and performers, where desire can never be satisfied but creates 'an endless network of replacements, substitutes, and representations of the perpetually absent object' (Grosz 1995: 176).

The inability to accept the primal loss of separation between mother and child to acknowledge that there is perpetually an always-lost moment that can never be replaced, gives rise to the constant need for self-realization and self-recognition through an 'other'. In psychoanalysis, the search for the true object is never satisfied, but that does not diminish the search. Peggy Phelan, who links the spectator's desire for meaning in performance to the need for self-identity, proposes that the impossibility of realizing self-identity '*maintains* rather than cancels the desire for it' (Phelan 1993: 14, emphasis mine). Drawing on Lacanian theory, Phelan says 'the relationship between the real and the representational, between the looker and the given to be seen, is a version of the relation between self and other' (1993: 3). One's own origin of self is both real and imagined, one looks continuously outside oneself for verification of one's own identity: 'self-identity needs to be continually reproduced and reassured precisely because it fails to secure belief' (Phelan 1993: 4). Looking for one's identity in another always requires the loss of 'self-seeing', since looking 'both obscures and reveals the looker' (Phelan 1993: 16). Limitations of both language and vision prevent recognition of oneself in the other, encouraging desire in its relationship to loss, institutionalized by conventional psychoanalytical theories and embedded in the binary code of subject and object. If it were possible to acknowledge the loss and accept the constant tension between real and imagined, 'we would not have to press quite so hard on the visible configurations of the other' (Phelan 1993: 26). Psychoanalytical narratives of self in relation to other and the perpetual search for the ever-lost original object suggest the possibility of *searching* as a constant activity. Performers and spectators in ballet adhere to the search through the oscillating cycle of real and illusion. For performers, the goal of perfection remains temptingly out of reach, wrapped in a cycle of success and failure, and therefore always desired. For spectators, the beautiful body of the ballerina remains temptingly out of reach, and therefore always desired. In ballet, performers work their real bodies to reach the illusion, while spectators look through the illusion for a glimpse of the real. The dancer is the illusion of the fabricated real of the desire. Spectators and performers search for what they cannot have.

The feminist perspective on psychoanalysis emphasizes the Oedipal narrative as the impulse that drives and generates narratives in film, theatre and media presentations. For DeLauretis, narrative itself is structured upon the question of desire, geared to the quest to know the answer, to satiate desire: 'Thus not only is a question . . . always a question of desire; a story too is always a question of desire' (DeLauretis 1984: 112).

For feminist theorists who expound the theory of the male gaze, all narrative is based on Oedipal logic and structured upon the question of desire (Mulvey 1975; Kaplan 1983; DeLauretis 1984; Dolan 1993). Furthermore, the Oedipus tale is focused on the 'hero as mover of the narrative, the centre and term of reference of consciousness and desire' (DeLauretis 1984: 112).[2] This is the hero's quest, to know the answer. He embarks on a quest to satiate his desire, 'for (self) knowledge through the realisation of loss, to the making good of Oedipus' sight and the restoration of vision' (DeLauretis 1984: 125–6).

I persist with the Oedipal narrative in order to understand its hold on young female bodies of beauty. The girl's story (an arduous one, according to the Oedipus myth, with the final reward being motherhood) is always a question of male desire. According to Freud, the phallus is the signifier of power and desire; the bearer of the phallus (man) is the subject of desire and woman, who lacks the phallus and therefore is not the subject, cannot desire. According to Freud, the girl actively loves her mother as a little man until she recognizes that both she and her mother lack the famous phallus. She then shifts from actively desiring to desiring to be desired, becoming feminine in her effort to get the phallus from her father – that famous phallus that never existed in the first place (Freud 1933; Benjamin 1988). This scenario brings DeLauretis to the conclusion that 'story needs sadism' and a woman's consent must be obtained, or forced, if necessary, in order for the Oedipus narrative to be fulfilled (DeLauretis 1984: 134). Within this context, the ballerina must consent to embody a feminine that is yet another fabrication of male desire. Following this narrative, I can see now how I consented to the struggle to embody the impossible (feminine) perfection through ballet, while the promise of reward was woven in the practice itself. I can see now what I did not know then – I was never supposed to possess the goal at all, but be the goal, someone else's prize – it was not my story at all.

I fought with my body on a daily basis. I was caught in a cycle of events whereby the more absent (thinner) I made myself, the more present I imagined I became. As I became thinner, in my mind I became more desirable. With becoming more desirable, I felt in control, I had an identity. But it was my bulimic body that had control. Bulimia, the food syndrome of starving, bingeing and self-induced vomiting, is an obsessive affliction. The ballet career is caught up with success and failure, where success is often nothing more than a 'correct' body, where women's bodies must remain girl-like. These pressures increase the likelihood of eating disorders among dancers.[3]

Rebecca Schneider describes the desire/loss narrative as having a secret service, becoming part of a perpetual and insatiable addictive cycle of exchange 'designed, packaged, and sold – marketed, outfitted, and set upon a runway of dreams where it is also marketed for gender' (Schneider 1997: 5). The important ingredient in this perpetual cycle is that desire, in its associations with loss, can never, must never be satisfied, or the cycle breaks. Therefore, the female body, as the idealized object in the narrative of desire, must always remain temptingly close but never grasped; a symbol always of what is forever lost:

> Fondly he holds the phallus in his arms, longingly he looks into his princess' eyes, and ecstatically he lifts her, his hands around her long, stiff tube of a body. Easily he holds and moves with her. Flying, she is his.
>
> (English 1980: 18)[4]

According to these dramatic feminist theoretical tales there is no escape. The ballerina has no choice but to meet a death in the arms of feminism. Certainly, there was comfort in the feminist psychoanalytical theories acting as an explanation for the perpetual domination of the male gaze and providing survival strategies for female bodies. I was able to step outside and objectify the patriarchal system that had dominated my ballet career in the 1960s. The theories of the gaze pursued the ballerina and her image relentlessly as the object of patriarchal phallocentric oppression (English 1980; Adair 1992; Foster 1996). As feminist discourse raged, the ballerina was drawn into its alluring psychoanalytical clutches with the promise of liberation from the clutches of the Oedipal narrative. I have drawn attention to the discourse here because 1970s feminism saved my life; because the emerging anger was positive; because re-embracing my body took place on a platform of feminist questioning and not from thin air. I write about the Oedipal narrative in order to move on.

But mine is not every ballet dancer's story. These theories belong to a certain era of feminism and were useful to a particular era of dancers. These theories, while liberating the female body from the clutches of beauty, also deny her agency. Alexandra Carter (1999) counteracts the feminist psychoanalytical perspective, proclaiming it as a negative stance towards ballet dancers. Carter offers a critique of feminist psychoanalytical writings on ballet, seeing that an image such as the dying swan had become 'a sitting duck' for feminist discourse (Carter 1999: 91). 'Not only was the ballerina rendered speechless but a whole history of women's creative endeavour was undermined' (1999: 92). The theories tend to blanket over and negate women's performance practice, their expressions of desire and subjectivity in Western dance traditions. They act to dismiss ballet performers themselves from discourse, negating their embodied intelligence of dancing.

9 AN ARTICULATE SILENCE

Then there is the pain of learning ballet. Through the pain of practice, the language of ballet became available to me. With the language came the freedom and the ability to express within that particular art form. With this skill came the pleasure of belonging, of owning, for a moment, the tools of power. It was a short-lived pleasure, as my body was conditioned to desire further knowledge and the cycle of pain–knowledge–power repeated. But with it came the ability to speak with my body – a silent language. There is something about the silent presence of ballet performers that haunts me. It is a silence that speaks volumes. It has agency.

Our re-thinking in the 1970s concentrated on giving the dancer a voice, verbally and politically. This is, undoubtedly, a feminist achievement. But there is something about a ballet dancer's silence that is not answered through feminist discourse. Silence is a vital element of a dancer's presence. Her/his silence is a symbol of his/her power of communication. I am playing provocatively here when I say that the secret of this power is in an internal dialogue with pain endured when embodying the language.

To speak of ballet and pain in the same breath may sound melodramatic. The pain of ballet is not comparable to the pain inflicted through broken limbs or by oppressive religious, political, legal and penal regimes. I am speaking of the pain that occurred when my body transformed itself from one shape to another, when it learnt to articulate a language through a codified technique that was alien to its pedestrian everyday existence. I am speaking about the pain involved when learning and practising an externally driven physical pursuit, challenging my body to enact extreme physical feats. I am speaking about an intense activity, repeatedly practised on or by my body where the language learnt required an engagement with a physical discipline at the level of painful somatic sensation in order to achieve its expression.

Ballet is not a performance that the dancer masquerades only on stage, at night, under lights. The language that is imposed on the body in turn shifts and constructs the shape of the body in order for the language to be further refined. Ballet dancers practise their language for many hours each day in the studio. The rest of the time they practise living their body within the confines of its code. The muscular discipline is not taken off when they leave the studio; it is perpetuated on a daily basis through the day-to-day functioning of the body. Many of us slept with our legs turned out. The bodies of ballet dancers are recognizable as they walk down the street with their turned-out legs and feet, muscular calves and thighs and long stretched necks. The ballet dancer lives an extraordinary existence even before the performance begins, when the constructed becomes real, the codified becomes the normal; the crossover between the two can no longer be defined clearly. Inherent to the construction of these bodies are the relations of pain and silence.

Elaine Scarry (1985) analyses the inexpressibility of human pain and its associations with destruction and creation in the world: 'The closer something is experienced somatically, the closer it comes to pain' (Scarry 1985: 166). To have pain is to be owned by something that is difficult to describe because of its immediate presence, its silent hold over the body. Owning a pain, or being owned by pain, provides a certainty, a vibrant present, and a fixed point of security, full on the body, inseparable from the body and therefore absent in its representation in language. Pain, as a physical state, has no access to representation in worded language. For the ballet dancer, this results in a double silence, for not only is s/he unable to communicate verbally, as the pain is inseparable from, and inherent to, his/her language, but the discipline permits no sound: consequently s/he is construed as doubly powerless by the silence. However, s/he is *not* powerless. To argue the power of silence, I turn to Michel Foucault and his bound relations of pain and power.

For Foucault, knowledge is power and knowledge is created, disseminated, produced and refined through language and discourse. Each power system constructs its own discourse and the physical body becomes the focal point for constructing that knowledge. A power system operates on the body through the persistent inscribing of its language on the body.

> The classical age discovered the body as object and target of power . . . It was a question not of treating the body, *en masse*, 'wholesale', as if it were an indissociable unity, but of working it retail, individually; of exercising upon it a subtle coercion, of obtaining holds upon it at the level of the mechanism itself – movements, gestures, attitudes, rapidity: an infinitesimal power over the active body.
>
> (Foucault 1977: 137)

The body is both the tool of production and the object produced, constructing and carrying the language on itself. Moreover, while each system's particular language works on the body, it also infiltrates and feeds the body's desires and ambitions, willing each body to comply, to impose its own inscriptions, producing and refining the knowledge that perpetuates the power system.

> A 'political anatomy' which was also a 'mechanics of power' was being born; it defined how one may have a hold over others' bodies, not only so that they may do what one wishes, but so that they may operate as one wishes, with the techniques, the speed and the efficiency that one determines. Thus discipline produces subjected and practised bodies, 'docile' bodies.
>
> (Foucault 1977: 138)

Because bodies resist, power exists. Young dancing bodies are resistant and unpredictable, making ideal vehicles for the imposition or expression of power. Bodies fall back, flail and fling. Bodies are sexual and hungry. They drop downwards. Bodies hurt. The knowledge/power system both creates and feeds off the dancing body. A system of power is employed to discipline and mould bodies into a particular shape: these bodies then self-perpetuate the need for knowledge and therefore the power system. Power is needed, and is expanded to control, precisely because of the resistance: bodies spill out and exceed the confines of the discipline. The power/knowledge disciplines define sanity from madness, order from chaos, docility from rebellion. In parallel, the power/knowledge discipline of ballet creates the very subjects over which it has control. The symmetry of ballet draws attention to what it is not – the presence of chaos. Chaos defines order, and bodies are chaotic – just there, below the surface.

Human bodies do not transcend naturally; gravity pulls the body down to earth. Consequently, the body itself must be inscribed incisively to represent and signify ballet's meanings and values. Legs do not usually turn outwards or lift above hip height, necks do not lengthen naturally, backs do not arch easily and spontaneously; they must be trained, persuaded, day in and day out, through years of practice, to conform. And it cannot be done without pain. Through pain, muscles and bones are moulded to create the system's persuasion of 'normal'. The pain diminishes when the body has learnt its lesson, memorized its position, increased its capability and transformed its shape. It will return when there is a new lesson to learn.

The pain is not imposed only from outside. According to Foucault, the power system perpetrates the dancer's desire: that which will bring the reward of success, with the dancer imposing the pain upon him/herself. The dancer, now a tool of the system, supports the system through a cycle of self-inflicted pain, inducing the power, which brings success.

Foucault's strategies are inspiring but also negative for dancers. As with the Oedipal narrative, his theories deny agency to the dancer. According to Elizabeth Grosz, for Foucault 'the body seems to be the passive raw data manipulated and utilised by various systems of social and self-construction, an object more or less at the mercy of non intentional or self-directed, conscious production' (Grosz 1994: 122).

Clearly, a political strategy to change the power system requires the verbal expression of the pain: 'Verbally expressing pain is a necessary prelude to the collective task of diminishing pain' (Scarry 1985: 9). However, the silence of pain also connects to the articulation of ballet language, the life force and currency of the language, revealing itself to the dancer and between dancers in the embodied work itself. The ballet dancer's articulation of movement requires his/her silent acknowledgement of pain. Her/his physical, not verbal, expression announces his/her presence in the world.

Ballet dancers practise the sensation of pain in the exact opposite of its purpose. Biologically, pain is a signal, a warning that something is wrong. For ballet dancers, somatic pain is a signal that things are right, a warning signal to continue. For dancers, pain is the point. Dancers invest in the pain. Rather than attempting to diminish the pain, dancers frequently strive to increase the pain. If verbalizing diminishes it, then dancers recognize, collectively, that it is more valuable to stay silent. Dancers know that the experience of 'pain', this immediate vibrant presence of feeling on the body, is an essential element of dancing. As a *measurement*, pain provides the performer with an internal tool for judgement, degree and memory of movement language. The silence is maintained, because pain is necessary to achieve the language, and it is through articulation of the language that the ballet dancer expresses his/her powerful presence.

'Work' is the synonym that Scarry gives to the phenomenon of pain and imagination as they move out into the world. The performer's silent pain is fed by his/her imagination and s/he transforms the imagination, through physical work, into movement language. Pain and imagination work together to transform his/her body, bringing him/her the power of articulation. Often, in the process of training, the more intense and extreme the pain and imagination loop at the body site, the more powerfully projected and articulate is the performance of language that emerges.

> Man could never do without blood, torture, and sacrifices when he felt the need to create a memory for himself; the most dreadful sacrifices and pledges . . . all this has its origin in the instinct that realised that pain is the most powerful aid to mnemonics.
>
> (Nietzsche 1969, cited in Grosz 1994: 13)

10 DYING TO PLEASE

Arguing for the practice of somatic pain as power and as a form of agency comes provocatively close to suggesting there is an element of pleasure to be experienced in that dynamic. Yes, this is the embodied eroticism of ballet, the interweaving sensations of pain, pleasure and power. The hierarchical teacher–pupil dynamic establishes a pattern of reward and punishment, praise and criticism to encourage the physical disciplining. At stage school, I experienced a particularly dramatic embodiment of the teacher–pupil relationship. The stereotype of Madame Dragon, which epitomized the dance academy, was founded on very real experiences for many young girls. It was an intense partnership, driven by success and failure, wonderful in its intimacy, and dreadful in its power.

Madame is the grand dame of suburban stage schools. She wears her experiences of the Ballets Russes on her body like medieval armour, an architecture of formidable gothic design.

Each morning, she stomps through our tiny cold dressing room that is clouded with stale talcum powder. She strides through her smoke-filled office and into the dance studio. Footsteps of clicks and thumps warn everyone of her approach. Her stiletto heels frequently catch between the floorboards. Her entrances and exits are grand, theatrical events, pervading every inch of available space, throwing us wispy girls breathless against the walls. Her presence, both gloriously loving and utterly terrifying, fires each girl's desire to become one of her chosen girls. Like a haughty dominatrix performing her moods, Madame, as Jekyll and as Hyde, lauds it over her young protégés.

On Friday afternoons, Madame holds private lessons for the chosen few. On good days she opens the door to welcome me in . . .

'Louise darling – today we will have such a happy time. I am certain you understand how the hard work that ballet demands is all worthwhile. Now you must work even harder for a truly brilliant career. I would like you to put on your pointe shoes right away. We'll work on your ballet dance, especially those darling little *pirouettes*, and then we'll carry on with your Greek dance. Do you remember it? Sweetheart, you are such a dear dear girl.'

On a good Friday I emerge dripping with sweat, feeling very special, loved and intoxicated with dreams and ambitions.

On a bad Friday there is no welcome. I wait
behind the closed door. She rings her bell from hell,
signalling my time to enter.

There she sits and glares; she presses on her
stick. Nothing is right. I try, keep trying, but my
feet are cold, my toes won't stretch, I can't get up
on pointe. 'Lift your leg higher, higher, higher. Now
hold it, hold it. Straighten your supporting leg, keep
your back straight, lift your arm to the side', the
stick swaggers around in the air gesticulating
upward-ness. 'Balance! I did not say you could drop
your leg. Now lower your leg slowly, slowly, slower –
no! Don't bring your foot crashing down to the floor
like a flapping fish. Start again.' I want her love so I
take more pain. I long for praise but her stick only
thumps harder and the abuse rages on. As I leave
the studio I feel her calling me, 'Come Louise, come,
come through the shame, I will reward you.'

Training, as a young girl, held an addictive attachment to this teacher–
pupil dynamic, a relationship of dominance and submission that coaxed
the desire to work. The internalized belief in an out-of-reach moment
was endorsed and goaded on by doses of pain and pleasure. In this
strange sadistic masochistic relationship, it became impossible to separate
the desire for praise from the desire for criticism, as the latter became
the essential ingredient of the former. This dynamic relationship maintains a strong grip throughout the profession, between mothers and
daughters, teachers and students, and choreographers and dancers. Both
sides of the dualistic partnership enter an all-subsuming relationship.
Ballet training reveals its eroticism here, in these intense pleasure–pain
power relationships.

For Bataille (1987), a person calls his/her being into question through
her/his lived erotic experience, without which a gulf of discontinuity
exists between one being and another. According to Bataille, eroticism
offers an experience for a body to meet with another and in so doing
answers the fundamental need for continuity. Erotic desire is a call to
become one with another being. Bataille's eroticism focuses on the
outcome of sexual desire, the orgasm of heterosexual reproductive
sex, which reflects the Freudian concept of *le petit mort*: 'We have all
experienced how the greatest pleasure attainable by us, that of the sexual
act, is associated with momentary extinction of a highly intensified

excitation' (Freud 1920: 62 cited in Bristow 1997: 121). To dissolve into continuity, a certain 'death' must be experienced (i.e. climax and ejaculation): 'Reproduction leads to the discontinuity of beings, but brings into play their continuity; that is to say, it is intimately linked with death' (Bataille 1987: 13). As continuity can only be found through death, the height of erotic pleasure always holds the violence of death at its core: 'The whole business of eroticism is to destroy the self-contained character of the participators as they are in their normal lives' (Bataille 1987: 17). For Bataille, eroticism merges the space between bodies. Erotic activity, whether physical, emotional or religious, offers life everlasting, through an appointment with death, where one dissolves into the other: 'The dissolution of the passive partner means one thing only: it is paving the way for a fusion where both are mingled, attaining at length the same degree of dissolution' (Bataille 1987: 17). This comes close to describing the relationship many young dancers have with their ballet teachers and mentors. Through erotic relations something dies but something new is supposedly created. And dissolution, death, pain and anguish are associated with erotic pleasure (Bataille 1987).

Within this framework, one or other of the partners will dissolve in erotic activity. Bataille relegates the female to a passive role, saying: 'Many women cannot reach their climax without pretending to themselves that they are being raped' (Bataille 1987: 107). In other words, a submission to pain is required by one person or the other to achieve this erotic state of 'ecstasy'.

Vancouver 1967. Danny is a dancer too. He knows all the words to the Dylan ballads. We are not in love. It's just sex. We get stoned and hang out together on tour. One night, after the performance, we drop acid and go swimming in the hotel pool. After the usual god-like-hallucinations-and-philosophical-outpourings-of-oneness-with-the-universe that I associate with acid trips, we have sex in the shower. I awake to find my left arm covered in bite marks from shoulder to wrist. As the day proceeds these turn into purple-blue bruises. By the time I arrive at the theatre for ballet class, they are not a pretty sight – but a site that blatantly tells its tale. The ballet mistress is visibly shocked. That night we are performing Swan Lake and I am one of the swans.

I look at my arm. I look in the mirror. I think about
the swan. I think about the night before. A swan
who has sex. A swan that proves she becomes
human at night. A swan who is alive on earth and
living in sin. An interesting performance proposition
maybe, but not tonight. As a fallen swan I take
stock. I will have to white up tonight.

The Bataille-esque eroticism of the little death and, in parallel, the hierarchical relationships of ballet training, play a fine dance with physical
violence. Eroticism as a relationship of pain, power and pleasure finds
its way into all aspects of the ballet dancer's life. It is built into the
choreography and the grand *pas de deux*. It is built into the classical
ballet stories, the consummation through death. Most of all, it is there
in performance between spectators and performers at the moment of
performing. In this timeless zone, where adrenaline rushes, a total giving
and taking occurs, a little death between performers and spectators. At
the moment of performing, held by the eyes of spectators, I could feel
myself dissolve through and transcend the pain to become something
else. In ballet, the moment of performing provides the climax: the height
of pleasure, the release of withheld desires, the loss of oneself into another
form. This is the reward for the sweat and tears. Here it might appear
that the ballerina is the one to dissolve in erotic activity. But she does
not. As Bataille says, the woman *pretends* that she is being raped. The
ballet dancer's so-called role of submission is not a weak and powerless
one, rather a role that has the ability to draw a spectator's eye, to manipulate desire, to command a spectator's response, to engage a dynamic
presence. The ballet dancer *performs* the act of submission from a position of power. She, like he, possesses the famous phallus – the language.

Zooming forward and looking back, stepping out of the clutches of
beauty and ballet, I am about to skim over the radical feminist deconstruction of eroticism, swerve to the side of X6, to a later time of queer
subversion. From the 1990s onwards, we could play, laugh and juggle
with the intense relations of pleasure and pain. Here I could acknowledge the seductive engagement in the eroticism of ballet, as a performer,
director and spectator.

In *Virginia Minx at Play* (1993), I explored the erotic desires behind
various personae including a housewife, a Latin lover, an opera diva and
a mad woman with knives.[1] In this last incarnation, in the section 'Sweet
Rage', I confronted the moment when self-abuse became pleasurable,
when horror became humour. Chris De Marigny described the piece:

The most thought provoking work is *Sweet Rage*. In this Claid appears in a scarlet-hooded cloak, a muttering bent figure that surreptitiously produces one knife, then another. Casting aside the cloak she reveals herself in a huge wig and white shift – a character who appears to be half witch and half naïve child, who delights in these gleaming deadly weapons. Sitting on the floor, looking much like Mary Wigman's witch in *Hexentanz*, she continues to wield these deadly objects in increasingly aggressive gestures, as she starts to cut and rip her flesh. In a mindless and dissociated state, this bloody figure starts a little skipping dance to the popular thirties' tune *I Love My Baby, My Baby Loves Me* – a chilling spectacle.

(De Marigny 1993: 5)

Performing 'Sweet Rage' offered me a cathartic erotic play as I took charge of the pain–pleasure experiences that had been a part of my ballet youth. By 1993, these inherent memories were tools with which to play in performance.

As choreographer, I directed *Across Your Heart* (1996), for CandoCo Dance Company, an integrated company of disabled and non-disabled performers. The performance begins with Helen Baggett, her back to the audience, naked except for a white loincloth, boy/girl classical androgynous innocence. At the end of the piece, Helen hangs upside down from scaffolding, blood dripping from her belly, above the dinner table. Her classical androgyny is exposed as mortal flesh and blood. At the table sits Celeste Dandeker in her wheelchair, drinking Helen's blood and laughing. Kuldip Singh-Barmi wears a tight-fitting, long grey/brown dress; he is a grotesque/beautiful figure whose movements are accentuated by distorted quirky, fractured gestures. He shifts deviously through the spaces between other characters, a shadow of lurking chaos. He becomes other figures – clown, gigolo and dead body – returning in the gaps to the grotesque unidentifiable creature. He fills the chalice with Helen's blood and hands it to Celeste. Kuldip pulls Jon French out of his wheelchair, leaving him on the floor unable to move, completely vulnerable. Sue Smith performs as a hunched, hooded creature, a figure in pain, leaning forward on two long thin sticks as extended arms. She hunts Kuldip. As John lies on the floor, Kuldip and Sue cross the back of the stage. Kuldip, in his tight-fitting dress and distorted movements, is gripped within the frame of Sue's hunched body and long stick arms, becoming an insect in a spider's jaws. These two surreal and monstrous creatures appear and disappear, juxtaposed against more identifiable events of funeral, carnival and wedding. Celeste poses for wedding photos, standing, out of her wheelchair, wearing a long, full, white lace dress, echoing Frieda Kahlo's paintings.[2] The dress is removed revealing Celeste, strapped into a walking-frame machine that looks like a leg calliper for a whole body which holds her upright; invisible pain is externalized as a physical trapping. Celeste stands and walks independently, but within a contraption that encases her. There are two flat steel feet and, as she thrusts her weight forward with her shoulders and arms, the steel feet rock forward, slowly and painfully. We see Celeste alone on stage, facing the back, walking upstage precariously, and rocking from side to side as she goes, summoning enormous effort to move the steel frame. She is singing gaily, joyous and innocent, her pain and pleasure made vulnerable to our voyeuristic view.

As a spectator I allow myself knowingly to collude with the eroticism of ballet. I watch a class at the RBS. I face a row of young girls standing at the barre wearing skin-clinging pink tights and pale lilac leotards: clones of each other – almost. I look at the girl closest to me; I read a petite delicate innocence on her body. After six years of training, her tiny, constructed, jewel-like image has become inseparable from her real body. With her hair drawn away from her pale face, I observe a sophistication of expression way beyond the vulnerability of her body. She steps towards the barre into *arabesque* and her left leg rises behind her. The rest of her body remains delicately poised and shows no sign of tension. Her face transcends the effort. At the moment when her leg goes beyond hip height, beyond all natural possibility, I feel violence like a knife cutting her/me. My gut is fired by a display of flesh and sword, the young girl's body and her sharp technical virtuosity. Something like a memory seeps through her body/my body, speaks through the image. There is the edge of violence, stealing through the sweetness. I feel the thrill of pain and pleasure run through my body as my eyes grasp her vulnerability. My gaze pierces her image and my eyes burn. I feel a wrenching shock open an abyss between tenderness and violence. Her leg lifts as an unfolding quietness of violence, she is a demure diamond exposed to glaring sunlight; a fragile smile stretched into a screaming grotesque. The effect on my body is sudden, gut wrenching and breathtakingly wondrous as I take charge of the dissolution of her body into my memory. Performing, watching, directing and writing, I re-claim pain and pleasure with an ironic awareness of subversion and performativity.

But collusion came later. As I grew up in the 1950s and 1960s, the myth of beauty enticed us, simultaneously tantalizing and cruelly deceitful. Rise above the madness, chaos and self-destruction (to a sanity that was madness in disguise) or fail. Surviving as a dancer required a constant negation of my own body; fight its hunger, ignore the fear, reject its downward pull, seek its pain, change it, re-construct its shape, exist for the dazzling image that was always just over there. The dualism was right inside the bodies that were feeding Western aesthetics of beauty. It was also what made the ballet presence so seductive. The spectator's engagement with real and illusion was teased continuously by the persistent dualism between flesh and blood physicality, and spiritual beauty. For many of us, the chaos that was our real bodies would sooner or later stake its claim, as it did for me in the 1970s.

After leaving the National Ballet Company of Canada in 1969, I live in New York for two years, studying at the Martha Graham School. I perform with members of the Martha Graham Company, modelling and baby-sitting to earn a living. I tend Martha's garden in return for a scholarship. She taught class just once. I sit with my legs open wide to the side. I lift my arms above my head, open my hands, palms up, lifting my face to look at the ceiling. I say, 'My name is Louise', in time with the movement. I am told that if I have more sex my dancing will improve. I wonder how much more that could possibly be. I have classes with Helen McGehee, Mary Hinkson, Bertram Ross, Dick Kuch. I am invited to join the newly formed Martha Graham Company but I cannot. It is too late. My body can no longer lie: emotional and physical chaos is cracking the surface. I am treading the waters of cockroaches, drugs, sex and bulimia. I leave New York in 1971 and return to Toronto. Here I am swept along for another sex crazed, stoned-out year where dance does not feature. I work in a porn cinema.

   At the age of 21, I return to London. I ask my father for advice. He suggests secretarial work. He pays for a gruesome operation for my osteoarthritic toe joints. I learn to type and never regret it. I get a job as a secretary at the Physiological Flow Studies Unit, a medical science laboratory at Imperial College, London.

   I learn fairly accurate shorthand, organize a conference or two, sleep with doctors, learn how to feed punch cards into a room-sized computer and

see a greyhound dog splayed out with its throat
pulled back and its aorta dissected. At this point
I think I will try a few dance classes. I struggle into
footless tights and leotard and take a somewhat
lumpy body to the back row of an evening class at
the London School of Contemporary Dance. Within
a short while I find myself back in the contract-
and-release of it all, as Jane Dudley's
demonstrator of the Graham technique.

It is 8 a.m. on a Monday morning, Studio 3,
The Place, London, 1973. Jane Dudley is teaching
me the combinations of movements that she wants
demonstrated in the advanced Graham class she
is teaching at 9.30 a.m. Her hips will no longer
allow her to dance. We both face the mirror. She
holds me close, in front of her body. I have my left
leg lifted and wrapped around her waist. My back
arches against her chest, her arms clasp around
my torso. My arms are raised above my head; she
presses me firmly with her hands. She uses my
body to remember her own, to become her own.
She comes alive through my body. I feel her body
transformed. We both look into the mirror. I am
working to understand her demands. She wants
a flat line from thigh to ribs. I want to get it
right. She is meticulous; our eyes meet in the
mirror. I understand her urgent desire to transfer
knowledge. We are locked in a passionate
teacher–student embrace. As I look at our bodies
in the mirror, I foresee that this will be the last
time I submit my body, as a dancer, to another's
demands.

No!

Figure 3 Emilyn Claid in *5 Saturdays* (1975). Elephant and Castle roundabout, London.

Photographer: Geoff White.

II No!

Coming down to earth as dancing subjects

11 EXPRESSIONS FROM THE LIFEWORLD[1]

You'll find us down in the docks, by the river, a mere stone's throw from Tower Bridge. Walk across Shad Thames, a cobbled street with Dickensian walkways overhead. Walk up Lafone Street. When you find the warehouse marked X, climb the six flights of rickety narrow wooden staircases. At the top push open the door and enter. You'll find a vast space with a high-beamed vaulted ceiling. You will see skylights and detect the smells of tea, dust and cinnamon. The tongue-and-groove maple wood floor streams away in front of you. It's stained dark brown and polished smooth from tea trampled into its pores over many years. Look to the left past the heavy wooden double doors with the monstrous steel electric-powered winch with which we hauled up the old piano. You will see the five of us sitting at the table in the corner. Electric heaters surround us, creating a tiny oasis of warmth. On the table is an old brown teapot, mugs of tea, packets of biscuits, *Golden Virginia* tobacco (for those of us who smoke). We are talking. It's 1976; we do a lot of talking here, making up for many years of dancer silence. Come, sit down. We are discussing plans for a Radical Summer Dance Course.[2] We offer you a cup of tea and introduce ourselves: Jacky Lansley, Mary Prestidge, Maedée Duprès, Fergus Early and myself.[3]

Jacky was one of the first wave of artists to leave The Royal Ballet to make her own work. With ironic wit, critical intelligence and rigorous analysis, Jacky challenged every X6 procedure. Drawing on feminist philosophies, she questioned each proposal, refusing to compromise. I remember her in *Women Dancing* (1978) as she crawls slowly down the length of X6 against a shimmering image of the ballerina Anna Pavlova (Lansley 1978: 10). I remember her in *Zena Mountain* (1979) wearing a glamorous blond wig and Wellington boots as she re-works theatrical traditions from a feminist perspective. No ballet step or performed gesture was left unturned, but each must be examined, considered for its patriarchal, capitalist, hierarchical dependencies, deconstructed in its composition, cut through and re-figured – but not necessarily discarded. I remember Jacky Lansley performing with Rose English in *Romeo and Juliet* (1979). They adopt masculine characteristics in their body images, reversing gender roles, fighting a duel, wearing doublets and lying on their backs with their legs in the air. Their sardonic humour and cool objectification of the audience convey a refusal to conform. 'I was a little disturbed by a feeling of underlying aggression', writes dance critic Nadine Meisner (1979: 20).

Mary, British Olympic gymnast and ex-Ballet Rambert dancer, roller-skated fast around X6, exploring speed and balance (*Latest Release* 1979). Thinking in the gaps between fixed time and space, Mary remained motionless rather than repeat old patterns of movement. X6 provided Mary with the context to explore alternative ways of moving: contact improvisation, release technique, Alexander technique and t'ai chi. I remember her walking on stilts under the archways of London Bridge, and balancing upside down on the handles of a trolley in a disused car park down in the docks (*By River & Wharf* 1976). Quietly perceptive, always seeing two sides of the argument, Mary spoke to an internal dialogue, attending to kinaesthetic knowledge. She walked as easily on her hands as she did on her feet.

Fergus also looked to reconsider his earlier dance experience, both with The Royal Ballet and at the London School of Contemporary Dance, to seek out a supportive environment for his choreography and performance. Knowledgeable about dance history, culture, funding and politics, Fergus had an articulate, confident command of writing and speaking to the point. Being the only man in the collective was not a privilege that Fergus flaunted. In fact, he was more feminist than I was. I remember him, balanced in *arabesque* on a chair, wearing a vest, shorts and tap shoes (*Dances for Small Spaces* 1977), while I played Satie's *Gymnopedies* on the piano. I remember him as he cracked a whip across

Figure 4 Jacky Lansley in *Dancing Object* (1977). X6 Dance Space.
Photographer: Geoff White.

sheets of corrugated iron in the middle of the night (*Dance of the Hours* 1977). I remember him playing a flute, walking slowly down the length of X6 wearing a long white dress (*Sunrise* 1979). For Fergus, dance was for everybody. He paid attention to the dynamic of the collective, to the equality of people's time and space, encouraging us to share in all aspects of dance production.

Maedée was vibrant, sparkling and dynamic. She approached life and dancing with joy and an efficient get-on-and-do-it attitude. Her slightly sideways glance at feminism was refreshing and her refusal to enter into what she considered the intense 'turn-out-your-pockets' wasteland provided a light touch to our often heavy proceedings. I remember dancing in her X6 extravaganza, *A Dance Score* (1979), where she invited her students and the audience to join her in a participatory performance while fruit salads were being prepared on the side of the stage. She sang, played the piano and laughed often. I admired her generous spirit and passion for dancing as I watched her in choreography by Rosemary Butcher (*Pause and Loss* 1977) and Richard Alston (*Doublework* 1978). While other members of the collective had already accomplished pro-fessional careers in conventional performance traditions, Maedée was embarking on hers; she used X6 as a platform from which to fly into a successful career as a solo artist.

Our survival tactics at X6 took many forms. Flooding to the front of my memories is the sense of anger and rebellion. Falling down to earth, letting go of that externally directed upwards search did not happen easily. The pattern of desire in its relations to loss and lack was thor-oughly embedded on our bodies and in our practices. The pattern penetrated the very core of the body and all of the language. Stripping off the layers did not happen without a fight. We rebelled. I was angry and I guzzled greedily from radical 1970s feminist politics to feed that anger. I rebelled against the previous years' powerlessness to effect change; the lack of creative encouragement within established traditions; the exploitation of my body as a choreographer's 'tool'; competitive structures; crippling training and obedience to silence. I rebelled against the cultural pressure to construct my body to fit an aesthetic mould, together with the ensuing lack of confidence, eating disorders and my wasted youth. I rebelled against the naivety of the dream, the 'turn-a-blind-eye politeness' of my middle-class background. I wanted no part of the slippery hierarchical universal notion of transcendence. I no longer trusted institutions. I rejected my identity as a ballet dancer. By 1977, my body had re-constructed itself as a non-desirable object that no longer conformed to the aesthetic of beauty, with a body weight at least a stone

Figure 5 Mary Prestidge in *By River & Wharf* (1976). Butlers Wharf, London. Photographer unknown.

heavier than the ideal. I performed a series of introspective autobiographical solo performances at X6 including *Going Back* (Szczelkun 1977:
14–15) and *Solo* (Green 1977: 10). *Solo* took the physical expression of
anger as one starting point for devising material. Dressed in boots and
a plastic anorak, I begin the performance hidden under a blanket on a
mattress, rocking to the sounds of the Everly Brothers singing 'Blue
Venus'. Many were the images of 'graceless' girls stomping around the
X6 studio, running, rolling and kicking our feet. X6 Dance Space was
full of women reacting against the status quo, reversing the romantic
image of a lithe, petite and forever-submissive sylph. Though lithe, we
were no longer thin, long-legged, hairless or under 5'5" in height.

Rebellious anger was a driving force for the creative process and
dynamic presence. Being passionately angry about past politics and practice offered positive resistance, a rich resource of starting points for ideas
and ways of working.

History, family, school, dance-training institutions, work, culture and
class had constructed our bodies. The 1970s dance rebellion – where the
expression of anger was a creative force for independence – re-conjured,
re-juvenated and re-shaped our bodies. We did something with our
anger, manipulated through the art practice: we began to shift the
baggage. At X6 we devised ways to make and show performance that
would collapse the binary power dynamics between choreographer and
dancer, spectator and performer. We explored how we could displace the
power imbalance between these roles. We began to discover devising
tools and methodologies for collaborative performance. We physically
invented and experienced shifts in aesthetics – coming down to earth
from the vertical transcendent. We experimented with embodying
feminist principles, replacing the dying swan with person-as-political
agendas – empowering female bodies as subjects of their own work. One
of our first performances was a re-working of *Swan Lake* devised by Jacky
Lansley (1976, after Marius Petipa/Lev Ivanov 1895). Dressed in boiler
suits and bare feet, we stomp, stamp and charge round the space as large
and rather noisy swans. Improvisation became performance as we
rejected the fixed and formal use of space and time. We presented our
own work and that of others. These were intimate events, with audience
seated on the floor in close proximity to the performers. We focused on
process not product as a strategy to shift the past and invent the future.
We explored relations between dance, performance art and theatre,
defying the narrow conventions of the silent dancing body. Jacky led
women's consciousness-raising groups and women's theatre groups.
Mary re-figured gymnastic training by rejecting competitive goal-oriented

Figure 6 Fergus Early (standing) and Julian Hough in *Manley Struggles* (1978). Riverside Studios, London.

Photographer: Geoff White.

ideals. Fergus led Alexander-based ballet classes. We encouraged artists and colleagues to write about their own and each other's work, which was then published in the *New Dance* magazine (1977–87). We founded the magazine. We wrote, edited, typeset and designed the layout sitting around the X6 table. The magazine took a broad cross-cultural perspective and encouraged an innovative widening of boundaries for what constituted contemporary dance performance at the time. We taught each other how to take charge of dance management and funding applications, initiating and organizing the Association of Dance and Mime Artists (ADMA) (1976–84), an activist pressure group that gave independent artists a voice.[4] Our angry rejection of what had gone before gave us the positive dynamic drive to make change.

Out of these dynamic shifts emerged new liberated images of men and women dancing.

12 FIGURES OF PARODY[1]

From the anger came parody, a vital postmodern, feminist performance tool through which 1970s artists channelled their anger and rebellion. The most amusing, hysterically funny performers were often the angriest. Juno and Vale's interviews with live art performers Annie Sprinkle, Karen Finley and Holly Hughes, describe anger as a positive passionate creative force 'for cutting-edge theory, linguistic re-construction, adventurous sexuality . . . Anger can spark and re-invigorate; it can bring hope and energy back into our lives and mobilise politically against the status quo' (Juno and Vale 1991: 5).

I am sitting on the floor in a gallery at the Museum of Modern Art in Oxford in 1977 watching Jacky Lansley, Rose English and Sally Potter perform *Mounting* (1977), an inter-disciplinary performance of theatre, dance, text and visual art. The performance takes place within a gallery exhibition by American artist Frank Stella. I watch duels fought by two women dressed as boys, with a third figure (Sally Potter in a white dress) running 'like a frightened rabbit, posing as "Fear", "Distress" in the spotlight' (McRitchie 1977: 22). Tracks from *West Side Story* (Bernstein and Sondheim 1961) give an extra charge to the humour. One-sided interviews take place between Rose English and the absent Frank Stella. Rose wittily comments on Stella's technique whereby the 'sensually delicate surface belies the nature of the medium on which it is presented – very heavy sheets of metal' (McRitchie 1977: 22). Sally Potter verbally directs a hapless ballet *pas de deux* between Jacky and Rose. The three women's banter throughout is full of political irony and subversive wit. As spectators we laugh – our laughter is then undercut by the final violent images of blood trickling from mouths and legs accompanied by the music from *Jaws*: 'Slipping out quietly she went to the sea to wash herself. In the darkness she saw the sharks high and dry, basking for the last time: relics for the museum' (Lansley *et al.* cited in McRitchie 1977: 23).[2]

The three women presented urgent statements of radical Marxist feminist politics. '"Art" is revealed as allied with ruling class interests in the assumption that it exists "above" materialism' (McRitchie 1977: 20). But the performance was so funny.

Becoming subjects of our own work, we quickly embraced the use of parody as a subversive tool. Laughter, like tears, is a healing agent for emotional pain. The excitement and expulsion of laughter brings a thrill of pleasure through the body. Shared laughter brings an immediate bonding between oneself and others. Laughter is suppressed, controlled and contained by Western culture, which denies its driving force for change. For French feminist Julia Kristeva, laughter is one of the first expressions of semiotic impulse between mother and child:

> Oral eroticism, the smile at the mother, and the first vocalisations are contemporaneous ... During this period of indistinction between 'same' and 'other', infant and mother, while no space has yet been delineated, the semiotic chora ... relieves and produces laughter.
>
> (Kristeva 1980: 284, cited in Grosz 1989: 44)[3]

To a large extent in Western culture, the pleasurable release of laughter is restricted to the realm of jokes. Freud tells us (1905) that three elements are required to excite pleasure for a tendentious joke: the one that tells the joke, the one who reacts with laughter and an object (subject) of derision, to be copied or parodied, which both parties recognize.

Our parody performances also had three elements: a performer who told the joke; a spectator who received it; and an object to be mocked, recognized by both performer and spectator. Performers and spectators feed off the tendentious joke. Through laughter, not only can politically subversive statements be made but also the object of anger can be disrupted and displaced.

There was no shortage of hostile objects waiting to be subverted by feminist artists in the 1970s. Many stereotypes of women's roles were parodied in *Helen Jives* (1978) a women's theatre group at X6, directed by Jacky Lansley and *Blood Group* (1979) directed by Anna Furse (Furse 2000). Jacky Lansley performed as *Zena Mountain* (Prestidge 1979: 10). Zena was a glamorous interview hostess in a blonde wig one moment and a suited male executive the next who could ridicule and parody her guests with fast, cutting, bittersweet wit. I found myself parodying Martha Graham's style of contemporary dance – riding a bicycle through south London, carrying a wooden staff in one hand, wrapped in an abundant length of white cloth, gyrating my body through a series of pelvic contraction-and-releases while sitting on the bicycle saddle looking very serious (*5 Saturdays* 1975).

In parallel, male performers at X6 were also using parody, displacing heroic machismo, particularly Fergus Early, Julian Hough, Craig Givens, Tim Lamford, Julyen Hamilton, Phil Jeck and Doug Gill. Tim Lamford and Julyen Hamilton employed two footballers to join them in their performance at the ADMA Festival (Drill Hall 1977). Tim and Julyen stand facing each other. 'The footballers likewise, just looking. Then staring. Eventually coming together and poking each other as if to fight, pushing each other out of the door. Tim and Julyen were doing a ridiculous laughable tap-stomp, in comparison' (Meehan 1977: 12). In *The Ballet of the Night* (1977) at the same ADMA Festival, Fergus, at 2 a.m., is 'wearing a white cloth as a nappy with a baby mouth stopper in his mouth. Sounds created by rolling and thudding on the rug, holding a rattle between his feet' (Claid 1977: 13). Pre-empting X6, Dance Organisation rehearsed and performed at the International Arts Centre at the Elephant and Castle in South London. Dance Organisation was an umbrella structure for a group of artists who worked individually and together. One particular piece was entitled *High Window* after the novel by Raymond Chandler (1947). The piece was performed by Fergus Early, Craig Givens, Maedée Duprès and me. At one moment, Craig is dressed in a long black cloak, carrying a bunch of white lilies and a paperback version of the novel. He walks slowly down the length of the warehouse space to lie down on the cold concrete floor in the far corner – a non-heroic tribute to Chandler's murders and the Wilis of *Giselle*. Performing *Passionate Fools* at X6 in 1979, Doug Gill and Phil Jeck act out a story about their adventures to capture and release two pigeons. In the re-telling, Doug becomes the pigeon that Phil is attempting to catch in a cardboard box. Doug nests up in the X6 rafters and Phil joins him and they coo together. It is a humorous and often ironic take on the dis-appearance of 'birds' and the ineptness of men to capture them (Green 1979: 14).

Balletic stereotypes were not to be spared, frequently becoming the tendentious object of the feminist joke. I was particularly interested in the contradiction between the purity of the ballet image and the reality of women's sexual, fleshy, bloody and ageing bodies. I exposed the red-eyed edges of the male gaze through parody. I created a tutu strip (1979) that metamorphosed into various performance guises over the following years.[4]

Standing centre stage in a spotlight, wearing a white tutu (the same tutu I wore as a teenager for ballet competitions), I begin by practising a series of stereotypical ballet gestures, exaggerated by a childlike innocence. Raunchy stripper music interrupts (*Harlem Nocturne*, Earle Hagen and Dick Rogers 1940). Trapped in the spotlight, I begin to strip awkwardly, simultaneously getting out of the tutu while attempting to cover my body. My transcendent expression becomes a confrontational stare. I shift from awkwardness to abandoned sexuality. Finally, I swing the tutu over my head by its elastic shoulder straps, then turn upstage, flinging the tutu over my shoulder.

The audience laughed with recognition at the moment the ballet stereotype was trapped in the stripper music. Their laughter pleased me as performer, as a measure of my ability to parody, to install and to subvert the convention. Of course the audience was 'in-the-know', for that is how the subject becomes a parody – both giver and receiver must recognize the object of derision. I was performing within a white, British, feminist, post-modern dance context that fully understood the rejection of transcendence.

The art form of ballet, however, was never the object to be parodied; it was the lifelong performative practice of the images of beauty that had distorted our bodies. We used exaggerated ballet stereotypes to climb out of that history. The infamous image on the front cover of *New Dance* magazine was of a romantic ballerina with the words 'bleeding fairies' emerging from her sweetly smiling mouth (Issue 5 1978). On the back cover was an image of a classical ballerina wearing a white tutu, her leg high in *arabesque*, with blood scribbled onto her crotch with a red pen. These crude images had been used as publicity material for the performance *Bleeding Fairies* (1977). Jacky Lansley, Mary Prestidge and myself took images of sylphs, whores and witches from traditional ballets and subverted their mythical properties through feminist principles. We sang a little ditty. Here is the first verse:

If I had known about the blood when I first saw a fairy,
I would have made her dew drops red instead of pearly white.
I would have dreamt her all with tits,

And made her wand of tampons.
She would not have been a fantasy, but very much more
   like me.

CHORUS

Who invented fairies, were they bleeders first?
Do we need a fairy, or will a bleeder do?[5]

I returned to balletic parody over the following years. *Laid Out Lovely*
(1994) explored beauty and death: the death of the beautiful body and
the beauty of the dead body.[6] The parody emerged through a representation of the ageing ballerina.

   I mince across the stage wearing pointe shoes and a pink net skirt.
I carry a gin bottle and smoke a cigarette while attempting to preserve
the image and retain the status of a 'prima ballerina' – despite a severe
limp. I reminisce on the days when I performed in the great ballets,
flirting with the pianist in the corner. I put the gin bottle between my
legs and mark out ballet steps with my hands. I use and abuse two boys
(Russell Trigg and Brenton Surgenor) as they partner me through some
rather ungainly lifts and I swear and curse at them for their incompe-
tence to lift me higher.

   The laughter that this figure evoked threw a revealing glance at the
tragedy of ageing and the death of beauty. Laughter is a crucial element
of spontaneous play, releasing the fear that blocks desires for change.
Laughter evokes subversion, chaos, courage and creativity. The cathartic
pleasure of laughter is an engaging component in performer–spectator
relations that is far too often denied by dance makers and performers in
Western culture's efforts to establish dance as an art form of the highest
order.

   Parody has a slippery surface.[7] I am aware of a theoretical point of
contention. Feminist artists have found parody to be a useful postmodern
tool for making performance. However, feminism and parody spar with
each other across the wrestling ring. For feminists, there will always be
the danger that parody simply perpetuates the systems it tries to displace
through its strategy to install and subvert. Postmodern use of parody
requires complicity with the past and, although the techniques to install
and subvert canons and conventions are clearly disruptive, the complicit
conditions limit the extent of radical change urged by feminist politics.
Theoretically, feminist artists can use postmodern strategies but only as
a first step towards a political goal. Feminism is a political movement,
while 'postmodernism is not; it is certainly political, but it is politically
ambivalent' (Hutcheon 1989: 168).

umburaanaul

However, for us, the postmodern tools of install and subvert did not dominate feminist politics, they enhanced its messages, allowing us to observe the distance we had travelled. In practice, as was seen in *Mounting* and *Bleeding Fairies*, women artists' bodies had been radically re-shaped by 1970s feminist liberation. By conventional standards our bodies were in the process of re-constructing differently, being robust in image, language and expression. We worked hard to re-present our bodies as subjects of our work. We no longer conformed in body image or language. When we installed the conventions, we did so from a place of difference. In other words, re-turning to install the convention had become, and could only be seen as, a mask of subversion on our bodies.

So the question of whether or not fetishized costuming, for example, served a political objective or whether its sadomasochistic appeal played straight back into the clutches of a patriarchal economy of desire even as that economy was rejected, was not X6 artists' immediate concern. Our strapping, strong, angry and outspoken bodies beneath the costumes ensured there was no danger of us perpetuating the convention. This danger only emerges when performers have not shifted out of the conventions they wish to subvert. The shift has to be made experientially, physically and emotionally, inhabiting a different mind and body. That was the work at X6. The figures of presence we wished to subvert emerged from our lived experiences, histories and personal agendas. But we had to step out of those histories in order to successfully subvert them. We had to be brave, to let go of the feminine ideal, not only academically and politically, but also on and in our bodily desires. For the experiences to become parody, the performer's 'I' had also to be the 'eye'.

In other words, the presence of parody as a subversive tool for performance carries a double entendre. Parody requires performers to have inhabited the experiences to be subverted, while the creation of the parody happens from outside those experiences. Parody is cathartic for performers and spectators when they can position themselves inside and outside the tendentious object. This is the key to the communion of laughter.

I consider myself very fortunate to have met the other X6 artists, to have had the opportunity collectively to question my previous dance history in order to re-figure the future. The liberated angry figures of feminist parody that emerged in our performances were raw. But they were survival tactics. Lurking within and behind the most successful figures of parody lies the frightening potential of human tragedy.

The performer's own experience gives the presence of parody its crucial pathos. For many dancers re-emerging from a career in ballet, the object to be parodied was not external to us; it was parasitically living on and in our flesh and bones. Ballet tattoos don't rub off. They had thoroughly marked my body.

13 SUBVERTING TRAGEDY

I am writing about the performance tools employed in 1970s dance performance practice to deconstruct the conventional images of beauty and transcendence. I look at our use of the personal as political and auto-biographical strategies for creating a performing presence. I remember the ways we engaged the audience through complicity, humour and laughter. Now I am going to divert slightly, to ponder for a moment and think about the underside of parody.

The dynamic for parody is the drive to subvert tragedy, and tragedy in performance offers an intriguing perspective of performer–spectator relations of engagement. Theatre director Augusto Boal writes how classical tragedy 'imitates human acts' (Boal 2000: 12) and is directed towards the failing of humans to achieve the metanarrative of happiness, goodness, virtue, justice that 'consists in obeying the laws' (Boal 2000: 24). Boal references Aristotle, for whom tragedy is a form of 'catharsis' for those unable to attain this virtuous happiness (Boal 2000: 27). However:

> It is not in the tragic characters that pity and fear manifest them-selves – but rather in the spectators. *Through those emotions the spectators are linked to the heroes.* We must keep this clearly in mind: the spectators are linked to the heroes, *basically*, through the emotions of pity and fear, because, as Aristotle says, something *undeserved* happens to a character that *resembles ourselves*.
>
> (Boal 2000: 29–30)

For tragedy, performers and spectators enter into a complicit relation-ship, a mutual recognition of an abysmal conclusion to an inevitable course of events that stands in the way of attaining goodness. Tragedy becomes a tragedy because there are witnesses who observe the action, witnesses who empathetically do nothing to stop the inevitable slide into the foreseen abyss. In tragedy, the performer enacts a hero/ine who goes naively and inevitably towards his/her destiny. Whatever happens to the performer happens to the spectator. The further the performer enacts the fateful journey of the flawed victim, the more the spectator feels the overwhelming sense of pre-destined fear and pity. The spectator does not intervene to halt the course of events. It is a cathartic event for spectators. Boal quotes Milton to explain:

> 'In physick medicine, things of melancholic hue and quality are used against melancholy, sour against sour, salt to remove salt humours'. In effect, it is a kind of homeopathy – certain emotions or passions curing analogous, but not identical, emotions or passions.
>
> (Boal 2000: 30)

There lies the tragedy, in the witness' own grief at his/her own inability to find happiness. Tragedy is there to purge the spectator of his/her own imperfections. The spectators are silent, complicit witnesses, bound by their own knowledge of events. Their presence is important; their presence makes the event a tragedy. Their act of witnessing evokes the tragic element.

Postmodern parody begins with tragedy; then another layer is added. Parody is tragedy but also parodies tragedy by subverting the notion that there has ever been a supreme and virtuous goodness. In parody, the performer enacts the tragic victim who goes naively towards the inevitable destiny but is in fact knowingly performing the victim from outside the role. Using a range of choreographic and theatrical techniques, the performer lets the spectator know that s/he knows the pretence while continuing to enact the fateful course of events. The spectator buys into the ambiguity. There lies the parody, as both actor and spectator *watch* themselves performing the tragic roles of victim and witness. In the relief of a shared but subverted tragedy, laughter erupts. In this relationship, performer and spectators are bonded by complicity, an understanding of the cultural context: race, gender, sex and class (the laws) within which the tragic failing occurs. Being complicit in these details increases the performance of tragic humour. Spectators and performers can then acknowledge the double entendre of parody: they experience the purging of the imperfect element that stands in the way of their lawful happiness while also subverting the idea of lawful-ness and 'supreme goodness' as being happiness in the first place.

Feminist strategies in the 1970s allowed artists to break out of their own tragic pathways in order to parody them. At X6, we were devising methods to emerge from our so-called inability to maintain the upward path to happiness. With collective spirit, we cared and cried about people's oppression; we got to the roots of things; we wanted to know why; we looked for meaning; we looked for the causes of things; we cared about liberation. Acknowledging this, we stepped out of our tragic pathways to use parody as an important political tool for change. I had a particular tragedy to subvert that lay deep under the surface images of ballet stereotypes. Bulimia was a private tragedy but shared by millions of young women, and men, across cultures, age and race. The first performance of the parody, *Raw Hide*, was at X6 in 1979.

I sit at a table downstage right, wearing a pale green stretch-nylon dressing gown, a blond perm and a pair of glasses. 'Eleanor Rigby' plays on a tinny tape recorder. I sit still, looking at the bare table. Behind me is a fridge. My eyes shift sideways slightly. The audience laughs knowingly. I know that they know I am enacting a woman, at home, on her own, thinking of food. My eyes shift sideways again, the spectators know I am going to go the fridge and begin to laugh. My glance tells the spectators that I know, that they know I know, that this character I am playing is on her own, stuck-on-an-inevitable-course-of-events-towards-loneliness-and-overweight-or-worse-starvation-and-death and at some point I am going to get up and go to the fridge. So, when I eventually do get up to go to the fridge, there is more laughter. At the fridge I take out a plate, a carrot and a grater. I return to the table, grate the carrot on to the plate, sit down and look at the carrot. I eat the carrot shavings. Another glance straight ahead – I know they know that I know all about the other food in the fridge. I return to the fridge and take out one biscuit. I flick the carrot off the plate giving the biscuit centre place. I sit, clasping my hands together, looking at the biscuit. Lightly, almost singing, I put the whole biscuit in my mouth and my eyes glaze over. Spectators laugh at this moment of exaggeration as they recognize the beginning of an inevitable slide towards the abyss . . . Later I throw myself about on the fridge to the sounds of Lonnie Donegan singing 'Raw Hide'.

Taking a stand outside the personal tragic pathway while retaining its embodied memory is a key to parody. The spectator knew (and knew that I knew) that I was unfolding yet subverting the tragic course of events, a tragedy made more poignant by the acknowledgement of the West's obsession with dieting. The spectators' laughter became the means for me to measure how well the subject was both installed and subverted. Laughter acts as a healing force for both spectators and performers. As I was the choreographer and performer of *Raw Hide*, this relationship of action and reaction between spectator and myself was cathartic for us both.

While I was director of Extemporary Dance Theatre in the 1980s, Lloyd Newson choreographed *Beauty, Art and the Kitchen Sink* (1984).[1] The piece subverted conventional images of masculine heterosexuality by drawing attention to the vulnerability of men in their struggle to attain the ideal masculine image.

I watch Lloyd, who appears downstage left, wearing a towel, looking at himself in an imagined mirror (the audience). He dries his body with the towel and wraps it around his waist. He examines his face while Donna Summer's song 'Love to Love You Baby' is played on a tape recorder. He peers forward, dances to himself in front of the mirror, and stabs the air with disco pointing gestures. With exaggerated narcissism, he draws the towel around his neck and into his mouth, turns and looks at his back in the mirror over his shoulder. He sees a big pimple, stops dancing, unwraps a plaster from his trolley, and sticks it on the spot. Examining his bald head, he gets the shaving cream, squeezes a blob onto his head, puts deodorant under his armpits, uses the deodorant as a mike, singing to himself, while spreading the shaving cream on his head, until it resembles a bathing cap. Upstage in silhouette, fashionably dressed heterosexual couples dance at a disco. They laugh and kiss; they are in love and in opposition to Lloyd's lonely private ritual. He shaves his head, shaves his eyebrows. He turns the tape over and Elvis Presley's 'Are You Lonesome Tonight' blares out. Addressing the audience throughout, obsessed with his blemishes, he covers his face with plasters. He sits in a chair, legs apart, towel wrapped loosely round his hips, and continues sticking plasters on his cheeks, eyebrows and chin. Excessive and grotesque, Lloyd's character draws attention to the obsession to conform to the Western aesthetic of the handsome conventional male body. In admitting the impossibility of upholding that image in flesh and blood reality, Lloyd reveals how the 'normality' of masculinity is itself a performance – a thesis rigorously argued by Judith Butler: 'There is subversive laughter in the pastiche-effect of parodic practices in which the original, the authentic, and the real are themselves constituted as effects' (Butler 1990: 146). Later, in *Beauty, Art and the Kitchen Sink*, Lloyd wraps his penis in bandages.

The audience witnessed Lloyd performing a character who was obliviously carrying out his (private) ablutions before going to the disco. The spectator saw Lloyd installing and performing the role of someone who was naively unaware of the media-perpetuated masculinity trap in which he was ensnared. Audience and performer witnessed the inevitable journey along which this bedraggled featherless peacock was heading. Both performer and audience recognized the tragedy in store when the character realized that idealized beauty was unreachable. Lloyd's performance skills of exaggeration, repetition, distant focus and delayed timing allowed spectators to know that he knew that the tragedy was subverted into parody. This was Lloyd's accomplishment as the performer, to construct the tragic figure, the illusion of a character unaware of his fate, through which the spectators could bear witness to the tragedy. Yet, simultaneously, Lloyd had his attention in the present, he was parodying that figure, being inside and outside of it, subverting its tragedy through techniques of excess and timing, evoking the spectators' laughter.

The strategy that links these two performances is that there is no separation between performers and makers. The performers own the material to be performed; they are inside and outside the work. For a parody to have its greatest affect, with laughter as the ultimate measurement, then performers and spectators acknowledge the failure to conform that lies behind. Recognizing and understanding the tragedy that is being displaced, through the laughter, by these surface images, is parody at its best. For artists at X6, parody became a political tool for change. Parody depended on our ability to work through the tragedy to the parody; to create a surface from the depth; to look forwards and back; to remember and let go simultaneously.

14 FEMINIST BATTLES WITH ANDROGYNY

Withdrawing from the expression of object of desire and re-figuring desire as subjects, re-working gesture, focus, muscular strength and body image, inevitably provoked the play of masculine qualities on female bodies. Looking back at the female performers whose work was driven by the positive dynamic of anger and rebellion, their images now strike me as being androgynous. But classical androgynous imagery (the union of feminine and masculine on the male body), was far removed from our 1970s feminist reclamation of beauty. Moreover, for feminists, the high-art aesthetic of classical androgyny represented a denial of the female desire, feminine sensuality and eroticism: 'The ascetic position is one of the highest fear, the gravest immobility. The severe abstinence of the ascetic becomes the ruling obsession. And it is one not of self-discipline

mirisalgauriul
but of self-abnegation' (Lorde 1984: 57). My feminist consciousness could not, in the 1970s and 1980s, enthusiastically embrace the potential in the ambiguous play of gender performance that androgyny would later offer me from a queer perspective. Weil argues that the androgynous figure denies the bodily and psychical difference of a feminine autonomous sexuality. Bringing the feminine, excluded body to the forefront of the scene of representation is important in order to 'dislodge the androgyne and the sexual, aesthetic and racial hierarchies it establishes from the universal, revealing its givens to be constructions of patriarchal ideology and not the results of divine or natural law' (Weil 1992: 11).

From a feminist perspective, the classical union of feminine and masculine in a male body provides Western culture with access to transcendence through a much 'safer sex object than a woman' (Walters 1978: 15). Avoiding association with the adulterated sexual act between men and women (alluded to by Plato), the androgynous male figure allows spectators to access the femininity of smooth curves without having to consider a woman's sexual difference. To express mythical concepts of divine unity, concepts of the mind rather than the body, the represented image has to be disassociated from notions of real mortality – flesh, blood, procreation, motherhood, ageing – of which the female body is a constant reminder. For feminist female performers in the 1970s, fighting sexually, socially and politically in order to ground our bodies, the unifying signification of androgyny was not a feasible option. Feminist artists were re-claiming the realities of mortality and reproduction from the transcendent desires of patriarchal spectatorship.

There was a positive 1970s androgynous voice in writing. Carolyn Heilbrun's manifesto (1973) encouraged androgyny as a liberation for men and women, allowing each a wide range of experiences and human impulses that in Western culture had systematically been constrained to one or other sexes:

> Androgyny suggests a spirit of reconciliation between the sexes; it suggests, further, a full range of experience open to individuals who may, as women, be aggressive, as men, tender, it suggests a spectrum upon which human beings choose their places without regard to propriety or custom.
>
> (Heilbrun 1973: x–xi)

Heilbrun investigated literature. She charted a path from Oedipus in Greek myth to the Bloomsbury Group and Virginia Woolf. She considered the androgynous qualities of female characters such as Diotima in Plato's *Symposium*, and Sappho in Plato's *Phaedrus* and *Antigone*. She wrote at length regarding Shakespeare's androgynous ideal, particularly in the plays, *As You Like It* and *Two Gentlemen of Verona*, where 'a boy plays a girl who plays a boy who pretends to be a girl, but few realise that the beautiful ease of the passage from boy to girl is part of the point, if not the whole point' (Heilbrun 1973: 29).

Heilbrun devoted a whole chapter to 'The Woman As Hero' (1973: 47–112), considering the androgynous characteristics of writers such as Charlotte and Emily Brontë, George Eliot, Jane Austin and Georges Sand. Of Katherine and Heathcliff's tragic relationship in Charlotte Brontë's *Wuthering Heights*, Heilbrun wrote: 'the miracle consists in her ability (Brontë's) imaginatively to recreate in art the androgynous ideal which she perceived within herself on the loneliness of those moors' (Heilbrun 1973: 82).

Heilbrun (1974) envisions an androgynous world where 'we would stop referring to the minds of brilliant women as masculine' (1974: 147) and where a range of possibilities are open to any individual body, regardless of gender.

Positive response to Heilbrun's manifesto was based on the notion of wholeness, essential to each human being, giving women the power of language equal to men. Several articles in *The Androgyny Papers* (Secor 1974a), focus on the androgynous vision, where masculine and feminine unite 'for the Rebirth of the new human being and the new society' (Bazin and Freeman 1974: 212) and for 'psychic unity' (Gelpi 1974: 152).

Heilbrun's writing was ahead of its time. Feminists were busy re-discovering their own female bodies as different and separate to male. Heilbrun's manifesto is written 17 years before Judith Butler's *Gender Trouble* (1990), which explores the cultural construction of gender and sexuality. Heterosexual feminism was not ready for a performative recon-ciliation between the sexes. Heilbrun's manifesto was, for the most part, severely contested. Showalter opposed her positive references to the androgynous attributes of Virginia Woolf, asserting that 'androgyny was the myth that helped her evade confrontation with her own painful femaleness and enabled her to choke and repress her anger and ambition' (Showalter 1977: 264, cited in Weil 1992: 149).

A complete volume of *Women's Studies* (Secor 1974a) was dedicated to *The Androgyny Papers*, providing an important critique to Heilbrun's mani-festo. For Secor, androgyny represented an ideal utopia, an image with no means of getting there. While images of the witch, Amazon or lesbian 'suggest energy, power, and movement, they are active, self-actualising images'; the concept of androgyny, however, offered only 'images of static completion' (Secor 1974b: 165). Secor's apprehensive observations included the notion that androgyny sets personality structures as givens for man and woman, that the 'constant reference to femininity and masculinity functions subtly to keep the focus on genital differences and on sexual union' (Secor 1974b: 166). For Secor, androgyny focused on heterosexual love, which inhibited women bonding with women, and its focus on union between man and woman hindered women fully identifying with themselves. In good, honest, angry 1970s feminist style, Secor suggested the harmony offered by androgyny did not take into account men's fear of woman/mother. She saw this fear as central to Western culture's artistic expression and, while androgynous images do nothing to shift this fear, at least the images of witch and Amazon face the fear directly.

Weil summarized Heilbrun's project as being 'inappropriate for women wishing to advance themselves or to promote the new discipline of women's studies' (Weil 1992: 151), saying that *The Androgyny Papers* salvage the ideal of androgyny 'only by reinstating the mind/body dualism and the concept of wholeness that have constituted the underpinnings of patriarchal ideology' (Weil 1992: 152).

Criticized to the end, Heilbrun withdrew to a defensive position, stating that androgyny may only be a 'necessary stopping place on the road to feminism'. The liberating place of androgyny would inevitably be overtaken, when a woman 'has become her own person and found her own voice, her self' (Heilbrun 1980: 265).

At least the feminist negation rooted androgyny back to the site of embodied sexuality for male and female bodies. Feminism of the 1970s did bring the myth down to earth, pitting androgynous male/female merging and spiritual transcendence against agendas that focused on empowering the essential woman. Art practice in this decade focused on *female* mythical images, representing images of *feminine* sexuality, in recognition of the *feminist* ideals of woman's liberation. Judy Chicago describes her *The Dinner Party* (1979) as 'a symbol of our heritage' and 'goddess worship, which represents a time when women had social and political control' (Chicago 1979: 53). The long triangular dinner table is set with ceramic dinner plates, each one illustrating a different three-dimensional design. For Chicago, this work is a celebration of women's achievements, both historical and mythological, each woman being symbolically represented by an image on a ceramic plate. Symbols representing Virginia Woolf, Georgia O'Keefe and Emily Dickinson appear explicitly sexual – the female anatomical imagery of vagina, labia and clitoris are closely represented through butterfly iconography. Chicago writes that she used the iconography of the butterfly, together with 'blending of historical facts . . . symbolic meanings and imagination. I fashioned them from my sense of the woman' (Chicago 1979: 53). *The Dinner Party* illustrates feminist essentialist art practice at its best through the real identification of woman and her different female sexuality.

The feminist ideals and politics of 1970s art practice appeared to reject the concept of androgyny, unable to foresee the potential of androgyny as a play of gender for artistic expression and performance for female bodies. The notion of embracing androgyny as an imaginary concept, whereby the human body is not *being* androgynous but *playing* androgyny was not on the agenda. The 1970s were a busy time for *being* female and *being* real: performing illusions were out. But remembering the X6 performance practice, our feisty bodies certainly appeared androgynous in our big boots and baggy clothes.

I watch Kirstie Simson moving in contact improvisation sessions at X6 in 1977. Kirstie is tall, with short-cropped hair, a long, strong, anatomical bone structure with a powerful physical presence that could never be contained within the conventions of contemporary dance. Her body breaks out of formal training, her energy defies all the rules, and her expanse of movement has no patience with stylized steps. There are no physical boundaries for Kirstie, no feminine pretence, no primness; she is out in the open, free from constraint. A positively aggressive, masculine use of space and physical attack emerges from her muscular female body. She runs, falls, turns upside down, takes herself to the precipitous edge as fearlessly as she laughs. I watch Kirstie dance on the X6 roof on a rainy winter day dressed in cotton dress and track shoes (*Splendid Dance* 1978).[1] I see her throw herself precariously at Julyen Hamilton's (smaller) body, which swerves so that Kirstie can catch her own fall (*Musk: Red* 1983).

> What makes me most angry is seeing what is alive get broken. Not just how women's bodies fix, lose their passion because of the fear of being taken over, but how the dance world needs to package that spark when it emerges. I get mad at the packaging of women's bodies, packaging of goods. Performers stop being open and letting go. The spark goes. The package gets fixed, used and then discarded, whether that is a ballet body or a body–mind centring body. Fame will never be as important to me as this openness; it's about a passionate force.
>
> (Simson 2003)

Our rejection of femininity as transcendent object of beauty, to claim the flesh and blood reality of our female bodies provoked an aggressive held-back quality of presence: 'In emotional terms, performing maleness means reducing facial expressiveness, reining in exuberance, holding back' (Solomon 1993: 148). Our androgynous images were provoked by the rejection of beauty and appeared as masculine neutrality on female bodies. Yet politically, as a feminist, I was rejecting the idea of androgyny. Seen from this perspective, re-claiming the essential feminine, becoming female subjects, surfaced on our bodies as the very figure feminists were seeking to avoid.

The grounded figures of androgyny became integrated into 1980s and 1990s independent dance. The presence of the muscular, down-to-earth female body in high heels and underwear or boots and dresses was familiar in *Hoopla* (Anne Theresa de Keersmaker, Rosas 1983); *My Body, Your Body* (Lloyd Newson, DV8 1987), *Flag* (Lea Anderson, The Cholmondeleys 1988).[2] The image re-surfaced in the performing bodies of Jowale Willa of Urban Bush Women; Lindsey Butcher and Annelies Stoffel in Extemporary Dance Theatre. In the Divas' performance of *Torei en veran Veta, Arnold!* (Liz Aggiss and Billy Cowie 1987), the women were dressed in sharply cut women's suits with severely buttoned jackets, high-heeled shoes and cropped hair. These women were not smiling. Independent performers such as Yolande Snaith and Kathy Krick (*Can Baby Jane Can Can* 1987) and Liz Aggiss' re-appropriation of German expressionist rebellion (*Grotesque Dancer* 1986) presented hard-edged, strong, feisty androgynous figures.

Embryonic in the 1970s, emerging fully in the 1980s, was a presence of feminist androgyny in the body image, expression and physical language of women dancing. Moreover, I saw the androgynous presence as a direct outcome of the rebellious anger and subversive parody – a positive force that refused to please or conform to conventional femininity. As a physical manifestation, anger marked the body in certain ways. The feminist androgynous presence was not about *being* angry per se; rather, how the anger was translated and emerged through language, image and expression. As histories construct bodies, so anger transformed the flesh, gave it a muscular, unbound, expansive, I'm-looking-at-you power (conventional masculine characteristics). The female anatomical body merged with the expressions of masculinity to create the solid grounded, fearless, feminist androgynous presence.

So, there she is – the liberated female body – dressed in Doc Martens boots, cotton dress or oversized tracksuit, short haircut, and unshaven armpits and legs. She doesn't smile unless she wants to; in fact, she doesn't have to smile at all. She looks at her fellow performers and she looks at you. When Jacky Lansley, Maedée Duprès, Yolande Snaith, Kathy Krick, Kirstie Simson, Gaby Agis, Liz Aggiss or Annelies Stoffel danced in the 1970s and 1980s, they looked, not up to some longed-for ideal, but straight out, directly, proudly and defiantly. Our feminist anger translated to our bodies as a positive, androgynous force full of robust, dynamic energy: strident, big, female bodies with unrestricted movements that cut and covered large quantities of space. This was political and personal. For me, this was the outcome, not of reconciliation or union between the sexes, but rather, a rejection of male-defined, fetishistic femininity on our bodies: a subversive statement of a passionate, inspiring, liberated presence of female subjectivity. This androgynous quality was engaging, intriguing. Performing and watching held an ambiguity and contradiction. What the performer was doing (becoming woman) was not what the spectator was seeing (feisty androgyny). The 'eye' of the spectator and the 'I' of the performer were seductively deceiving one another.

Fashion markets were quick to appropriate the art movement. Frocks and boots became a familiar trademark for the new, liberated woman of the 1980s. Even now, female androgynous fashion continues to have its highlighted moments. In 1997, the magazine *Style File* depicted an image of bare female legs wearing male brogues: 'Style pundits are predicting that by spring heels will be gone and androgyny will be the next buzzword' (Macleod 1997: 17). However, there is a big shift in meaning between the 1970s and 1990s androgynous look, just as there is between the classical and feminist images of androgyny. *Style File* in the 1990s catered to the conventional fashion market while the feminist artist look of the 1970s signified a rebellion against that same market. The 1970s embodied image revealed unshaven 'not-so-thin' legs, opposing *Style File's* image of very clean-shaven thin legs, which was accompanied by the caption: 'brogues are really cheeky and boyish to me, and look so sexy with a bare leg . . . After all, the heaviness of a man's shoe shows off the delicacy of feminine proportions to great effect' (Macleod 1997: 17).

Style File's 1990s interpretation of androgyny was appealing to the queer economy of desire, which 1970s feminism did not embrace. The discussion – defining androgyny within a queer context of desire as different to that of classical and feminist interpretations – continues later.

15 WITHIN THE FRAME OF
NEW DANCE

New dance is the prevalent term that describes the context for the shifts
in 1970s dance forms. Initially, however, we gave the term to a dance
magazine – providing a means for dance artists to write about their
art/performance practice.

> Dance like any other art form does not exist within a social or intel-
> lectual vacuum. It is subject to the same societal pressures and stimuli
> that impose on all areas of our lives. We can never exclude thought
> from our practice ... Writing is necessary, as a creative extension
> of our work, in order to project outwards, receive feedback, and
> communicate in depth to others.
>
> (Lansley 1977: 3)

Jacky's words in the opening editorial of the first issue of *New Dance* magazine declare the genealogy of the term. New dance was about the
relations between performing, thinking and writing dance. The term
framed our awareness of a set of discourses, processes and ways of
thinking that arose out of our practice of that time. New dance was never
intended to represent an identifiable *style* of performance work.

I write in a notebook for the period 1973–9. I begin
with comments about the electricity blackouts, a
consequence of the miners' strike, and end with
details of my son's first weeks of life. Interwoven
are teaching and improvisation notes, dance class
exercises and anatomical descriptions of the bones
of the feet. There are no separations on the pages
between performance notes, Christmas shopping
lists, tasks for teaching and thoughts about re-
evaluation co-counselling. Insights about race,
class, gender and eating criss-cross the pages.
Dance technique sequences sit alongside recipes
for bread, love notes, writings on sex and passion,
my relationship with Stefan. There are snippets of
information about the X6 collective and individual
performance reviews. Angry ranting at

gynaecologists mixes with arrogant philosophical
statements. Each page contains lists, large
writing, tiny writing, circled phrases, underlined
words, divided off sections and gaps.

Art process was life experience and life experience was the art process.
London, in the 1970s, was a time of radical experiment in the arts.
Marxist feminism, psychoanalysis, postmodernism and minimalism provided theories and practices through which artists questioned Western
dance culture. We were living these theories directly, in practice, on and
through our bodies. These practices affected our lives with an immediacy
that led us to investigate the institutions, the patriarchy from which we
had rebelled. They led us to an inquiry of hierarchical systems of production. We were not a system; we had all exited systems and we were
creating a non-system. We were defining the change in order to survive,
to survive from all our ex-systems. Stefan Szczelkun, artist and writer,
was a frequent collaborator at X6, working on *New Dance* magazine and
taking part in events. He remembers:

> There was a sense that we were radically challenging culture, society
> and ourselves with these events. This was the counter culture – the
> beginnings as we saw it then, of a new alternative society. Our efforts
> were imbued with tremendous hope, optimism and utopian zeal.[1]
>
> (Szczelkun 2002: 17)

I wrote in *New Dance* magazine that the cultural movement of new dance
emerged through the creative relations that each dance artist made
to the social, cultural, environmental and economic context/climate
within which they were working: I wrote that the new was the now
(Claid 1977). So new dance, to me, was about ways of connecting things,
a generic label for work that emerged within socio-economic conditions;
work that simultaneously connected, reflected, shifted and created new
cultures for dance.

Foucault (1969) re-figures the histories of the great European systems
of thought (medicine, madness, law and psychology):

> What are they? How can they be defined or limited? What distinct
> types of laws can they obey? What articulation are they capable of?
> What sub-groups can they give rise to? What specific phenomena
> do they reveal in the field of discourse?
>
> (Foucault 1969: 29)

Foucault

This is a set of questions that aptly parallels our questioning of dance conventions at X6. Re-writing events, Foucault speaks of the 'unities', the meta-systems of power that construct the bodies over which they have power. He goes on to speak of a different construction of a 'unity' as a cluster of discourses that will be founded not on 'the constitution of a single horizon of objectivity' (Foucault 1969: 36), but rather

> the interplay of the rules that make possible the appearance of objects during a given period of time. The unity of the discourses . . . would be the interplay of the rules that define the transformations of these different objects, their non-identity through time, the break produced in them, the internal discontinuity that suspends their permanence.
>
> (Foucault 1969: 36)

Thinking of new dance in this way holds it away from being identified as a particular style or technique of dancing, defining it instead within a wider and political framework as a range of movement forms and performance activities crossing styles and disciplines.

As we sat around our X6 table drinking tea, liberation, not new dance, was the term that drew us together. Liberation from fixed forms and structures was our key to making performance. Whether the performance works were minimalist, parody, autobiographical, inter-disciplinary, traditional, ballet or contact improvisation, men dancing together or women dancing together – the attention to liberation from convention united them to new dance, not for their similarities but for their differences. We freed up any possible unity of style because that is what liberation is about.[2]

New dance, as a cluster of discourses, never intended to draw all 1970s dance experiments under one roof nor reduce them to a single structure. The activities of new dance were unified by the interplay; how artists' different statements appeared and disappeared, bounced off each other according to their relations with a much broader set of cultural and political issues. New dance was a framing device for dance artists' liberation. New dance was always a becoming context, always in the moment of now, and the performance forms were influenced by our developing awareness of context and place. The dance performance and the artist's awareness of the social, cultural location within which it was constructed were crucial to the artist's formation of both. New dance is better known now as independent dance.

16 LETTING GO OF THE MIRROR

As the 1970s and 1980s fold through time into history, absorbed into documentation and categorization, there is a style of contemporary movement practice in Britain that *has* come to be called new dance – a genre of dance practice that traces its genealogy to the 1970s era. Parallel to our cathartic feminist explorations were our investigations into the performance of stylized coded dance languages, leading to re-thinking how the body moves at a deeply embodied level. We deconstructed the physical patterns of coded conventional performance techniques: ballet, contemporary dance and gymnastics. We found ourselves in a continuous process of interrogation and reappraisal, deconstruction and re-construction of the codified techniques. Our new tools with which to do this were body–mind centring, Aikido, Alexander technique and release-based knowledges.

The codified dance performance techniques have brand names such as Cecchetti (ballet), Russian ballet, Cunningham and Graham. Each training technique is also the performance form, the training being a compilation of adapted phrases of movement from already performed and dated choreographies. Dancers learn each technique by embodying the external representation of the performed language. These are the mirror-reflected languages, working from the external images to the internal kinaesthetic. In contrast, body–mind techniques focus on the internal anatomy of the body where there is no externally constructed performance form as such. Studying Cecchetti ballet or Graham, depends on learning set movement designs and an external image. Body–mind techniques encourage functional, anatomically determined, improvised movement with an internally focused sensitivity. Our goal at X6 was to strip the performance techniques of their transcendent mannerisms to see if they could offer an efficient, healthy, empowering method for training performers. We did not intend, necessarily, to give up on these techniques, particularly ballet and gymnastics, but to re-figure the teaching of them influenced by the body–mind knowledges such as release and Alexander technique.

X6 artists practised body–mind techniques to un-fix the coded methods of training and allow our bodies a much wider range of movement possibilities for performance. We used them as pre-performance preparations for the body, as process not product, through which we could discover our individual movement vocabulary for performance.

First, we gave serious attention to letting go of balletic and gymnastic muscular tension, hyperextension of legs and arms; pulling upwards on the surface of the body, the external presentation of form, lifted chin, arched back, locked knees. Letting go required a rejection of the *desire* to be the beautiful image and all the paraphernalia that comes with external praise – a far harder challenge than letting go of the technical feats themselves. We challenged ourselves to let go of the need for outside approval and criticism; pain as a measure of correctness and articulation; formal designs and fronted shapes; the hierarchical structures embodied in the techniques themselves and the emphasis on static pose and two-dimensional fronted movement. Mary Prestidge wrote about her teaching at X6 and her methodology for re-thinking the process for achieving the handstand:

> I found far greater pleasure in the process of getting to the handstand than in achieving the handstand itself. I was less inspired with teaching people to do tricks and more with the qualities and subtleties of moving that could be achieved. I have found a way to rotate my body 180 degrees from one vertical plane through the horizontal and back to the vertical with the minimum amount of muscular strength and tension . . . First of all I attend to the hands and wrists. I often use another surface, the floor or wall to sensitise and activate those areas. This usually develops into 'padding' on all fours which sends the weight pouring from the tail along the spine and into the arms. Freeing and supporting the pelvis in this way is a start to feeling what it's like to be upside down.
>
> (Prestidge 1999: 67)

Fergus Early had already begun re-thinking ballet before X6 began. In the early 1970s he taught ballet to contemporary dancers at the London School of Contemporary Dance:

> As a teacher I had to work out what would make sense for some one who did not want to be a ballet dancer. This was quite a challenge as ballet is so much about wanting to be a ballet dancer. I was finding the things that could be construed as good for the body, rather than fitting the particular aesthetic model. I wanted to find a way that was not overly rhetorical or stylistic, stripped back so the technique could apply elsewhere and make sense to people who wanted to dance in another way. At the same time I wanted to give them something that was ballet.
>
> (Early 2003)

Re-thinking a performance technique such as ballet or gymnastics was based on a hypothesis: if it was possible to re-learn the basic body–mind pedestrian actions of everyday life through the application of a technique such as Alexander, then it must be possible to re-learn the fundamentals essential to the language of ballet through the same method. We re-learnt how to sit, stand, roll over, crawl, hold a pen, walk and run. We then drew certain elements from the body–mind techniques and applied them to re-thinking the basics of ballet such as the turnout of the legs, lifted extensions, linearity, upward flow, jumping and turning, and pointed feet.

By applying body–mind techniques, it became possible to strip the ballet language of its performance mannerisms. Focusing on the anatomical framework and directional pathways of the body rather than on muscular tension to execute movements, artists at X6 developed a new system of teaching and practising ballet that did not harm our bodies.

Stripped of its external affectations and ways of learning, ballet, with its technical strategies, provides a balanced, intelligent way to train the body. It offers a wide range of movement through using the vertical stance and the turn out of the legs. The emphasis in the training on strengthening and lengthening the legs and feet provides the dancer with an ability to jump high in the air. The lift of weight out of the hips facilitates fast, intricate footwork and the ease to travel fast through space. Co-ordinated use of legs and arms around an upright spine allows for a still centre, and economy of movement that is precise and clearly defined.

Alternatively, body–mind techniques provide the dancer with downward skills: flying horizontally through the air, catching another body while falling to the ground, working upside down, balancing on hands and head rather than always on the feet, dancing from an awareness of the balance of bones and joints rather than the muscles, and an economic efficient use of energy. Intelligent focus is given to the in-betweens, the flow and the gaps between fixed identifiable images.

There were no mirrors at X6 so we had to let go of external images. Re-working the language of ballet at X6 required each of us to re-claim an intelligence and philosophy about the language, not to be reliant on outside judgement. We aimed to achieve a quality of upward line through knowledge of Alexander technique, a fluidity of movement through release technique, a balanced spine and co-ordination through body–mind centring. We re-worked the duet form and partnered lifts through contact improvisation. Where previously we had picked up our legs and arms using hyper-extensive muscle tension, we re-learnt how to lift our limbs drawing on the power of gravity. We figured out how to move

Figure 7 Eva Karczag (1996).
Photographer: Nienka Terpsma.

fast while remaining still in the centre and to stand still while listening to fast-moving internal action. We learnt to be economic with movement, clearing away excessive tension and exaggerated gesture. Our aim was to redefine clarity, precision and articulation of detail, re-discovering them through listening to internal body intelligence rather than depending on an external master. We inhabited mirror-reflected languages, removing them from their externally focused performance forms. As an achievement of the 1970s research, ballet became a generic technique alongside those of body–mind centring, an efficient, bodily economic pre-performance training for dancers. Letting go of the mirror we became real people, with back, front and sides, thinking dance movement from the inside out.

X6 artists were not alone. Influential in the development of these crucial shifts in dance practice was the movement philosophy at Dartington College of Arts in the UK. The head of the dance department was Mary Fulkerson. Mary came to Britain from the University of Illinois. She invited visiting artists from the USA to work with her students. Among these artists were Steve Paxton, Lisa Nelson, Simone Forti and Trisha Brown. These practitioners introduced post-modern dance methodologies – minimalism, chance procedures, improvisation, the use of pedestrian movement and timing, release technique, contact improvisation, and body–mind centring – familiar to the context of Judson Church in the 1960s. Emphasis was directed towards 'the center of the body (the torso), the weight and momentum or energy flow of the body, and the ability to lose one's balance, to fall off the vertical' (Novack 1990: 129). With an emphasis on somatic study, Fulkerson developed teaching methods that aimed at clearing away habits and mannerisms, releasing muscle tension, working with breath, stillness and internal imagery rather than external posturing. The work allowed each student to find authentic physical movement and from there allowed her/him to develop a personal movement vocabulary.

Working with improvisation rather than set material, the emerging movement forms read as non-linear, fragmented, fluid and weighted downwards: movements that are physically sensual to perform rather than, as in ballet, metaphorically sexual to watch (Novack 1990). Employing Mary Fulkerson's movement direction and that of the visiting staff, students aligned, co-ordinated, balanced, strengthened and conditioned their bodies. The training worked at a deep unconscious level, influencing basic pedestrian movements of the body before the adoption of any particular performance-driven style of training. This training opened the space for human-ness to re-emerge. Kirstie Simson talks about the role of 'honesty' in practising body–mind work:

> The work is in opening to what is genuine. In this state of openness the joy comes through, the sensuality and passionate energy emerges. It began when I was in Steve Paxton's workshop at Dartington in the 70s. It was the 2nd class and it was like a spiritual revelation. I realised that everything I needed to perform was already in me, that I didn't need to continue down that well-worn track of training in the dance world, to try and match someone, to fix a technique. The intelligence was already in me.
>
> (Simson 2003)

Many practitioners working in the UK, including Laurie Booth, Yolande Snaith, Rosemary Butcher, Richard Alston, Sue MacLennan, Eva Karczag, Kathy Krick, Kirstie Simson, Miranda Tufnell, Dennis Greenwood, Gaby Agis and Kevin Finnen, worked with Mary Fulkerson. An articulate, careful, imaginative and intelligent teacher, she helped craft the direction of emerging choreographers in the 1980s.

Rosemary Butcher trained for three years at Dartington. Her prolific body of work, ranging from *Landings* (1977) to *Inner Voices* (2004), consistently reveals the performing body as anatomical presence undertaking movement achieved through internal kinaesthetic attention to the task: 'What I have to offer must be purely in a task form and they [the dancers] must use that task and move in their own way in order to achieve the sort of results I want' (Butcher cited in Crickmay 1986: 10).

Analysis of Butcher's early work is more likely to discuss the structure and the architectural use of space, than the externally expressive presence of the performer: 'Lines, circles, spirals, diagonals, squares, corners, edges, directions, dimensions, are a constant feature of the choreographic language' (Crickmay 1986: 11).

These elements took precedence over any concern for illusion, fantasy or seductive relations between performer and spectator. Architectural and visual space between bodies came into focus for the spectators; bodies were defined 'by' rather than 'in' space. Butcher's performers consciously resisted conventional elements of timing, narrative, suspension, climax and repetition and the I-see-you relations between themselves and spectators.

As Alexander, contact improvisation, release and body–mind centring were incorporated into movement forms for performance so the new thinking dancer and new dance style emerged. They emerged as dancing that appears as a non-linear, non-spectacular, non-hierarchical, improvisational, loose-limbed, internally focused, release-based and pedestrian-informed movement language. I say a new dance style – but this is more of a non-style style. Not exactly a formless-ness in movement; rather, a rejection of fixed conventions of space/time forms, a non-form form.

Sue MacLennan is another choreographer whose work has also been informed by training with Mary Fulkerson. MacLennan's *Venus Hurtle* (1990) has seven bodies working in different groupings: solos, duets and group sections. As choreography derived from improvisation, each body has an individual language of eccentric gestures, a clear but always understated sense of humour. Each dancer is focused to the internal body–mind work, yet each body's external expression of this work is different, sharp and quirky, or fluid and fractured.

I watch explosions of hurtling off-centred movement; dancers scattering throughout the space. As each movement is performed, it sets off reactions in other performers' bodies, producing continually shifting patterns and changing directions. Something in one space sets off something elsewhere; bodies bump, crash, push, lift and fall. Movement is unpredictable, catches me by surprise and breaks the expected formal codes of choreography. Bodies move in many different directions and are always in the process of change. Before one movement is complete, another has begun. An elbow lifts, knees fall, a foot circles, hands clasp, a back tilts – all in fast succession – then a sudden stop, complete stillness. Bodies pause in strange quirky poses, then re-embark on journeys that go nowhere in particular. There are no straight lines, no grand statements and no linear narrative: movement tickles; it goes nowhere and everywhere. But there are minuscule fragments of narrative in each meeting between the dancers, as one body balances for a breath of stillness on the thigh of another. I am aware of the shapes of the spaces between bodies and how these spaces are filled and emptied.

As the key to discovering individual interpretations of movement language, new dancers look inwards to the body and outwards to the intelligence of improvisation. Performers listen to anatomical and muscular workings of their bodies while making decisions in time and space. Here, improvisation is a spontaneous putting together of arbitrary things and letting them go again. Improvisation releases the fixed sediment trapped between body and mind. The first step towards improvisation is the ability to get lost (Paxton 2001). Getting lost requires courage. Courage overcomes fear. Overcoming fear trusts the body's intelligence. Trusting the body's intelligence is listening to the body. Listening opens the space for play. Opening the space for play allows for the imaginary to surface. The imaginary is the body's key to improvisation. Improvisation in performance offers a performer and spectator a unique sense of self. A self in immediate relation to others is about presence in the world.[1]

X6 Dance Space and Dartington, as two experimental dance environments in the 1970s and 1980s, travelled on paths with identifiably different but parallel trajectories, exchanging ideologies and knowledge. X6 was a research laboratory for professional artists creating a political framework for emerging subversive performance work. At Dartington, Mary Fulkerson was providing movement training for students across the disciplines. At X6, we worked outwards from conventional dance forms to explore dance in relation to other disciplines. Students at Dartington, a cross-disciplinary arts college, were looking inwards to a study of movement that could inform theatre, music and visual performance. The focus at X6 was not on training beginners, for its artists were already professionally trained, but rather on employing person-as-political strategies to re-figure each performer's practice. The X6 experiment involved dance artists who were re-thinking their bodies while Dartington was training emerging artists who were thinking their dancing bodies for the first time. For artists at X6, re-thinking dance was a feminist, political statement, necessary and urgent, stripping away dance and life patterns in order to go forward. For artists from Dartington, such as Laurie Booth and Yolande Snaith, dance was the initial and innovative development of a personal movement language and aesthetic.

Undoubtedly, Dartington and X6 influenced each other. The ideas and artists in both contexts met and merged through the Dartington Festivals (1978–87) that took place each spring. X6 artists were invited to show work and lead discussions at these events. Dartington offered body–mind techniques; X6 offered a political, feminist context for new performance work. Dartington was influenced by American post-modern minimalism in the visual arts and eastern philosophies; X6 was framed by European theatrical traditions. X6 provided a London venue for guest teachers and performers from Dartington, where their work could be seen and shared through workshops and performances. Mary Fulkerson and Steve Paxton were frequent visitors to X6. In 1978, the X6 collective invited Steve Paxton to run the first London contact improvisation workshop. He wrote a letter of confirmation asking participants to practice 'forward and backward rolls done very gently' prior to the workshop and to wear 'loose cotton clothing, bare feet' (Paxton 1978).

X6 and Dartington shared three main objectives. One, to establish the dance artist as subject of her/his own work, foregrounding the choreographer as performer explosion of the independent dance scene in the 1980s and 1990s. Two, both contexts were developing a different aesthetic, one that moved away from the upward thrust towards the downward fall of weight. Three, to open up the boundaries of what might be defined as dance, to include site-specific performance, performance art, time-based visual performance and cross-disciplinary collaboration.

17 FIGURES OF *JOUISSANCE*

As a practice, I call non-linear, improvisational multi-directional, non-fixed movement '*jouissance* dancing'.

Jouissance is a challenging term to define. It is a term drawn from psychoanalytic/French feminist/post-structuralist theory, which describes something that goes beyond Freud's definition of the pleasure principle, whereby 'the psyche seeks the lowest possible level of tension. "*Jouissance*" transgresses this law and, in that respect, it is *beyond* the pleasure principle' (Lacan 1979: 281). The term refers to the fluid, formless, multiple, semiotic drives internal to the body as sensation.

Academically, I am playing provocatively here – intentionally. *Jouissance* is unrepresentable in language (Lacan 1979); it is formless, semiotic, internally erotic, pleasurable and infantile; it is internal to the body before language. If so, then how can I apply it to a dancer's body as a 'style' or expression? I do so as an analogy, to give imagery to a performing/watching relationship that cannot be fixed. I do so as a performer, remembering improvising dancing in the 1970s, attending to internal somatic sensations of dancing. I do so in writing, with a subsequent acknowledgement and perception of that dancing through feminist and post-feminist eyes. I remember that space of moving, between real and representation, between breathing and imagination, between being and playing, and between moving and thinking. I apply the term to the pleasurable sensation of dancing with the least physical tension that creates unfixable images in time and space – yet they were experienced and observed. I use the term *jouissance* to describe this dancing because when I encountered *The Laugh of the Medusa* (Cixous 1981) for the first time; when I read Kristeva's (1984) understanding of *jouissance* and semiotic forces; when I discovered Irigaray's *This Sex Which Is Not One* (1985), my body took an immediate, almost instinctive flight back to my new dance body. The dancing, the watching, the reading and writing are interwoven. I apply the term positively, to the dancing that instigated the vital shift that took place in the 1970s away from the fixed perspectives of formal patterns on the body and between bodies. I use the term to describe a physical sensational imagination at play internal to our dancing bodies – attending to an inward focus rather than a focus out. I use the term because of the challenge to articulate the feminine imaginary, described by Irigaray as 'a proper(ty) that is never fixed in the possible identity-to-self of some form or other. It is always fluid' (Irigaray 1985: 79). The male imaginary is described as linear, rational and pertaining to self-identity, while the feminine imaginary, the unconscious of Western thought, is perpetually yet to be realized (Whitford 1991).

Irigaray's feminist philosophy purposely brings the previously unrecognized real, sexual female body into philosophical discourse in order to disrupt that discourse. She describes the diffusible, multiple, fluid nature of female sexuality and imagination, which is separate from, and different to, the solidity and finality of male sexuality and rationality represented by phallocentric language (Irigaray 1985).

Familiar to gender studies students is Irigaray's (in)famous image of the two lips. As a metaphor for defining female sexuality, Irigaray's two lips illustrate how there is no single identity for female sexuality, no beginning or end, no definitive point between one or two or many erogenous zones. The image aims to dispel the myth that defines female sexuality as being located solely in vaginal penetration, as being one and the same as male sexuality: 'It is continuous, compressible, dilatable, viscous, conductible, diffusible . . . that it allows itself to be easily traversed by flow by virtue of its conductivity to currents coming from other fluids or exerting pressure through the walls of a solid' (Irigaray 1985: 111).

Julia Kristeva's writing concerns the emergence of semiotic drives within symbolic forms, closely linking the real body to language and therefore to art practice. Her notion of the semiotic suggests pre-linguistic, pre-Oedipal, multiple sexual drives, which are non-representational. These exist in the child before separation from the mother's body, before identification as a subject, before its entrance into the world of language and representation. Kristeva animates a notion of the semiotic as 'an anarchic, formless circulation of sexual impulses and energies traversing the child's body *before* sexuality is ordered' (Grosz 1989: 43). These drives of *jouissance* also signify as feminine and maternal. For Kristeva, they precede the unified binary oppositional structures and hierarchical structures of symbolic representation. She asserts that the pleasure-seeking semiotic drives, which return in adult life as a surge of *jouissance*, impassion the symbolic paternal language:

> Art – this semiotization of the symbolic . . . represents the flow of jouissance into language. Whereas sacrifice assigns jouissance its productive limit in the social and symbolic order, art specifies the means – the only means – that jouissance harbours for infiltrating that order.
>
> (Kristeva 1984: 80)

Cixous explores an expression of feminine pleasure in her writing that is more than orgasmic, as a kind of corporeal non-genital multiple pleasure:

> Almost everything is yet to be written by women about femininity: about their sexuality, that is, its infinite and mobile complexity, about their eroticization, sudden turn-ons of a certain miniscule-immense area of their bodies; not about destiny, but about the adventure of such and such a drive, about trips, crossings, trudges, abrupt and gradual awakenings, discoveries of a zone at one time timorous and soon to be forthright.[1]
>
> (Cixous 1981: 256)

Cixous' writing is described as 'open and multiple, varied and rhythmic, full of pleasures and, perhaps more importantly, of possibilities' (Tong 1989: 225).[2] This description could be an analogy for new dance movement language and its non-hierarchical fluidity of phrasing, as performed and observed with joy and pleasure by male and female bodies in the work of an artist such as Sue MacLennan.

French feminist writers such as Kristeva, Irigaray and Cixous advocate a feminine imaginary to counteract that prescribed by the rationality of language. They desire, in different ways, to open the space of written language to the force of libidinal, rhythmical, anarchic drives of the pleasurable internal impulse (Grosz 1989).

Jouissance requires external sites to emerge as an expression. I am suggesting dance as one of those sites – a site that can be felt, experienced and imagined between performers and spectators but cannot be fixed. The deeply found joy of an emerging subjectivity for women and men dancing began with recognition of the embodied process/practice of *jouissance* sensation. Yes, the term is provocative, for it exists in experience yet it cannot be represented. As dancers, we took hold of the experience as subjects of the dance, yet this dancing could not be fixed, it could not be described or written down. I use the term 'figures of *jouissance*' because we found ourselves present and absent, as a subject within and without of language: 'Violent silence, instinctual drive, collided void; and back again – the path of jouissance' (Kristeva 1980: 179).

A physical inner force of imagination erupts through the dancer's body to influence the movement, creating dancing that is multiple, fractured, varied and non-hierarchical. Moving in this way, the inside becomes the outside. Dancing involves a process of un-learning, making gaps, allowing an effervescence of *jouissance* to flow through, rather than a process of constructing a stylized play of surface illusions. Listening internally, the *jouissance* dance performer negates outward projection. The language and the dancer's body converge through a vulnerability, formless-ness and anatomical intelligence.

We, both men and women, were returning to a pre-lingual movement quality and physicality but with the knowledge of language. There was a flip side. For women, *jouissance* dancing was a 'pharmakon' (Derrida 1981), a term of '*differance*', a remedy and a poison for performer–spectator relations of presence. This new dancing gave and denied us agency, feeding subjectivity and invisibility. Later, but not yet, I shall pin down this dilemma.

18 K/NO/W BODY OF ILLUSION: SEDUCTION IN REVERSE

vorgotar

I wrote earlier of the seductive relations in the conventions of ballet, working through the oscillating play of the illusive surface and real body of a performer's presence. The illusion (the technically formed geometric body) engages spectators by a suggestion of the real, teasing without revealing, evoking possible meanings for the spectator while the real identity of the performer remains a secret. The desire to search the illusive surface for the meaning of the secret on the part of the spectator and the performer's skill in presenting a surface appearance as a secret that never reveals its contents, sets the scene for ballet's seductive hold over its patrons.

The new dancer turns all this around. New dance switches seductive relations between performer and spectator into reverse mode whereby the spectator remembers, and simultaneously rejects the illusion, which becomes an absence on the real body of the performer. The work initiates an era in dance when knowledge of convention informs the absence of convention in the work.

In the 1970s, as performers and as spectators, we radically re-thought the expectations of performance. At the Dartington Festivals, I watched for hours while dancers rolled slowly or walked endlessly backwards and forwards across the vast grass lawns, focusing internally on the act of rolling and walking. I watched because it was necessary to watch, because presenting the slow roll, as a statement in time and space, was a radical re-education for the performers and myself as spectator, and was a practice of un-learning time and space for performers and spectators. As we understood the emergence of the practice, we re-figured the practice of watching.

Together, performers and spectators broke habits and predictable patterns of moving and watching:

> There's a lot of debate about how contact improvisation can be performance. Well it can't, in that your focus is so *in*; when you are working really fast with someone, you have to deal with that person around you. There are elements of virtuosity that can be seen, but the intimacy of the touch that you have between you is so inward, presence, as such, doesn't come across. But at the same time, that engagement with the body – and the engagement with sensation – for me are important in performance.
>
> (Prestidge 2003)

The practice of contact improvisation in performance prompts Sally Banes (1977: 18) to write: 'the primary focus in the dance is the dancer's physical sensation and awareness, a focus that threatens to remove the work from the realm of art altogether, by making the spectator obsolete'. Cynthia Novack (1990: 47) sums it up as she contrasts social dance with post-modern minimalist theatre dancing in New York in the 1960s: 'everyone would go to a dance concert to watch people stand around, and then afterwards everyone would go to a party and dance'.

Significant to the movement experiment of American artists at Judson Church in the 1960s is Yvonne Rainer's 'strategy for denial' (1965) as a manifesto for American post-modern minimalist dance performance: 'No to spectacle no to virtuosity no to transformations and magic and make-believe no to the glamour and transcendency of the star image no to the heroic' (Rainer 1965: 178).

The 'manifesto' was written by Rainer as a response to her particular performance, *Some Sextexts . . .* (1965). It was not her intention at the time to write a manifesto or to make any kind of a universal statement about post-modern dance (Rainer 2003). Encouraged by her challenge to the presence of illusion, artists began to cultivate performer–spectator relations based on a denial of seduction. The post-modern performance culture cultivated a specific audience away from the conventions of the theatre towards galleries, studio spaces and site-specific venues more often associated with the visual arts. In this specifically white Western art context, engaging with *absence*, as presence, became the key to performer–spectator relations.

Rainer's *Trio A* (1966), is claimed as the signal work for 'the entire post-modern dance' movement (Banes 1977: 4).[1] Rainer rejected the always out-of-reach qualities of the ballerina's presence, and the deep and meaningful expressive-ness of modern dance. Instead, she opted for a neutral body in action, the revealed, non-mysterious subject of the dance. One section of *Trio A* consists of a four-and-a-half-minute solo composed of pedestrian movement, task-like actions and broken lines, 'violating nearly every canon of classical dance conventions' (Banes 1977: 44). The emphasis was given to the physical dynamics of an active anatomical body rather than to the conventions of narrative, climax and virtuosity. These were rejected in favour of an anti-metaphorical pedestrian language. When she made the piece, Rainer challenged herself not to repeat, not to make variations, never to look out front, but instead to democratize her body and to deal with her body's weight. Gestures were made into minimal tasks; for instance, 'left hand pulls right arm and head looks to knee' (Rainer 2003). Similar to the practice of t'ai chi, the most challenging aspect of performing *Trio A* is in learning how *not* to attack the movements, allowing one movement to dissolve out of the one before. The effect is one of 'unmodulated continuity' without 'playing to the overt spectacle of watching' (Rainer 2003).

Post-modern minimalist dancing runs as water through the fingers of post-structuralist theorists such as Deleuze and Guattari (1988), who offer enticing analogies for dancing bodies and the feminist quest for subjectivity in performance. Their propositions focus on overturning all theoretical models that claim desire to be predicated on lack. Their spirited controversial discussions rebel against state philosophy, against psychoanalysis and the death wish, against Marxism, against organized movements, identities and subject/object binaries. Their idea of a 'Body without Organs' (BwO), together with motifs, such as becoming, nomadic thought, planes of consistency, smooth plateaux of immanence, rhizome networks and assemblages, well describe the post-modern dance experiments. The motifs intrigue; they refuse identity as a single truth and they offer creative potential for transference, networking and connections to other events and mediums. BwO is described as a set of practices, not a concept; a body in a state of change; an experiment that is unfixed, unrooted, always moving, always on the way somewhere; a body in the practice of desiring: 'You never reach the Body without Organs, you can't reach it, you are forever attaining it, it is a limit (Deleuze and Guattari 1988: 150). We are informed, as readers, that we have one, make one, cannot desire without one, but to recognize its practice we must let go of 'the three great strata concerning us . . . the organism, significance and subjectification' that bind us, stopping the free networking of movement between bodies (Deleuze and Guattari 1988: 159).

Similarly intriguing are the concepts of rhizome networks and becomings. A rhizome, as a horizontal network, 'connects any point to any other point. It has no beginning nor end, but always a middle from which it grows and which it overspills' (Deleuze and Guattari 1988: 90). Becoming evokes movements of bodies as a process of transmuting, making, doing, trans-crossing, never being, always on a journey with no final destination, junctions of creative change. A BwO is an attractive analogy to apply to post-modern minimalist dance. As Yvonne Rainer says of her own *Trio A* (1966):

> One of the most singular elements in it is that there are no pauses between phrases. The phrases themselves often consist of separate parts . . . but the end of each phrase merges immediately into the

beginning of the next with no observable accent. The limbs are never in a fixed, still relationship . . . creating the impression that the body is constantly engaged in transitions.

(Rainer 1968, cited in Copeland and
Cohen 1983: 329)

To appreciate *Trio A*, to engage with the practice of BwO, requires prior knowledge of the 'great strata' of conventions that this piece shakes loose and overturns. In other words, to appreciate the piece and its minimalist pedestrian approach to presence, spectators must buy into the deconstruction and reconfiguration of dance language for performance from a place of knowledge. The *Trio A* performer is what I like to call a 'k/no/w body of illusion'. In other words, the *Trio A* performer is watched by spectators who know what she is not doing. As the work continues to be performed, the *Trio A* dancer engages with artists and spectators who know the history, context and source of the choreography, audiences who seek out an alternative to conventional seduction in performance. They know what came before and reject it. The engagement with watching *Trio A* is through my (the spectator's) deconstruction of the classic text on the dancer's body rather than the dancer's dazzling virtuosic ability to impress. The *Trio A* performer becomes engaging as she diffuses the metaphysical properties, negating stylized, coded language and transcendent representation of the human body.

Within this context of k/no/wledgeable engagement, the *Trio A* dancer seduces her spectator by a reverse strategy. The real/illusion strategy for seduction is turned inside out. In ballet, I watch the surface illusion for glimpses of the real body. Watching *Trio A*, I search the real body for glimpses of the performed surface of illusion – which is present only in its absence, in my memory. *Trio A* opposes the convention so radically that it draws attention to the convention's absence. I find myself watching *Trio A* for glimpses of the (absent) universally recognizable virtuosity of Western dance. In this way, Western dance audiences engage with the performed illusion, where the performed illusion recalls itself through its absence – in memory. The k/no/w body of illusion – as a figure of *jouissance*, as the post-modern minimalist experiment, as the reversal of seductive strategy – questions the habitual codes of performer–spectator relations in dance performance.

Performer–choreographer Eva Karczag was a visitor to X6 in the 1970s, having worked with Jacky Lansley and Richard Alston in Strider Dance Company (1971). She went on to work with Trisha Brown. Her work is influenced by improvisation and Alexander technique.[2] Returning to London in 1997, she performed the solo *Anemomenotactic*

Orientation (1997) at the Dance Umbrella Festival. She evoked an engaging presence for me as a k/no/w body of illusion.

I watch her in *Anemomenotactic Orientation*. Eva appears, running out from the front of the auditorium onto the bare stage, dressed in a flowing cotton tunic over loose trousers. She runs to upstage centre, turns and runs down the centre line to stop directly in front of the audience. Eva's feet are bare and she wears no make-up. The stage is lit with open studio lighting. She looks directly out front. She is not actively engaging with the audience, she embodies the task of looking with her attention concentrated to the moment of listening:

> My father had introduced me to these particular Scarlatti piano sonatas. The piece was tracking my personal journey, from a close use of music and a more 'formal' way of moving and using the space in the first section, to music acting as an emotional trigger in the second, to a play between music and silence, where movement becomes more quirky, and music and dance run parallel and influential, but not entirely intimate in the third, to the sound of moving, mostly in darkness, in the last.
>
> (Karczag 2005)

She dances, incorporating tiny loose-limbed gestures of isolated body parts, expansive waves of movement combined with running in wide circles with abrupt stops. There is a long, slow section performed in silence close to the floor, incorporating rolling, sitting, crawling and stillness, where Eva delicately and precisely positions her body, arms and hands in specific yet non-heroic poses.

Eva's presence was vulnerable, honest, with no illusive surface to hide behind. She rejected stylized glamour, feminine fetish, make-up, jewellery and tight-fitting clothes. She refused evocative smiles, the tilt of the head, frivolous gestures. I was invited to watch her as if she was in a studio practising, not performing. There was an intimacy of familiarity, of shared understanding, of taking part in an experiment. She was sharing with me what she did every day in the studio. Her performance collapsed the conventional real/illusive seductive space between spectator and performer with a style of non-performing real body presence. The real body of Eva became the language performed. As I watched her dance; I identified with the pedestrian actions, her internal concentration on task. Simultaneously, I was seduced by the gap of what was not there in performance. This was the gap left by the absence of stylized, codified vocabulary and performed expression; it was a gap full of promise, an absence of presence. I was seduced by the k/no/w body of illusive presence between us. Yet, in writing this, I am drawn up against the different perspectives of performer and spectator. For Eva, the work was not one of absence but of being physically present with her whole body–mind in the moment now. Her full attention to the task evoked the ambiguity of a k/no/w body of illusion.

19 DERRIDA'S PRESENTS

As a spectator, performer and writer of new dance I am intrigued by the dichotomy between being there and not being there – the seduction of presence as absence. It is not possible to speak of absence and presence without bringing the philosopher, Jacques Derrida, into the performing space. Post-structuralist theories and dance performance might seem an odd collaboration. The theory attends to that which is not apparent within a text, while dancers inhabit bodies that exist in time and space. Post-structuralist ideas are romantic in their dissociation from embodiment and my mind dances its own imagination. It is easy to forget I have a body that articulates through physical practice when my imagination is caught up in the seduction of 'becoming'. But perhaps because post-structuralist theory slips through the gaps of material identity, it submits itself to manipulation as a way to watch and write about new dance performance.[1]

Derrida's attention to presence and absence appears in his deconstruction of classic texts. He deconstructs Plato's *Phaedrus*, exposing the logocentric bias of speech over writing (Derrida 1981). Plato's writings are important to Derrida as they inaugurate the metaphysical approach to presence and origin that, with its bias on the spoken rather than written word, has passed down through the history of Western thought. First of all, Derrida establishes how metaphysical logic assumes that speech, not the written word, provides access, through the speaker speaking, to the presence, soul and essence of the speaker. Then Derrida reveals how 'Plato is inescapably condemned to writing, even as he seeks to denounce its effects and uphold the authority of self-present (spoken) truth' (Norris 1987: 33).

In other words, only through speaking can presence be acknowledged to exist, but only through writing can speaking be preserved. Only through representation does presence exist. Writing represents presence

in its absence. Writing and speaking function by a process of differing and deferring, where the notion of presence 'sustains itself by differing
from itself and that, as such, presence is always deferred' (Kearney 1994:
119).

'*Differance*' becomes an open-ended play of meanings in language
(before definition and preceding identity). Here, presence becomes a goal
rather than an origin and is a presence that can only define itself by its
absence, its representation in language. As such, it becomes a goal that
can never be attained. Because presence or truth is always deferred,
Derrida suggests that Plato is persistently drawn to search for it, to search
through the writing for the ultimate truth of presence. So presence
re-stimulates the desire for itself:

> Only words that are deferred, reserved, enveloped, rolled up . . . only
> hidden letters can thus get Socrates moving. If a speech could be
> genuinely present . . . offered up in person in its truth, without the
> detours of a signifier foreign to it, if at the limit an undeferred logos
> were possible, it would not seduce anyone.
>
> (Derrida 1981: 71)

So, what are the parallels here for performer–spectator relations in
dance? Derrida's writing attends to a deconstruction of classic texts
revealing the impossibility of a single truth or presence. He is engaged
by the play between truth and non-truth. For spectators that know
the classic dance convention, Eva Karczag's performance provides the
deconstructed text that Derrida seeks. Her dance presented me with
an absence of the single truth of the classic dance text. I am engaged by
this absence, reading multiple thoughts, meanings and identities into
that absent presence. Compared to watching ballet, her performance
engages me through a reverse strategy of seduction.

Thirty-five years after *Trio A* is conceived, the post-modern strategy
of denial as a seductive play of absent presence is still going strong.
I watch Jonathan Burrows and Jan Ritsema perform *Weak Dance Strong
Questions* (2001). They meander about the performance space at the
Institute of Contemporary Arts in London as we, the Dance Umbrella
audience, enter. They are dressed in casual trousers, T-shirts and shoes.
The stage is stripped of theatrical trappings, brightly lit with non-
theatrical working lights; the seats are arranged intimately in a half circle.
Jonathan explains that they are going to work for 50 minutes and then
the performance will end.

Jonathan and Jan start moving. Jonathan walks backwards and stum-
bles over his own feet, creating a clumsy limping effect as he walks.

He begins a step, hesitates, changes direction before completion, and pauses mid-movement before reaching any identifiable line or position. Each arm gesture is unfinished, undefined, never resembling a recognizable style or extended image. The movement language is stripped of climactic phrasing and expressive depth, shifting away from a stylized performance presentation towards pedestrian movement. On a surface level, Jonathan's image resembles that of a drunken man emerging from a pub, stumbling and bumbling in a non-articulate manner around Jan. The two men rarely acknowledge one another in an empty space. Yet the work is thought-provoking, precise and intelligent. I am engaged with Jonathan's presence more for what I know is not there than what is there.

Jonathan is intent on embodying pedestrian, task-like, non-performed movements, actions that draw attention to an empty space of presence. But the emptiness carries the fullness of his history. He performs this piece now, at a certain point on a long journey and after many years of performing with The Royal Ballet, independent choreographers and as author of his work. In his body memory, he carries a wide range of techniques, styles and histories. The experiment he now undertakes is in finding the spaces between identities of his own history. He inhabits negative space, where negatives provide the shadows and reversal of positives. In *Weak Dance Strong Questions*, Jonathan moves negatively in positive space; he becomes absent, unfixes his history. As spectator, I bring with me the memories of his past performances, different personae and eras of time. He rejects the full realization of ballet and conventional choreographic skill but this history reveals itself on his body. In this London-based context of independent dance, many of us who are engaged by Jonathan's stripping-away of years of layers of experience also carry our own rejection of convention. We, as spectators, are k/no/w bodies of illusion.

I see Jonathan return to a child-dance after years of technical sophistication, a return that requires intelligence and a conscious unfixing of images, working backwards in time. Jonathan's experiences as a ballet body and his skills of choreographic craft are being denied by his own body in this performance. There is nowhere else to go but towards the undoing of what has come before. For moments, I wonder if I am watching the second act of *Giselle* performed backwards or a dance without its outside shape – like talking in one's sleep, when no consonants are pronounced that might define the words. I look through Jonathan's actions for glimpses of a highly skilled virtuosity that is there as a trace.

The work triggers expectations in my watching body. As one move-ment gesture happens – perhaps a leg lifts slightly off the floor – I can feel my body expect the line to be extended to completion. As in *Trio A*, my body memory expects a particular flow of movement, but that memory is abruptly broken. Jonathan's arm gesture dissipates as he turns his torso against that flow of movement. As my intuitive body patterns are broken, so my thinking takes over. Like Derrida's 'hidden letters' that are so seductive, so Jonathan's past identity is like a secret:

> When it is the call of this secret, however, which points back to the other or to something else, when it is this itself which keeps our passion aroused, and holds us to the other, then the secret impas-sions us.[2]

> (Derrida 1995b: 29)

I am reminded of the k/no/w body of illusion in Rachel Whiteread's sculpture, *Untitled (Upstairs)* (2001), where the staircase itself is absent, yet the space around the staircase is filled, drawing attention to the stair-case in its absence. Similarly, Martin Creed's *Lights Turning On and Off* (winner of the Turner in 2001), where an entire gallery of the Tate Britain is devoted to this artwork. The gallery is empty except for the action of lights being turned off and on. I notice the vast space and the positioning of other viewers to myself. I am drawn to the Victorian architecture of the room that is empty of the artworks – an absence of presence. I am engaged by the strategy of seduction in reverse whereby I look at the real with a memory of the illusion.

Memory and imagination interweave for k/no/wing performers and spectators of new dance. Recognizable dance conventions are displaced but the memories of the dazzling spectacle remain there as echoes. The performer's denial of illusion becomes the seductive strategy in reverse for the spectator. No longer searching for the real body through the illu-sion, the spectator searches for illusions (meanings/images) through the real body.

I have this conversation with a neighbour.

What are you writing about?
  I'm writing about presence.
  Do you mean birthday or Christmas? Presents with ribbons, bows and baubles, or brown paper packages tied up with string? Precious ones? Fragile ones? Bulky, cheap or fun ones? And what

about those with curious shapes? Or those that
you don't have time to wrap? Or those that are
passed over casually, the unimportant ones? Do
you mean giving or receiving?

What I mean is performing presence.

Oh, you mean jack-in-a-box, wind-up toys, dial-a-
clown, musical boxes with ballerinas that go round
and round.

*No, I mean what goes on between performer and
spectator.*

Oh, you don't mean real presents then?

Well, yes and no.

Why do you want to write about it?

*Good question. Because presence is a wrapped-
up secret, the pleasure is in the unwrapping.*

But if you unwrap a secret it's no longer there.

Maybe.

20 PARALLEL EMERGENCES

The feminist, post-modern attention to the absence of presence was a
white privilege – the consequence of a white inquiry and experimenta-
tion, a re-figuring of presence in a white, Western post-Enlightenment
crisis of identity. But the absence of presence is not necessarily a
destabilizing or a weakening of white supremacy. In a sense, the attention to absence strengthens white elitism by making power invisible.
White elitism perpetuates itself through its own invisibility, having pre-
established itself as a universal identity to make invisible: 'Whites must
be seen to be white, yet whiteness as race resides in invisible properties
and whiteness as power is maintained by being unseen' (Dyer 1997: 45).

In parallel to the post-modern, feminist liberation concerns of white
artists in the 1970s was the emergence of the voices of British black
contemporary dance artists. However, the 1970s feminist, post-modern
liberation movement did not necessarily speak for African, African–
Caribbean and South Asian artists – particularly in regard to the issue
of subjectivity and identity. As black and white dance artists, we worked

in parallel to each other with love and respect, but our agendas were also different. Black artists strove for *visibility* as practitioners of a range of different black dance forms – within the same European culture that white artists were attempting to reject. While white artists were busy rejecting the European aesthetics and colonial heroism of dance culture, black British artists were working to establish individual and different identities of presence that would be recognized within that context.

Each year at stage school, Madame choreographs my solo for the 'national dance' category of dance competitions. The solos supposedly represent national dance from a plethora of nations: Armenia, Egypt, Mexico, Spain, Portugal, Italy or Russia. Naturally, Russian dances are conveniently split between court dances and folk dances, though there is no mention of the difference or the Russian Revolution of 1917. Madame's inspired, Westernized appropriations are drawn from her own experience of the exotic dances that she performed during her time with the Ballets Russes. The dances I learn are not different dances, each with its own code, technique, rituals, history, aesthetic and performer–spectator relations. No, Madame creates an 'in-the-style-of' dance, where all differences of rhythm, style and language are absorbed into English stage school stiff-upper-torso dance. I perform an Egyptian dance inspired by a vase, with feet turned out ever so beautifully. I win. I am invited to attend classes given by the South Asian dancer Ram Gopal but African dance forms are never mentioned. These dances are deemed to develop (along with horse riding, swimming and skiing) the wrong muscles for the white dancing body.

No romantic or classical ballet had attempted to subsume African dance forms into the ballet aesthetic. Even though Les Ballet Negres (1946–52) had rehearsed and performed in London, and the New York Negro Ballet had toured Britain in 1957 (Horwitz 1996), I never learnt of these events as a young dancer:

The origin of conflict here is the clash between Europeanist and
Africanist views regarding the relationship of body/mind/spirit . . .
From an Africanist perspective, a pulled-up, aligned stance and
static carriage indicate sterility and inflexibility in the performer. In
the classical Europeanist view, the movement exists to produce the
(finished) work; in the Africanist view, the work exists to produce
the movement. As assessed by Africanist aesthetic criteria, the Europeanist dancing body is rigid, aloof, cold, and one-dimensional. By
Europeanist standards, the Africanist dancing body is vulgar, comic,
uncontrolled, undisciplined, and most of all, promiscuous.

(Gottschild 1996: 9)

The white elitist rejection of black body aesthetics has perpetuated a
continual denial of black dancers into ballet companies. Brenda
Glassman became a soloist with Dance Theatre of Harlem, the first all-
black classical ballet company based in New York. She shares her
experiences of the 1960s and 1970s:

My first love was tap. But my teacher, Joyce Butler, decided other-
wise for me. She didn't see why I had to go the way of other black
dancers. She wanted me to be a classical dancer. I was the first black
student she had ever had. I auditioned for the Royal Ballet School
and was accepted. They said, 'We will take you because you have
talent and we will train you but you will never be able to join the
Royal Ballet.' Being 16 years old, I thought that's fine; let me take
what's offered. The School performance that year was the ballet
La Fille mal gardée [Frederick Ashton 1960]. Jennifer Jackson was to
do Lise and I was not chosen to take part, not even as a peasant!
My friends all questioned the fact that I was not in the performance
as they all thought I was as good or better than a lot of those chosen
– they didn't see me as a black person. Immediately, I remembered
that first interview. It suddenly dawned on me. My god, it's because
I am black I am not in this. As luck would have it I became fourth
understudy to a peasant and one by one people got injured and I
did the performance. I rang my mum and said, 'Mum I am going
on!' and she put on her dress and came down. She saw me dance
on the Covent Garden stage. The Royal Ballet School sent me to
The Place to study contemporary dance. They paid for me to go.
I should have been grateful but I didn't like contemporary dance.
Dance Theatre of Harlem was my lifeline. I was a real ballet girl,
I could jump and turn – but I couldn't do it in this country. Monica

Mason said that if it were the same situation now I would have been in the company like a shot.

(Glassman 2003)

Western dance forms hide their white elitism well, safeguarding their power against a number of dangerous intruders: black bodies, dark bodies, disabled bodies, sexual bodies, leaking bodies, fat bodies, wrong bodies. The hegemony of Western dance traditions is well couched in a discourse that would never

insist on the pre-eminence of the ballet tradition (or on the apposi-tional forms of American and European modern dance) but on such common sense criteria such as the pursuit of technical excellence and aesthetic standards. It does not *impose* racist values but the formal requirements of a uniform corps de ballet preclude black bodies in white European companies ... The criteria that identify elitism, racism and sexism are simply not the criteria used by the consensus whose raison d'être is the production of and identification of art and whose standards are couched in artistic terms.

(Burt and Huxley 1985: 150)

White superiority, as racism, is deeply ingrained in Western classical dance traditions. African, Caribbean and South Asian bodies shout out through the silence of transcendent aesthetics. Against this background, in the context of race politics, the terms visible and invisible have explo-sive connotations for black artists.

MAAS Movers were contemporaries of the X6 artists. In 1977, MAAS Movers initiated the African–Caribbean British contemporary dancers' struggle for identity (Thorpe 1989). Greta Mendez, founder member and rehearsal director for MAAS Movers tells me:

I grew up in Trinidad. I trained there in modern interpretative dance, African, Scottish and Irish dance, and ballet. Every two years there was a national school/college arts festival in which we were judged on these dance forms by judges from the United Kingdom. When I arrived in the UK, I trained at the London School of Con-temporary Dance. I danced with several dance companies including Scottish Ballet junior team, Basic Space, Cedar of Lebanon, Nin Dance Company Trinbago and at the Royal Opera House. I could have gone on to work with companies in Europe and the USA but I put my own aspirations on hold in order to help set up MAAS

Figure 8 Greta Mendez in *Shattered Eye* (Michael Quaintance 1981). Riverside Studios, London.

Photographer: Dee Conway.

Movers. There was no vehicle for UK black contemporary dancers; they were voiceless at that time. There were few black dancers in mainstream dance companies. There were too few images of ourselves, insubstantial visible presence.

(Mendez 2003)

Evrol Puckerin, Ray Collins, Louis St Just, Jan Murray and Greta Mendez set up MAAS Movers. Evrol and Ray were the original directors. Dancers who performed with MAAS Movers included: Michael Quaintance, William Louther, Cathy Lewis, Patricia Banton, Tracy Ajose, Martha Gilpin, Vivien Rochester, Jacqui Simm and Holly Allen. These performers came from very different backgrounds, Caribbean, Caribbean British, African, African–American, African British and Indian African. The company was committed, energized and talented. Claire Hayes reviews a performance at Riverside Studios in 1978, describing

> six choreographer's visions, from the personal, emotional statements for soloists by Patricia Banton (*Save Me*) and Greta Mendez (*In Limbo*), to the group pieces of 'social comment' both domestic (Cathy Lewis' *Holliday*) and grandiose (William Louther's *Peace be Still*). Drawing on their heritage of Afro-Caribbean, jazz and modern, the choreographers created a rich texture of associative imagery, varied dynamics and rhythm. In Louther's piece, ritualistic group movement served as a base for solos just as his tape collage used soul music as a base for spoken rhetoric. In *Save Me* Banton directed tension through psychologically emotive repeated motifs.
>
> (Hayes 1978: 5)

Louther's *Peace Be Still* (1978) was influenced by Malcolm X and was a politically motivated piece focusing on black pride. Evrol Puckerin's work, *Spirits* (1977), focused on Caribbean dance traditions. Greta Mendez's two solos, *The Chair and Me* and *In Limbo* (1978), explored female sexuality. *The Chair and Me* took place in silence, with just Greta, the chair and an overhead spotlight. African–American Michael Quaintance brought macho rage into his choreography. Where Greta saw 'the laughter side of life' (Mendez 2003), Michael saw brutality. His intense psychodramas, in MAAS Movers, then NIN Dance Company, were drawn from his experiences of the violently sexist oppression of black women in his own African–American history. Similarly to Lloyd Newson and DV8, but five years earlier, Michael was making issue-based physical theatre work, stretching the boundaries of dance, exploring the darker side of male–female relations. He pushed the physicality of his dancers, particularly the women, towards a taut and dangerous edge. *Racks/Mingus 1* . . . (1981) was a piece that featured four women, 'it was tough, fast, brutal, vibrant. Michael wanted to choreograph works that had the same vibrancy as the streets of Chicago where he grew up' (Mendez 2005).[1]

Greta Mendez acted as rehearsal director for MAAS Movers. Everybody took on other jobs in order to survive. Greta describes the ad hoc availability of dancers to rehearse, and the accompanying exhaustion and frustration of holding the company together. After two years of being 'looked at' by the Arts Council of Great Britain, the promise came of revenue funding for the company. Performers such as Bill Louther and Evrol Puckerin re-appeared with the hope of establishing a funded dance company. There were frictions and differences between company members as the many different voices struggled to be heard. Despite all the hard work, the grant never materialized. The company disbanded just as Phoenix Dance Company was rising and a new generation of young British black dancers were training at the Northern School of Contemporary Dance. MAAS Movers set the path, opening up an awareness of black dance politics and the many different emerging black British artists.

Talking to Greta (Mendez 2003) about the years of MAAS Movers, I realized how our experiences of visibility politics co-existed but were different. In the 1970s and 1980s, many white post-modern performers were letting go of established dance structures and styles in order to re-figure subjectivity in performer–spectator relations. But this was not necessarily the same for black dancers. In the 1970s, there was no identifiable established black dance presence in the UK of which to let go. MAAS Movers' struggle for identity required setting one up in the first place. This was difficult when there were so many different identities to be realized. Greta talked about the company and I sensed that the objectives of each member of the group conflicted in the need to establish an identifiable style of black dance for the company. She confirmed this in an article in *Time Out*:

> We've had wonderful artistic rows at company meetings about the rep. The dancers who were trained in Graham technique want to do modern pieces. They did not want to be labelled as cliché black dancers, all wriggling hips, undulating shoulders, exotic. The other dancers wanted to do dances from the folk tradition. MAAS Movers, work incorporated the contemporary and the traditional, the real power of Shango rites, Limbo and calypso. I'm not talking

about a wailie-wailie-wahla ethnic stuff. I'm talking about folk dances that have deep symbolic meaning and poetry. Tradition is an empowering thing, all that we have today is built on yesterday, we shoot at comets to enrich our knowledge of today. In dance we can also explore some of those traditions, combined with trained bodies to create works that explore contemporary narrative.

(Mendez 1978: 15)

Greta's search for a company identity is echoed in the writing of bell hooks. hooks addresses the visibility issue 15 years later in her powerful and negative critique of Jennie Livingston's film, *Paris is Burning*. Describing the invisibility of African–American people in the film, she says:

Colonised black people . . . worship at the throne of whiteness . . . The 'we' evoked here is all of us, black people/people of colour, who are daily bombarded by a powerful colonising whiteness that seduces us away from ourselves, that negates that there is beauty to be found in any form of blackness that is not imitation whiteness.

(hooks 1992: 149)

The task of establishing identities for British black dancers became increasingly complex. The many different African, Caribbean and South Asian dance forms sought visible identity but were simultaneously suppressed under the efficient, economically viable, white, Western, all-encompassing category, 'black dance'. As Peter Badejo, Nigerian artistic director of Badejo Arts, affirmed:

African and Caribbean dance practitioners in this country and in the Diaspora are fighting an ongoing battle to increase the understanding of our dance forms and of their cultural contexts. To draw together that multiplicity of dance forms and call them Black dance only serves to reinforce the impression that there is only one culture, only one dance form. It makes the colour of the practitioner more important than the content of the art.

(Badejo 1993)

Under the all-consuming umbrella title of black dance, white institutional power was able to instigate a policy of divide and rule among the different genres, whereby the practitioners of different cultural forms competed for visibility and funding. Backbiting tension took artists' attention away from artistic endeavour and experiment and on to the need to fix identity. MAAS Movers performers met this crisis as they attempted to organize themselves for revenue funding, which consequently slipped past their grasp.

21 DIFFERENT VISIBILITIES

Given the ongoing challenge to define different cultural identities, the white post-modern fascination with the terms 'ambiguity' and 'absence' were not frequently applied by different black artists who were working to assert visible identities within the dance art context.[1] In the 1970s, we were aware of the equal and parallel emergence of black dance. We did not theorize in the same way, being more concerned with the all-embracing liberation politics of race and class than with the in/visible agendas within that frame. Claire Hayes (1978) indicates the different embodiments of visibility politics as she compares the work of MAAS Movers and Rosemary Butcher Dance Company, who shared a week of performances at Riverside Studios in London in 1978.[2] 'They shared the same performing space, the same auditorium, even the same type of audience. Yet the differences were extreme – not just in externals, but also in that inner dynamic of audience/performance relationship' (Hayes 1978: 5). Hayes describes basic differences 'in costume, lighting and music – Butcher's plainness and formality, MAAS Movers expressive theatricality' (Hayes 1978: 5). She goes on to describe the expressive qualities of the dancers. In MAAS Movers

> the emotional involvement of each dancer communicated itself to the audience in an exciting and involving way. Rosemary Butcher also demanded intensity from her dancers, but the intensity of simply performing a task, not interpreting ... MAAS Movers entertain ... Rosemary Butcher works from the periphery of our communication system.
>
> (Hayes 1978: 5–6)

I was reminded of these different approaches to performing presence in 2002, when I met Bharatanatyam dancers, Vena Ramphal and Mavin Khoo, at the Performing Arts Labs Dance Lab.[3] They told me how South Asian dance follows a long tradition that encourages identity and visibility, not an absence of presence:

Bharatanatyam has such a strong technique. My sense is that Western contemporary dance training has various techniques but the emphasis is on training the body to do what the choreographer requires. It is more about a way of moving than a technique. In repertoire, Bharatanatyam improvisation happens within the boundaries of the form. You are taught to smile and use your eyes. You are taught presence.

(Ramphal 2002)

I watch Mavin Khoo in *Phantasmaton* (Shobana Jeyasingh 2002).[4] Shobana Jeyasingh's choreography combines South Asian dance forms with Western contemporary forms. She respects their different identities even as she develops a new form between them. Her movement language shifts with ease between Bharatanatyam, contemporary dance and ballet without losing the contradictions between them. The performers are articulate, fast, dynamic, precise, energized and contradictory. The movement is a complex assemblage of different languages. There is no homogeneity among the dancers' bodies. Using the *mudras* from Bharatanatyam, the extension of legs from ballet and the use of weight from contemporary dance, the performers shift from two-dimensional to three-dimensional movement in space. Particularly influenced by Bharatanatyam's rhythms, performers emphasize the precise detail of movements and gestures performed with speed. In *Phantasmaton*, I watch as performers' backs shift fast from side to side, hips jut, feet slap down into wide positions, feet beat out rhythms, arms gesture with wild precision, legs cut in and out away from the body. The movements are deliciously distorted, energized by disharmony. A dancer's weight is thrown forward onto her hands, her head straining to look up, tail bone in the air, one leg straight, the other crouched, animalistic and bird-like. This is the attraction of the movement language; conflict, not ease, provokes the dynamic, jangling movements against each other. The pleasure is in its unpredictable nature, its complexity of different, identifiable, cultural forms.

Mavin appears behind the vast metal scaffold of chaotic steel strands. He stands in a square spotlight just to the side of the structure. He begins to *bourrée* around the side of the structure, performing small balletic steps usually performed by girls. The image of Giselle emerging from the grave is immediately recognizable. He *bourrée*-s forward, occasionally extending a leg in *arabesque*. Downstage centre, he performs a classical *ronde jambe en l'air*, balancing on the ball of one foot, and then slams both feet down with a slapping sound into Bharatanatyman stance – legs wide apart, knees turned out and bent – holding his arms straight, hands in

Bharatanatyam gesture. Mavin Khoo is petite by Western standards. He was born in Malaysia and has trained in ballet, Bharatanatyam, Odissi and contemporary dance. His stylized trainings construct and hold his body strictly within the confines of their traditional forms. Mavin exists within the codified techniques; he is totally in his body of languages, each of which leaves its essential, yet performative mark on his body. He walks with his feet turned out, chest forward, shoulders held back; his hands are expressive, his eyes wide, his leg extensions impressive. His feet are able to extend into a balletic point and the next moment hit the floor with a slap – precision and abandonment equally defined.

Mavin fills the space not with one identifiable style but with an embodied play of four full styles. He is fully present in his identities. His skills are recognizable in their contrasts. Mavin's body cuts the space; he is never *not* there, never performing absence. If Mavin is on stage, then every fibre of his body vibrates with the muscular tension of being, exuding the dynamic energy of his Western and South Asian identities.

The slash within in/visibility is a space of a complexity of meanings as the terms visible and invisible are applied to different social contexts. As feminist women become subjects of their own work, so they also become absent within the economy of the gaze. For lesbians and gay men, becoming visible has been a positive 'form of resistance to the negative implications of the lesbian/homosexual categories' (Dyer 1993: 21). Constructing a lifestyle of behaviour and dress has brought lesbians and gay men together with a code that is visible to them, but invisible outside the community. Drag king performance artist Diana Torr, discussing transgender rights, says, 'it's so obvious to me that transgender people are the next group that should become visible. After all, they pay their taxes. They're quite a force' (Chauchard-Stuart 1996: 6). In all of these cases, becoming visible is associated with the positive act of liberation, gaining power and claiming a place as subject. Phelan's critique of the film *Paris is Burning* (Jennie Livingston 1993) points out that one of the aims of the black, gay transvestite and transsexual bodies that parade in drag at the Harlem Balls is to pass as white, heterosexual women. To be successful – the highlight of visibility for drag artists – is to pass as invisible, as a white woman in a white world. Here, there is a complexity of contradictions. *Visibility* within the transvestite drag culture of the balls is attained through invisibility to the outside world, where 'the "secret" codes, the iconography of dress, the movement, and speech . . . can be read by those within the community, but escape the interpretative power of those external to it' (Phelan 1993: 97). At the same time as the black drag artists strive for visibility in 'passing' as white within a black culture, the act of passing as a heterosexual woman means being invisible within white culture.

I am intrigued by the visibility politics and contrasting approaches to performing identities in the pieces, *We Set Out Early . . . Visibility Was Poor* (1998), choreographed by Bill T. Jones, an African–American man, and *Bank* (1997), choreographed by Siobhan Davies, a white European woman. Remembering the different engagements with presence in the work of Rosemary Butcher and MAAS Movers in the 1970s, here again, visibility politics play out complex contrasting scenarios.

We Set Out Early . . . Visibility Was Poor involves a large cast of performers. They enter singly, in pairs or in trios. Bodies meet in the space, interact, take the focus for a moment, then disperse. Events happen – sometimes-pedestrian movement, sometimes-stylized technique; relationships and stories emerge and are played out. The stage is always busy with a range of different and contrasting scenarios. A playful dancing game occurs between performers while a woman's sexually provocative hip-thrusting solo is directed to the audience. Performers smile, project outwards and express emotions to each other. The energy is high; dynamic attack and exuberance are present in excess. The performers' individual expressions are outwardly focused, becoming the cause and reaction of unfolding events. Rarely does the entire cast perform group unison movement or a uniform language. Personal languages and styles are not compromised. Each performer stands out for her/his individual presence. Each performer's movements project a different history, culture, training, desire and sexuality. I watch a range of different personae, languages, images, narratives and expressions, all with sharp contrasting shifts of energy, quality and focus.

I see African–American, African–Caribbean, Caucasian, South American and mixed-race bodies. I watch male, female, gay, lesbian and transgender performances. I recognize themes of Aids, death, life and spirituality. I notice skirts, dresses, hot-pants, trousers, shirts, jackets, short hair, long hair, fat, thin, tall and skinny. I watch ballet, pedestrian movement, disco, jazz, contact improvisation and Cunningham. I experience phases of slowness, speed, tragedy, humour and joy. I sling terms together in different configurations on single bodies and between bodies: mixed race/girl/boy/skirt shifts to black/gay/ballet/tragic. All of these terms describe performers' identities. The piece moves fast; the combinations of performers never fix but spill out and change. Each performer portrays a different identity in relation to others in the group.

Watching *Bank*, my attention is drawn, not so much by individual performers but by Davies' finely tuned choreographic craft, its form and structures. I am not watching personal narratives but dancers working in unison, weaving in curving formations, moulding and shaping the space. I notice the use of weight in partnering work, the close proximity of darting bodies shattering the choreographed patterns in space. I observe the relations of movement to sound. *Bank* conjures the metaphor of the cavernous seashell, the inside of which remains an intriguing secret. The neutrality of the performers' expression emphasizes the choreographic patterns that become engaging for their spatial shapes. As spectator, I am invited to fill these shapes with my own interpretations. Critic Judith Mackrell writes:

> Davies knows how to make pure movement into theatre. So when we watch six dancers coiling and thrusting through fiercely muscular manoeuvres, while at the same time moving in formations so tight that they have to wheel and dodge each other with the skill of Italian footballers, we feel the exhilaration of lives being lived dangerously.
>
> (Mackrell 1997: 6)

The choreographed patterns in space, rather than the differences between personalities, engage me. *Bank* is a performance of seduction in reverse where I look through the beautiful empty shell of the choreography for glimpses of the dancers' performing presence.

My attention as spectator is different when watching these two pieces. In *Bank*, the performers share a language that is absorbed by the overarching choreographic shape. In *We Set Out Early* . . ., the choreography appears as an outcome of each performer's desire to interpret the material as individual expression. *Bank* suggests a repertory piece, where, through time, dancer and movement material could be replaced but the piece would still be recognizable by its choreographic form. In *We Set Out Early* . . ., the movement material seems to defy the choreography. In *Bank*, the dancers rarely engage with the audience or assert themselves individually. When they are dancing solo, their internal focus allows the shape of the gesture centre of attention. In *We Set Out Early* . . ., looking out, as the signal of desiring to see and be seen, initiates the movements performed. The choreography of *Bank* appears to fall smoothly, like a textured cloth, over each dancer. When the dancers perform *We Set Out Early* . . ., their real bodies and the language appear to clash, stimulating conflict and theatrical tension. In this piece, the performers present different visibilities, where each visible body is, in her/his own self, a complex body of race, culture, history, dance and sexuality. Speaking of African–American choreographers such as Bill T. Jones, Jawole Willa and Jo Zollar, Gottschild states how these artists are latter-day followers in the African American tradition of wearing many hats and inverting-subverting codes, descendants of folks who did so long before there were words like deconstruction or post-modernism. To know the mainstream culture and play its game, but also remember and keep one's own – that is and has always been the task.

(Gottschild 1996: 57)

The piece engages the spectators through the performers' play of iden-tifiable differences. In *Bank*, performers engage my active attention as k/no/w bodies of illusion, seduction in reverse. Race, culture, history and sexuality remain understated, framed within the white post-modern minimalist aesthetic. The performers become intriguing for their hidden identities within the choreographic shape.

Black traditions in jazz and improvisation have had a profound influence on the post-modern dance aesthetic. While white influences on black dance have always been made visible through racist oppres-sion, rarely have black influences on white dance been acknowledged and made visibly recognizable. Now, at last, Gottschild (1996) and Foster (2002) have drawn attention to this appropriation, revealing how Judson Church artists and George Balanchine assimilated the notion of 'cool':

The Africanist matrix of attributes known as cool was assimil-ated into a wide variety of white performances of the 1960s. Long cultivated within African and African–American artistic traditions, cool demonstrates the self's equilibrium in responding to the unpredictable flux of life. Its elegant stance, at once powerful, imper-turbable, omniscient, and relaxed, generates a perspective from which both criticism and humour can issue.

(Foster 2002: 31–2)

Flip. David Beckham, British football superstar, grows up in East London in the 1990s. He openly appropriates black culture in his dress, manner, physical gesture and hairstyle. A BBC documentary, *Black like Beckham* (Mckenzie 2003), interviewing black East Londoners for verification takes the ironic view that Beckham *is* a black man. This ironic reversal of in/visibility, re-appropriates Beckham into British black culture, suggesting perhaps that black and white cultural differences can become performative choices.[5] But apparently not. Tony Snow critiques the programme, saying:

Does the lifestyle of England captain, David Beckham, truly sum up the essence of black culture – or is it our perception of black culture, which is being misread? Piara Powar, national co-ordinator of Kick it Out, the national football anti-racism campaign, dismisses the proposition that Beckham is black – outright. 'David Beckham is David Beckham' he says. 'The fact that he is influenced by elements of black culture doesn't mean he is black. It trivialises and disrespects history and the way in which racism affects people's lives and it plays with identity in a negative way.'

(Snow 2003: 1)

Seemingly, race does not have the same postmodern performative freedoms as gender when it comes to the complex issues of cultural identity and visibility politics.

22 NEGATION OF SEDUCTION

Claire Hayes' (1978) review of MAAS Movers and Rosemary Butcher throws up the crux of the matter. The white Western post-modern attention to the absence of presence – a positive and necessary shift in dance politics – also provoked the possibilities of a non-engagement with female dancing bodies. I attempt to step outside the experiment to observe the state of play for performers and spectators in 1970s and 1980s dance.

The reverse strategy of seduction at work in post-modern minimalist performances, whereby spectators are drawn to the absence of spectacle, was not appreciated by a wide range of dance audiences in the 1970s and 1980s:

In a theatre presentation her [Butcher's] work seems distant . . . by setting the dance in a formal stage setting, I expected more than I was given. If I tried I could join the dancers in my imagination, but it was a big barrier to leap. Butcher's dances required a cerebral effort to enjoy them . . . I felt that the dance could exist without me, yet can a work of art have meaning without a two-way process?

(Hayes 1978: 6)

Outside the context of avant-garde art dance performance, a *jouissance* improviser with the appearance of a task-like embodiment of action did not always evoke an engaging connection between performers and spectators. For many spectators, the attention to absence of presence, as seduction in reverse, became a non-engagement with dance perform-ance. A crisis of presence loomed in dance performance, particularly for women. It loomed when the thinking-body dancers of the 1970s exper-iment met the performance packaging of the 1980s. It loomed as the new dance experiment became subsumed by the mainstream and was seen as performance rather than process. It loomed when our feminist dancing bodies, in denial of seduction, no longer concerned with *pleasing* the audience, infiltrated the middle-scale repertory dance companies (as my experience with Extemporary Dance Company will reveal). The crisis of performing presence loomed again when dance was no longer a form of entertainment but a subject of academic study. And again as dance artists sought to widen the boundaries of what was being labelled as dance. As these boundaries stretched and dissolved through cross-disciplinary collaborations, dancing as an identifiable choreographed form of expression began to disappear.

Chris Crickmay reviews the work of Miranda Tufnell and Dennis Greenwood as they perform at the Almeida Theatre in London in 1982. Miranda and Dennis were at the forefront of the new dance experiment, stretching the boundaries of the form to include pedestrian task-like movement, visual art and a conceptual awareness of moving with objects in space. Crickmay describes *Other Rooms* (Miranda Tufnell and Dennis Greenwood 1981), which involves 'a setting of two chairs and two tables arranged near a wall . . . The dancers move amongst the furni-ture, use it and rearrange it, in a manner that is sometimes natural and everyday; sometimes bizarre' (Crickmay 1982: 8). This review is part of a longer article for *New Dance* magazine (1982) in which Crickmay reviews *Other Rooms* alongside two other pieces, *Night Pieces* (Miranda Tufnell and Dennis Greenwood 1981) and *Fallout* (Miranda Tufnell 1981), and discusses the politics of invisibility for new dance work:

> What is it that unites all these three works? Firstly . . . a feeling of watching an evolving thought . . . the ambiguity and freshness resulting from the fact that the dancers continually change their minds in discovering where the action is going to go . . . To get anything from this work the audience must be willing to enter the same arena. If the work must first be categorized in order to be considered, then it will remain truly invisible.
>
> (Crickmay 1982: 8)

He is writing in response to reviews of the same work by established dance critics. He quotes the conservative and conventionally biased critic, David Dougill, as saying:

> 'an evening of British rubbish . . . In *Night Pieces* a man in an over-coat intones an interminable monologue of gobbledegook while sitting on and falling off a chair, and two dancers pawed the ground, pausing to switch hanging lights on and off. It was during *Other Rooms*, at the point where Miss Tufnell was crawling on all fours with a table on her back and a lamp dangling from her teeth that I realized these people have never grown up.'
>
> (Dougill 1981, cited in Crickmay 1982: 7)

As the 1970s experiment moved into mainstream theatres, audiences were being asked to read into absences rather than follow narratives, reject traditional gender roles and social hierarchies of dance. They had to open their eyes and minds to an esoteric and kinaesthetic under-standing. The work demanded that they put aside speculative fetishistic or voyeuristic desires, and be satisfied by performance that had no recognizable references to conventional structures and devices related to dance. As a post-modern minimalist dancing body, the practices of playing identities, expressing fantasies and desiring narratives was not stimulated or encouraged. For many audience members, this experimental style closed the conventional space of engagement and the space of mystery – the play of real and illusion between performer and spectator – was effectively collapsed.

As female performers avoided sexual objectification of their bodies (and male performers refused the heroic role), so dance performers appeared to adopt a presence that negated external expression in an effort to reject the binary code of the gaze. We withdrew from perform-ing, we even stopped dancing, concerned we might be seen as a desired object: we might overdo it, express too much, exaggerate facial emotions and project a meaning. Yes, theoretically, absence as presence is intriguing, but on our dancing bodies absence came close to disappear-ance within the conventions of theatrical performance. Rejecting this figure of non-performance, Fergus Early, albeit 20 years later, offers a very different perspective to Crickmay:

> I believe that you should *be* on stage, either communicating directly with an audience in terms of exchanging in some way, making them laugh or cry, or communicating with them through how you relate to other people on stage. If you want to communicate that you are

not 'there', then you still need to communicate that you are deliberately walled off and that is something to do with what you are
showing. But to pretend that you, a sentient human being, are not
there, are somehow just a form or shape or dynamic – I don't see
the point. I think that historically dance artists have always tried to
run after people in the visual arts, in terms of being avant-garde.
There is a wish to be as abstract as possible in a way that the visual
arts can be, which for me misses the point. I think of dance as part
of theatre. The visual arts can be abstract in a way that a person
cannot. There is something in that 'lets be cool' attitude. Why be
cool? What are you being cool about?

(Early 2003)

23 THE OTHER OF THE
   OTHER

I am attempting to analyse the dichotomy that has been my own practice of performing and watching. Feminist politics primarily focused
on bringing the real female body, as subject, to the performing stage
to establish subjectivity. Simultaneously, post-modern minimalist dance
agendas focused on deconstructing the narrative and virtuosity in movement language to establish a minimalist presence. These two historically
important strands of performance worked together to create a dilemma
for female performing presence in mainstream contemporary dance by
effectively closing the space of engagement for performers and spectators.
On the one hand, negation of conventional elements offered us the most
liberating and exhilarating features of feminist and post-modern new
dance practice, allowing for 'an appreciation for the possibilities latent
in nothingness, absence, the marginal, the peripheral, the repressed'
(Tong 1989: 233). In our studios, immersed in the creative process,
we enjoyed our freedoms of other-ness. On the other hand, within a
conventional theatrical setting, this presence was not met with wild
enthusiasm. Procuring audience engagement with dance languages
that were marginal, peripheral and repressed was no easy task; the
work attracted small audiences who were primarily composed of the
k/no/wledgeable performance and visual art community. Liberated, yes,
but beyond that intimate context, invisible.

Back to the theory. Peggy Phelan's feminist psychoanalytical perspective suggests that the conventional relationship between self and other in Western philosophy and mainstream culture, is a marked one where the self is marked with value and the other is unmarked. In a patriarchal economy of desire (inherent to conventional performance contexts), the marked term is the male subject and the unmarked is the female, which the subject then marks as his own: 'Unable to bear (sexual) difference, the psychic subject transforms this difference into the Same, and converts the Other into the familiar grammar of the linguistic, visual, and physical body of the Same' (Phelan 1993: 5–6).

The inability to accept the primal loss and concede to the perpetually lost moment that can never be replaced evokes the constant search for self-realization and self-recognition through an other. In Western mainstream performance media, an important contradiction is at work here that keeps seduction alive. The female body is marked or fetishized but the marking is never complete as the fetishization of an object never entirely provides the subject with an identity of itself. The real female body will always slip away. Within this context, the search for the other cannot be satisfied but that does nothing to diminish the search: the desire to mark persists and this desiring, as an active play, is seductive. In this way, all is well for the illusive fetishized body as she perpetuates the spectator's desire for the real. She (or he) is the queen, holding a prominent position centre stage as object of desire. But the *jouissance* dancing feminist subject emerging out of the 1970s and rejecting fetishistic representation did not have access to the same strategy of seduction.

The new dance artist's struggle to establish subjectivity in performance was an attempt to exist somehow *outside* traditional contexts of performer–spectator relations, to establish a relationship that negated identifications with narratives of desire. She resisted being the desired object, or desiring to be a desired object, refused and rejected all positions and expressions of desire within the performance context.

The (male) gaze of desire in Oedipal narrative found itself displaced by the *real* unmarked female body as female performers brought their real bodies face to face with the subject of that gaze. Artists such as Miranda Tufnell, Gaby Agis and Eva Karczag attended to the task of softly and quietly rolling across the floor, and their work stripped away constructed dance illusions. Certainly they were different, real subjects. Certainly they revealed pedestrian actions as dance movements. More importantly, they presented moments of process as performance. But, as a consequence, the performer–spectator relations of engagement in

Western theatre conventions could no longer be the context for such work. The markings, the familiar points of reference, were gone. Back in the 1970s and 1980s, audiences were knowledgeable but small. Artists rejected and were rejected by conventional venues as they sought new sites and new audiences, finding their work more suited to art galleries and external sites than theatres.[1]

In other art forms, strategies were found to address this dilemma between subjectivity and invisibility. Peggy Phelan (1993) recommends a tactic of 'disguise and displacement' for the feminist unmarked subject, emphasizing the political power for feminist artists in remaining un-marked in contemporary arts (Phelan 1993: 60). She describes the work of artist/photographer Cindy Sherman. Each of Sherman's photographs represents her body in a different disguise, whether as a young girl, a housewife, a film star, an image of herself situated within a subverted reproduction of an old master or as a mutilated body within the horror genre. These technologically sophisticated disguises encourage a multi-plicity and ambiguity of identities regarding the real body of Sherman, while Sherman herself slips away. Yet she continues to be the body of every one of her images and, as the artist, she is very much in control of her real body as subject. Sherman is both subject and object. Many images are fetishistic, parodic and ironic, where her real body remains disguised: 'The performative record of the disappearance of Sherman's body is the lure which keeps the spectator looking for Sherman' (Phelan 1993: 68).[2] Yet her body remains within every photograph 'like a ubiq-uitous ghost, she continues to haunt the images we believe in, the ones we remember seeing and loving' (Phelan 1993: 6).

No doubt the devices of parody, irony, characterization and theatri-cality were successfully utilized by feminist dance performers as strategies of disguise and displacement. However, when the site of the perform-ance was the moving body itself, the tools of disguise and displacement were not so easy to manipulate. Although Phelan claims that no per-formance can reveal a real identity, in the context of the new dance experiment, I disagree. There was no disguise for the figure of internal *jouissance*; the real body was not displaced. As she was not marked with fetishistic representation, she owned her body and performance presence as subject. In doing so, her dancing presence became a real identity but invisible to the conventions of the gaze.

The feminist dancing body of *jouissance* embodied the non-linear, fluid, multiple, diffusible and viscous signification of the feminine 'other'. There was the danger! In the conventional theatre context, the female body performing, because of her affiliation to internality, to feminine semiotic forces and female sexuality, did not read as appearance or illusion but as female essence. There was the challenge! How could the female body use the figure of *jouissance* for performance play? Paying attention to somatic sensation, dancing tended not to play on the surface of the female body as illusion. The movement did not disguise the female, it became the female: 'It is difficult for women to appropriate the image of the other for their own fantasy, as Lacan bluntly puts it, "There is no Other of the Other"' (Phelan 1993: 60).

Baudrillard speaks of a hyper-reality where the excess of illusion has become more original (real) than the origin itself. He suggests contemporary culture is experiencing a 'process of mourning the death of the image and the imaginary' (Baudrillard 1991: 7). Here, production itself is no longer a reality, but the greatest illusion of a reality long gone, which is simulated through the reproduction of elusive empty signs, signs that become all the more seductive for their empty form, their non-real-ness: 'The attraction of the void lies at the basis of seduction' (Baudrillard 1991: 77). In this hyper-real state, where the excess of illusion has suppressed the real entirely, the space of seduction is closed. I am saying that the very *opposite* closed the space of seduction in postmodern minimalist dance performance. As we questioned the illusive spectacle that was dance, turning attention to the movement processes, collapsing the space between real and illusion, conventional performer–spectator relations of engagement were challenged. Not, as Baudrillard says, by an excess of illusion but by *an excess of the real* (the thinking, moving body).

As the 1970s *jouissance* dancer stripped away the fetish of the marked female dancer's presence, establishing herself as subject, she also tended to strip away the precise, articulate, muscular, virtuosic, linear dynamics and external posturing of movement language. However, the virtuosity and external expression that were consequently negated have, conventionally, acted as a technique of disguise and displacement for the female dancer. The analogy of becoming and rhizomic networks (Deleuze and Guattari 1988) may be enticing to apply to dancing bodies. But it is perhaps indicative to note that a rhizome plant also produces powerfully articulated vertical shoots, each with an expressive identity. External articulations are the illusive markings that work in contradiction to the internal imaginary and hold her real body secret. These markings, in their oscillating relations with her real body, engage the spectator. In other words, take away the conventional virtuosities of dance and her body is unmarked. An important shift for female bodies but a costly one.

Dance artists in the 1970s and 1980s, in different ways, with different agendas across race and culture, challenged Western Enlightenment conventions. The feminist, post-Enlightenment achievements to establish embodied ownership and identity were problematic for artists who wanted to expose their work to mainstream audiences. We found ourselves enmeshed in a paradox, caught between subjectivity and invisibility.

24 KRISTEVA'S CRUNCH

Julia Kristeva's theory of semiotic drives and symbolic language offers a way out of the locked grasp of subjectivity and invisibility. Her philosophical writing spans psychoanalysis and linguistic theory. She focuses on the conflicting interrelations between the semiotic and symbolic at the site of the speaking subject, the flesh-and-blood body and phallocentric language. For Kristeva, the conflict between semiotic and symbolic, the ruptures of *jouissance* and erotic drives into paternal symbolic language, creates the clash necessary to impassion art practice:

> Art – this semiotisation of the symbolic – . . . represents the flow of jouissance into language . . . In cracking the socio-symbolic order, splitting it open, changing vocabulary, syntax, the word itself and releasing from beneath them the drives borne by vocalic or kinetic differences, jouissance works its way into the social.
>
> (Kristeva 1984: 80, cited in Grosz 1989: 56)

Kristeva claims that feminism should not struggle for a separate feminine being, different to men. She does not see masculine and feminine attributes as belonging to the binary code of the sexed bodies of male and female. She believes in the polymorphous sexual drives of the infant. Each subject therefore has access in him/herself to both masculine and feminine, as a subject in process – each child having access to its maternal body and paternal language. The feminist struggle should focus not on the 'sexual differences distinguishing subjects from each other, but a sexual differentiation internal to each subject' (Grosz 1989: 67). In other words, each woman should access her masculine and feminine, her potential for articulation in paternal language as well as internal *jouissance* in her own body.

The feminist project to establish subjectivity as other and different is considered here to damage the potential for a female presence in art practices:

> Feminist practice can only be negative, at odds with what already exists so that we may say 'that's not it' and 'that's still not it'. In 'woman' I see something that cannot be represented, something that is not said, something above and beyond nomenclatures and ideologies.
>
> (Kristeva 1981: 137)

The phallic centrality of the subject and the maleness of the symbolic order are endorsed by Kristeva. Provocatively, she suggests that men can subvert and change the symbolic, because they are the only subjects with a position to subvert. As Grosz explains:

> He . . . is able to say what she (the mother, the infant) experiences. Though a risk to his masculine, phallic identity, he can evoke the jouissance he experiences with her in a way that she cannot. He can transgress the boundaries of the symbolic, while she exists at its pre social margins. He can speak the jouissance which overwhelms her 'identity'.
>
> (Grosz 1989: 96)

Women are urged to position themselves similarly to men, arguing that the phallus, as signifier, belongs to both sexes, that the subject is neutral and is a position that can be and should be claimed by both men and women. Kristeva criticizes writing by women for women, implying that this writing takes up a position outside the symbolic. In this place/space, feminist struggles have no possibility of effecting change within the symbolic order. Women's position in the Oedipal complex is to be excluded from the paternal language; therefore they are unable to create ideological change.

When women also exclude themselves in a search for an essential feminine, they doubly deny themselves visibility and power. In other words, women must own the language before it can be subverted, and transgression can only happen from within:

> I believe two conditions are necessary if this course is to be followed. The first is historical; it involves throwing women into all of society's contradictions with no hypocrisy of fake protection. The second condition is sexual . . . it involves coming to grips with one's language and body as others, as heterogeneous elements.
>
> (Kristeva 1980: 164–5, cited in Grosz 1989: 66)

Kristeva's semiotic and symbolic provide an analogy for dancing women. Following her argument, I can see how women's agenda to establish another, different, feminine language for the female body dancing was unlikely to engage spectators.

Within the conventions of a theatre setting, women dancers must 'get to grips' once again with what they have rejected, the structures and external articulations of language. How can we do this and retain the feminine imaginary? I will return to that later. For now, an ironic twist.

The White Oak Project revives Yvonne Rainer's 1966 work, *Trio A Pressured No. 3* (2002).[1] Here, the issue of in/visibility is addressed head on. The solo is performed by Rosalind Leblanc and takes place centre stage. Rosalind is wearing tracksuit bottoms and a fitted T-shirt. She has a muscular body, liquid arms and no hard edges. As I expected, the solo never stops and it never repeats. There is no beginning and no end. Gestures are performed as tasks, without theatrical intention or expression. Hands flick her ears, toes tap the ground, feet circle and legs limp. The fragmented pedestrian movements, each one converging into the next, appear as if on a flat plane, without phrasing, without fluidity or glamour. If her body faces to the audience, her head is always circling or turned away. She never looks out.

But this revival is not happening in an intimate art gallery of the 1960s. Instead it is performed at Sadler's Wells Theatre in London, a traditional proscenium-arch large-scale venue. In this version, Mikhail Baryshnikov runs persistently around Rosalind, stopping, then fixing her with his gaze, trying to catch her attention as she constantly changes direction. This provocative choreographic framing device provides fixed and familiar points of perspective, gives the material a 'front' for spectators, for him, for her. Baryshnikov's framing helps to make this 1960s piece more accessible, by providing an identifiable frame (albeit a moving one) for the solo. His gaze provides the ironic statement that subverts Rainer's subversion of the voyeuristic gaze.

25 COLLECTIVE STRATEGIES

Issues of identity and subjectivity were inherent to the X6 collective as we questioned not only *what* to make but *how* to make it. Shifting the content of performance required a displacing of the hierarchical structures for making performance and, within that, the single revered voice of the choreographer. The discovery of new dance forms in movement and image reflected our strategies to re-figure how to work together. We embraced collaborative working structures and devising methodologies.

The following writing describes a learning curve that began with the embryonic collective experiments in the 1970s through to a reclamation of the role of director as equal but *different* to that of the performer–collaborators in the 1990s. Empowering the performer to participate in the creation of the performance brings clarity of intention that influences the material to be performed. However, understanding the necessity for the director's role as the link between internal process and external product, and as a critical eye, is also vital for the work to be read in a public domain. This fused relationship of power between performers and directors requires constant questioning to ensure the immediacy, alive-ness and unpredictability of the performance product.

At X6, we were eager to discover how collaborative methods of making performances affected what was performed. In the early days, we devised performances through *collective* collaboration, rejecting the notion of an outside director altogether. As five very different performer/makers, we were often compromised by each other's direction. So, for the most part, we did not collectively create performances. Rather, we supported a collective working structure to nurture our different personal development and directions.

A collective dynamic is more than the sum of its parts. The power of the collective to change cultural movements does not emerge through the voice of a single author. Neither does it emerge from the unity of the group. The outcomes of collective working occur in the weaving of a connecting web of processes between people and things. The web creates its own patterns of change that are invisible to established systems of production. Statements, events and creative outcomes dissolve back into the intricate network. Collective working is slippery in that its processes, not its products, have the power to shift cultural practice. These are processes that cannot be fixed because they cannot be caught in one voice. This is the creative tool of the collective. As long as the collective network is functioning, pumped by the lifeblood of its individual members, its invisible web cannot be absorbed by established systems into an identifiable knowledge. Likewise at X6, change happened without identifiable outward appearance. The X6 collective dynamic respected our different voices but did not fix on one voice of authority. There was no oeuvre by which ideas could be identified and categorized. It was, as Foucault might say, 'a discursive formation', whereby, 'it is not the objects that remain constant, nor the domain that they form; but their relation between the surfaces on which they appear' (Foucault

1969: 53). The practices that emerged at X6, the ideas that were caught in the web – in this fluid network between things – were rigorously bound by discourse, yet free from any identifiable system, and, for one moment, these practices existed as a bid for hope.

Within this collective structure we devised performances, interweaving the roles of director and performer. *Light Matter/Light Music* (1975) introduced me to the collaboratively devised process. The piece, which had been commissioned by the International Contemporary Music Festival in Royan, France, was directed by Jacky and Fergus, who also performed, along with Maedée Duprès, Tom Jobe, Janet Krengel and myself. The music was composed by Michael Finnessy.[1] The performance infuriated the French audience. Eggs and tomatoes were thrown at us and we were asked to leave France before the second performance.

Each performer had a story to tell, with the individual stories interspersed with group statements. We improvised our own dances from autobiographical starting points. In the performance, I was perched high on a ladder, facing towards an open skylight in the ceiling of the theatre. I performed Greek frieze lines and stamped my feet. At another moment I was sitting on a chair in a line with other performers. We wore long brown raincoats – we called them 'wanker-macks' because they had pockets that opened to the inside. Through these openings we produced baby dolls and union flags. Later I supported Tom Jobe,[2] holding long reins that were attached to his body by a harness. While I held the reins, Tom performed his story, running faster and faster round the outside of the stage. He ran until he literally collapsed with exhaustion. Every element of the performance rejected dance conventions of content and form. This work represented the raw, idealistic and cathartic beginnings to collaboratively devised methods of making.

Light Matter/Light Music was followed by *5 Saturdays* (1975), *Swan Lake* (1976), *Bleeding Fairies* (1977) and *Naples* (1979). The performances were vulnerable, fresh and awkward processes, revealing much more about people, time, place and culture than a polished choreographer-led product. In these collective collaborations, the content of the performance emerged through personally devised, improvised statements and through the spontaneously constructed relations between performers.

Collaboratively devised performance shifts the performer's presence from a silent body answerable to an outside director to someone who inhabits, manipulates and takes control of the material to be performed in relation to other performers and across disciplines. Collaborative performance is acknowledged not by the name of the director, the single origin or a single theme, but by the performers and the events. Encouraged by feminist person-as-political agendas, we saw ourselves as people first rather than as dancing tools. We were inspired by the notion that a compliant performer, whose role had been to imitate and interpret, a tool for the choreographer to manipulate, could, through collaborative devising methods, become a uniquely inventive voice. We wanted that empowerment. We made a conscious move to re-imagine what constitutes performance content. We were curious to experience the difference of performing our own material. We wanted to be fully alive in the process, in the present, without going through goal-oriented rehearsals. So much of our performance history had been spent in agonizing boredom, learning steps passed down or inscribed on us from outside sources, where the only, and longed for, highlight was embodying them in the moment of performance. We had known hierarchies where we were answerable to an outside eye to which different individuals became one. Now we wanted to be answerable to ourselves, through our own material, with interrelating intentions. We found that by working collaboratively, the relations between us identified the thing to be made. We spoke, improvised, contributed ideas and told our stories. We enacted pedestrian movements, performed in the streets, related to other performers, took hold, let go and parodied our pre-determined dance languages. We felt urgently alive – passionate – convinced that we could speak, sing, act and write text with the same articulation as we could dance. We collaborated across disciplines: musicians danced, visual artists spoke, dancers sang. Whether or not we had any skill in these different media was secondary to the drive to take hold of our own ideas and realize them in practice. We were hooked into the experiment. So, here in the 1970s, we researched, improvised, made music, taught our own classes, made costumes, props and sets, shared the financial outcomes, fused everything through and onto our own bodies. We were excited by process, not product. As Anna Furse remembers:

> Our search for a new theatrical syntax operated as a form of controlled anarchy. We worked with a kind of psycho-emotional jazz. We prepared our mind/body instruments by reading, research and physical training and then collided our imaginations together when devising.[3]
>
> (Furse 2000: 26)

The 1970s collective collaborative experiences pulled apart the fixed hierarchies between performer and choreographer. Directors became performers, equal to the others. We all mucked in, enthusiastically sharing ideas and ideals. Performance-making became a discourse defined not by a choreographer's specific language, its permanence, canon

Figure 9 Rosemary Butcher Dance Company in *By River & Wharf* (1976). X6 yard at Butlers Wharf, London. Dancers include Maedée Duprès, Miranda Tufnell, Dennis Greenwood.

Photographer unknown.

or category, but by its practice of process. And our externally learnt knowledge and practices of choreography were returned to us to emerge as our own.

Most exciting were the site-specific performances. Without the external director's gaze on formal perspectives of space and time, forms and structures shifted. Letting go of the single voice, letting go of the mirror, also meant letting go of 'front', leading us away from formal performance venues. Thinking differently about structures allowed us to think differently about space, time and ideas for performance, where to perform and how to involve the audience. We made site-specific perform-ances in London streets, wharves, car parks, play parks, Hyde Park, busy roundabouts and on bridges. Fergus Early, Maedée Duprès and I, as Dance Organisation, created *5 Saturdays* (1975). For five consecutive weeks, we performed each Saturday, using performance feedback to assimilate and develop the work during the weekdays, creating a loop system of continuity where performance and process were continuously and consciously informing each other. The performances took place around the busy shopping centre at Elephant and Castle in South London. In 1975, Dance Organisation parodied the entrance of the Shades in *La Bayadère*. The performance took place at the Serpentine Gallery in Hyde Park. Wearing cricket gear and carrying cricket bats, Fergus Early, Tim Lamford, Maedée Duprès, Craig Givens and myself performed this famous ballet entrance along the parapet of the Serpentine Gallery roof. *By River & Wharf* (1976) was devised by a range of artists including X6 members, Rosemary Butcher, Dennis Greenwood, Craig Givens, Eva Karczag, Martha Grogan, Julyen Hamilton, Miranda Tufnell, Dennis Greenwood, Sally Cranfield, Judith Katz, Kate Flatt and Tim Lamford. Fergus Early describes the event:

> An afternoon long festival of performances to be viewed during a pedestrian stroll around Bermondsey dockland one June day in the hot summer of 1976. Across Tower Bridge, down alleys, on old bomb-sites, suspended from Victorian girders, deep in Thames mud, on the grass of an urban square, beneath high-rise flats, a collection of dancers that now looks like a who's who in new dance performed new work especially created for their chosen location.
>
> (Early 1987: 12)

I particularly remember Fergus and his bush. He hid himself behind a moveable bush that presented itself to the audience at different places on the walk. Emerging finally from his hiding place, Fergus performed

a Morris dance with Tim Lamford. Mary Prestidge initiated a performance that involved a group of people making a very slow and continuous
walk across Tower Bridge on a busy tourist-full summer day. Again on
Tower Bridge – our local site – at the height of the tourist season, Maedée
Duprès organized an orange-passing event. A group of performers were
stretched at equal distances over the length the bridge and oranges were
passed continuously down the line from one end to the other.

Rather than working to a central focus or final climax, these performances were constructed in scenes with equal signification that were
assembled and juxtaposed one beside the other as fragments of a collage.
Collage displaces the notion of formal choreographic shape: a beginning,
middle and end. Instead, it is fractured, parts are linked by dynamic
contrast and practical, technical requirements rather than a unifying
theme. No fragment has hierarchy over another. Performers' stories
unfold in parallel; time dynamics are placed in juxtaposition: there are
no beginnings or endings, no major or minor roles. Collage, as a layering
of different assembled fragments laid next to each other, overlapping,
pinned together without hierarchy, defines a collaboratively devised
performance:

> Devised performance, as contrasted with conventional theatre,
> results from the identification, selection and accumulation of con-
> cepts, actions, texts, places and things which are composed and
> orchestrated in space and time according to a set of governing
> aesthetics, ideologies, techniques and technologies . . . What begins
> as a series of fragments is arranged in performance: dramaturgy is
> an act of assemblage. It then immediately falls to pieces as traces
> and fragments of a different order.[4]
>
> (Pearson and Shanks 2001: 55)

Inherent to 1970s collaboratively devised processes and products
was the potential for invisibility. Little of our devised performances
have passed down for posterity. In the 1970s we were busy empowering ourselves in the present moment – packaging, archiving and documenting seemed secondary: 'It felt exciting and dangerous and new and
deliberately unclassifiable. So somehow bothering to ensure our place in
any future canon of avant-garde theatre was irrelevant' (Furse 2000: 18).
With only restricted access to video, there was little record made of our
work other than personal archives, performance notes, the reviews in
New Dance magazine and the occasional overview of the era (Jordan
1992). As performers owned the material, they could also change it,

with no prescriptive repetition or fixed formula, from one performance to the next. Often there was only one performance and that had no documentation. As the work was created on and for a specific group, with relations between certain performers created by the particular material, work slid away when the performers dispersed. One performer could not be exchanged for another. Collective collaboration did not lend itself to named things but to the invisible in-between-ness of processes and relations. This is the nature of the lifeworld.

26 THE X6 LEGACY

Through the X6 collective structure, each of us developed our individual creative voice. We also developed confidence and an ability to observe each other's contributions with a critical eye. We learnt to do this without a hierarchical separation. We learnt how to lead but also how to listen. We were empowered to re-visit the performer's role without the constant need to rebel. However, collective management was challenging to sustain in an industry that was beginning to re-emphasize product over process. The collective's urgent and persistent mission to shift hierarchical methodologies became a detriment. The sitting-down-to-talk aspect of X6 lost its usefulness. The collective working process was slow. It required equally shared time to talk through ideas – talking that took the place of moving. It was important that the whole person came to the meeting table, complete with ongoing emotional states and day-to-day life stories. But wading through our personal stuff on a daily basis became a time-consuming event; feelings frequently got in the way of decision-making. I continued to turn out my pockets, I searched through the linings, ironed them flat, cut the pockets into small pieces, changed their colours, threw the bits about, reshaped them, sewed them back together differently and repeatedly. In the end, I realized that the contents had long been repositioned elsewhere. In time, the radical collective ideals so vital to the 1970s politics and experiment became unsustainable in a market economy that demanded fast turnover of product and, consequently, identifiable choreographers.[1]

The year 1980 marked X6's break up. We split up to follow our own paths. At the same time, Butlers Wharf was designated to be redeveloped as luxury residential loft apartments. Our will to fight for the space had dispersed into other directions.

The break up of X6 needs careful unravelling. I am pulled up by a contradiction. X6 offered strategies for alternative art practice through equal and shared communication of ideas and responsibilities. Conventional hierarchy was subverted as there was no single author, leader or 'oeuvre' to document. The collective structure inspired a horizontal perspective for making work with supportive systems connecting different voices and discourses with invisible threads. Simultaneously, this subversive collective practice nurtured feminist agendas that encouraged each of us to become authors and autobiographers. Through the collective networks and supported by these networks, the individual feminist voice emerged. The subjective and individual voice was as dependent on the collective network as the network was on the individual. The conflict between setting subversive collaborative strategies and supporting individual artists, between collective consciousness and the individual feminist voice, became a point of friction. This was the creative friction between the practice of collective working and the feminist strategies that the collective practice was framing. Feminist encouragement of performers as choreographers was at odds with the collectively shared ideals and ideas with no visible authors.

Or perhaps it was the other way round. Perhaps it was feminism that held us all at bay in a universal essential framework while the collective process encouraged our individual voices. Feminist agendas in the 1970s stressed women's equality with men, all women together – ignoring the different ideologies, cultures and creative potential of individual women. The liberation of women, discovering female subjectivity in a patriarchal society, was the challenge of the late twentieth century. The challenge of the third millennium is to realize and respect individual creativity and difference within that community. Liberation in the 1970s was about coming together in supportive groups – women, black people, working-class people, artists – all fighting for equality in the face of adversity. The notion of the genius as an isolated figure set apart from the masses was rejected by the group consciousness along with hierarchical leadership. Now, in 2005, liberation is about nurturing the voice of each individual within the group. We can return to the notion of genius, not as a lonely transcendent figure but as different, individual expressions of creativity that depend on, surpass and return to the group consciousness. This shift is something to celebrate.

Collective working and feminism, then, became each other's friend and foe, a dichotomy between singularity and community. We were hindered and empowered simultaneously.

Nevertheless, the 1970s politics and practices left a powerful legacy. The radical embryonic initiatives of the X6/Dartington contexts informed and influenced the development of a new contemporary dance culture. The necessity of working through collective and collaborative strategies indicated the importance for performers to take charge of the means of production, from writing grant applications to creating discourse. Learning those skills is now integrated into the professional development of artists, giving them the confidence to make and perform work outside the mainstream. The powerful role of the performer–choreographer that is now the backbone of independent dance is a direct consequence of feminist personal-as-political methodologies. The rejection of the choreographer-led vision and the emergence of devising tools and improvisational methods of making have encouraged a rich diversity of dance languages and performance statements. Working with personal autobiography, memory and emotion have now become valid sources of material for devised performance. Collaborative devising methodologies have led to the (now) familiar use of collage as a structural form for dance, theatre and physical theatre. Performers' practice of body–mind somatic techniques has now become central to contemporary dance training and is practised alongside and integrated into ballet and other mirror-reflected techniques. The 1970s awakened the respect for dancers as thinking bodies who can make their own decisions about training and professional life. Our recognition that improvisation, contact improvisation in particular, was a key source for movement exploration has led to extraordinarily exciting and innovative duet forms. The experimental practice of release technique by artists in the 1970s has now infiltrated the performances of ballet and contemporary dance, establishing an aesthetic of beauty that embraces gravity rather than transcending it. Parody, cross-disciplinary collaboration, site-specific performance and *jouissance* dance are all accepted now as threads of an independent performance culture. The experimental artists of the 1970s courageously opened up new venues and sites, and persisted in their belief that audiences could be engaged by new dance once the performance languages were made accessible. The first pressure group (ADMA) lobbied the Arts Council for funding for dance and highlighted the need for a political voice for dance artists. This has now been followed through by a range of different umbrella organizations such as Dance UK and the South Asian Dance Alliance. The ADMA Festivals provided performance opportunities for choreographers as individual artists rather than as company institutions, a criterion that Dance Umbrella Festival would also embrace when it began in 1983. *New Dance* magazine demonstrated the need for contemporary dance writing that was then addressed so forcefully in *Dance Theatre Journal*. The experiment initiated the independent dance culture, a framework for artists who direct, choreograph and perform their own project-based work independent of institutional companies and systems. All in all, these strategies instigated a radical shift in ways of thinking, watching and moving dance performance in Britain.

Late one night, to avoid the bailiffs, we return to
X6 at Butlers Wharf. We bring friends and lovers,
crowbars and hammers. Swiftly, silently, efficiently
and collectively, we lift every plank, tongue and
groove of the tea-stained maple wood floor. We
lower it down carefully in roped bundles to the
street below, using the old X6 winch. We load it into
a truck and take it away into the night. I imagine
the headline: 'Dancing thieves save floor from
developers jaws'. We take the wood to an old
factory building on Chisenhale Road in Mile End.
We lay the floor and in so doing prepare the
groundwork for the explosion of independent dance
that is about to take the UK by storm.

The 1970s ended and we took our newly empowered bodies out into the mainstream to follow different careers. The collective experiment had reached its sell-by date. The economic climate demanded product rather than process.

27 DRAWN TO THE MAINSTREAM

It is 1981. I have a shaved head. My son is two
years old. I interview for the job of artistic director
of Extemporary Dance Theatre. The company
represents established contemporary British
dance; it is middle scale, middle of the road. At the
interview, I talk about feminism, liberation politics,
innovation in dance theatre, men dancing, new ideas

on training, release-based ballet. I talk about
stretching the boundaries of dance; I enthuse
about giving performers power in devising work.
I teach the company class. I get the job.

I pause here to glance sideways at my time as artistic director of Extemporary Dance Theatre; first, because wonderful performers and choreographers worked with the company; second, because Extemporary performances reflected attempts to integrate new dance politics and movement forms into the mainstream. The following writing is an experiential account of what happened. It represents a personal view of the challenges to shift working methodologies and performer–spectator conventions. As director, this project proved to be much harder to accomplish in the mainstream than in the feminist collective context of X6.

The initial aspect that drew me to Extemporary was the repertory system of production. Here, a variety of pieces, each by a different choreographer, is presented within a single programme. Working with different choreographers allows dancers to build a range of knowledges about different ways of moving, permitting them to experience a variety of languages and styles. Ideally, a repertory system encourages performers to work against habitual patterns of movement and demands intelligent, thinking bodies capable of embodying differences. The practice of committing movement to body memory and the speed of learning required during the process of creating a repertory are useful skills for performers. Over a period of several years, by embodying a range of repertory pieces, each performer begins to discover an individual pathway. Individuality emerges between the many different styles of choreography: through the experience, performers make choices and form a personal future direction.

Directing Extemporary, I envisioned a company of performers who would do just this: embody a range of styles of presence, shifting from one to the other over the course of an evening. I imagined a performer's training that encouraged the extremes: ballet and improvisation with body and mind centring techniques, each practised with rigour, without hierarchy and without ending up as a homogeneous contemporary dance. I envisioned evenings of different genres of work, retaining the specificity of each work, yet performed by the same dancers. I hoped to encourage a company identity that did not rely on one codified contemporary dance technique as choreographic language but instead played creatively between a range of techniques, skills and styles. I planned to draw on 1970s devising processes and ideas for working relations between performers and directors. I was enthusiastic about change.

Certainly, there were some wonderful moments where innovation and convention met. David Gordon (*Counter Revolution* 1981) introduced us to the cause and effect of sequential gestures, how each pedestrian action becomes a reaction to the movement before, setting the timing and construction of the piece. Ian Spink (*Three Dances* 1982) opened our thinking to the three-dimensional potential of movement, opening stage space to multiple fronts. Karole Armitage (*It Happened at Club Bombay Cinema* 1982) and Michael Clark (*12XU* 1983) introduced punk to ballet, subversively manipulating and fragmenting ballet technique and displacing form from context. Katie Duck (*On the Breadline* 1985) encouraged the improvisational technique of 'journeying' – allowing performers' imaginations to move through anarchic connections between things, catching and revealing moments of outrageous behaviour and spontaneous surprise: get drunk, dance on a hospital bed, throw water from a bucket.

Over the years, an extraordinarily diverse range of performers worked with the company. There was the feisty androgynous-looking Swiss–German, Annelies Stoffel. In *Solo* (1983), Annelies understood how to access the physical expressions of emotional states on her body, embodying every detail of gesture, apprehending the relationship between internal and external manifestations of emotion:

> It's composed of body language and it reveals the variety Stoffel has as a dancer. Here she's maybe stretching her upper body to model for a Degas study, there she's executing a medley of everyday gesture. She's jocular or intent, proud or casual. A sequence of poses acquires its own rhythm, phrases are enlivened by numerous different inflections; and through it all, we see Stoffel's stage personality changing and shifting, always the same and always different. No heroics, just unassuming humanity.
>
> (Macauley 1983: 32)

Extemporary set up the BP Apprentice Scheme, to provide opportunities for young dancers at the beginning of their careers. Jon Smart, Chantale Donaldson, Hopal Romans and Fin Walker were apprentices. The scheme focused particularly on providing opportunities for British Caribbean dancers (Fin Walker being the exception). Chantale was the second performer invited to join the company as an apprentice. Her body was a river of melting treacle, swirling and circling, rushing, rising, licking the air with elegant curves, falling to earth with sinking softness.

In *As the Moon Rises* (Sue Broadway 1988), Chantale hung in a rope net high above the stage. Slowly she eased her body through the gaps of the net and dangled from the ropes by her hands, extending and arching her legs and back. She spilled out of her body into space, effortlessly, generously, allowing the fluid boundaries of her muscular body to expand as she spun fast, hanging to the rope by wrist and ankle. Her body shone and glistened. She was at ease in the air as she was on the ground. Chantale could observe a movement and immediately transfer it to her own body; she was inside the movement before it even left the choreographer's body. Chantale, British Caribbean, trained in ballet and Martha Graham technique, slipped through the gap of fixed identity. She was never where I expected her to be. Swiftly and silently she was always moving somewhere else.

There were others. Edgar Newman, quirky and complex, was in discord with himself and his body never appeared to be in one piece. In *It Happened at Club Bombay Cinema* (1982), each sculpted limb was in tension with another body part: arms with shoulders, legs with feet, spine with skull. His fractured body was constantly constructed into displaced symmetries creating such an intriguing quality, fragmented and so utterly displaced, that I was consistently drawn to watch him. Tam, a petite ethereal androgyne from Thailand, was a feminine balletic bird. In Daniel Larrieu's *Ombres Electriques* (1984), he walked delicately across the backs of Lloyd Newson, Jon Smart and Edgar Newman. Israeli born Yacov Slivkin was rehearsal director for the company. I remember him dressed in black dress and plimsolls, performing as the Italian widow in Fergus Early's re-working of *Naples* (1982), first devised for X6 collective in 1979.[1] Looking sultry and bored most of the time, Yacov broke out occasionally into Bournonville ballet steps, which he performed with a cool dismissive manner. Then he would stop and slouch off with a sullen, arrogant glance to the audience.

There will be more on Lloyd Newson, Fin Walker and the extraordinary Nigel Charnock later.

28 REPERTORY VERSUS PROJECT

In the end, the factors that had drawn me to Extemporary would also repel me. The repertory challenge of Extemporary was the determining factor in the decision to terminate my role as artistic director in 1989.

Extemporary became a compromise between the experimental and the established. It had become exactly what I had hoped it would not – an obscure medley of contemporary dance in performance. Ramsay Burt comments:

> The company, despite the individual attempts at new dance work, resembles a repertory company with a new dance style rather than representing a radical departure. The problem is in the repertory system itself. The supposed balance of work that makes up a company's repertoire is in itself an expression of hegemonic control by a liberal art consensus. The process of making dance collectively is replaced by the process of dancing the same dances night after night, and this has a tendency towards making a homogenous performance style . . . It has become possible to include new dance within a mainstream company programme because it is rendered safe, no matter how much it might have force in any other context.
>
> (Burt and Huxley 1985: 175)

The problems were illuminated as the repertory system of production clashed with performance as process. I had underestimated the *time* it took for bodies to re-learn through somatic attention, despite their willingness to do so. Letting go of single-track institutional dance training with its mirror-reflected languages left the dancers bodies vulnerable and exposed. Letting go of habitual movement patterns, using improvisation as a tool to discover language, was challenging territory for performers, requiring risk-taking confidence and patience to discover new ways of moving. Embodying a different style for each piece proved exhausting and unfeasible. There was no time to let go, undo, re-think and allow the body–mind knowledge to do its work. Production of a familiar product, a diet of accessible time-driven virtuoso choreography, consistently won out over the process-based innovation. The tell-me-what-to-do syndrome prevailed; I had underestimated performers' profound need for feedback and external direction. Extemporary, it seemed, was destined to produce, produce and produce with the performers fodder for the repertory machine.

At Extemporary, choreographers and performers were dissatisfied with the short periods for rehearsal time. A three-week rehearsal period with each new choreographer and each different choreographic statement proved insufficient time for the dancers to embody the choreographer's intent, leading to a lack of physical precision. An established repertory such as Rambert Dance Company maintains a company brand of movement language throughout each piece, even though the choreographies are different. In Extemporary, I was asking performers to embody a different movement language and way of moving for each choreography. It was just not possible. The contrasting ideas and styles of choreographers such as Tom Jobe (*City* 1981), Dan Wagoner (*Spiked Sonata* 1981), Steve Paxton (*Audible Scenery* 1986), Viola Farber (*Winter Rumours* 1987) and Katie Duck (*On the Breadline* 1985) were compromised on performer's bodies. As a result, each style was embodied superficially. Furthermore, the nuances and details of each different language became lost during a nine-month tour. Bodies slipped back into habitual patterns; unable to maintain the extreme differences, performers became jacks of all trades and masters of none. Pedestrian action and contact improvisation ended up looking like ballet, while contemporary dance ended up looking like jazz. Lloyd Newson was frustrated that technically skilled dancers could not reveal themselves as emotional and sexual bodies. David Gordon was amused as to why dancers continued to point their feet while running and falling into someone's arms.

In retrospect, Extemporary functioned in direct opposition to the artistic methodologies and the collective art-making culture I had come to appreciate through X6. X6 encouraged performers as makers; Extemporary commissioned outside experts. X6 functioned as a collective; Extemporary operated as a hierarchy. X6 encouraged performance as process; Extemporary made products to tour. X6 had very little funding; Extemporary had significant Arts Council grants. X6 did not rely on large audiences for its continued experiment; Extemporary required 'bums on seats' to ensure funding. X6's artistic plans developed and shifted in the present; Extemporary required a three-year artistic plan. X6 philosophies required research; Extemporary had no time for research. At X6 we were paid nothing and had plenty of time; at Extemporary we had no time and (comparatively) plenty of money.

Meanwhile, emerging in parallel to Extemporary were project-based independent dance companies with more direct links to 1970s politics and experiments. In contrast to the repertory system, project-based performance follows one choreographic voice.[1] Extemporary attempted to present many voices in one performance. In project work, dancers and director work together on a shared vision, delving deeply into a specific language and style of work. The success of the British independent dance scene is in its breadth and multiplicity of differences. Here today and gone tomorrow is the nature of project-based companies, while repertory companies can last indefinitely. Having something to say, saying it and moving on describes the independent project system; there is no need for compromise. This is its integrity, its alive-ness and honesty. Becoming mainstream, producing safe middle-of-the-road work, organizing company structures with a board, producing products that can be repeated ad infinitum are not the aims of project-based companies.[2] Extemporary's repertory structure turned out to be the antithesis of the independent dance theatre companies – a working structure I had helped initiate in the 1970s. Most of all, Extemporary was compromised between process and performance, making and marketing.

Acting as artistic director in a hierarchical company structure clashed with the X6 philosophy and the equality of different working roles. Moments in the studio, teaching, choreographing and rehearsing clashed with administrative and financial demands. I was torn between my responsibilities to the performers and those of the management, between rehearsal procedures and the administrative team that maintained the company's public face. shifting between studio and office, I attempted to switch my body and mind from living in the moment to the demands of strategic forward planning. I was driven by the need for change. But the company organization had rules and regulations, bureaucratic machinery that was slow to shift. Once an idea had been generated, the machinery was turned on; the wheels began to turn and lumbered along towards the fixed end goal. Change was likely to upset the system. This contradiction between living in present and future time, between new ideas and fixed goals, between process and product, was the basis for the repertory compromise.

My home life and work at Extemporary are also in contradiction. At home, I am a mother.
I begin sleeping with women. Living as a mother and a lesbian feels irresolvable with my role as the director of a middle-scale dance company. I thrash about between one role and another. I am never sure which part of my life is performed and which part is real. I wear a suit when I should be wearing an evening dress. I fight with a plastic Star Wars light sabre when I should be carrying a briefcase. As an artist, a lesbian and a mother, compromise is of no interest.

Historically, in the British context of contemporary dance, Extemporary was a place of ideas. In the early 1980s, it was successful in introducing innovative performances that pushed the boundaries of mainstream contemporary dance presented in provincial theatres. The company instigated the first apprentice scheme whereby young black dancers could gain professional experience in mainstream performance. The company proved that experimental work, given production budgets and supportive publicity, could engage audiences with thought-provoking, accessible and humorous performances. The company helped to break down the image British audiences had come to recognize as contemporary dance: angst-ridden, heavily symbolic, mysterious and transcendent, stylized, Martha Graham-derived and difficult to understand. Extemporary succeeded as a company of ideas, persistently challenging the comfortable predictability of performer–spectator relations in middle-scale theatre.

29 MIDDLE MUSH (own *Balk*)

Extemporary's demise *audis edan* resulted from its becoming stuck between the experiment and the establishment. This is a place I call 'middle mush'. It is everything that ambiguity is not, everything that seduction is not. It is the fixed, thick, solid place that dancing can become when movement is predictable and watching is endless, having lost the play between precise points. It is the dynamic I fear most in British contemporary dance.

Middle mush also happens in training. Dancing – I mean *dancing* as an artistic codified expression, as an articulate language – requires an in-depth training. However, institutional contemporary dance training in British postmodern, post-Enlightenment culture has became one of breadth, not depth. Ballet training works with the extreme limit of one technique but contemporary dance tries to incorporate all without any extremes. There are so many performance and body–mind techniques available that the dilemma facing contemporary dance is not the elitism of a particular system, but the mixture and merging of many. In universities, dance has become a thoughtful subject of study – something to write about and analyse rather than rigorously practice. Universities support a modular system of learning, enticing students to apply by offering an impressive range of goods – a little bit of ballet, a little bit of contemporary, a little bit of Kathak or an African dance fusion. The forms are studied for a term or two and then dropped for something else.

For many performers and performance makers emerging from academies and universities, moving the body in space and time has become one element of cross-disciplinary performance, where verbal texts, film and digital technology replace the expressive potential of the dancing body. Gill Clarke, who works at the forefront of professional development for dance artists in Britain, observes how performers are 'collaborating across styles, genres and cultures. They are making their work for many contexts, to be placed in bus stations, pubs and galleries, or transformed onto film, CD-ROM, or Internet – indeed their performers may even be virtual!' (Clarke 2003: 6). This is fine, but we need an articulate movement language with which to collaborate in the first place. Cross-disciplinary performance is sparked by the contradictions of specific differences, not the middle ground between disciplines.

Looking back at the 1980s, I remember how we took our new bodies of dance knowledge into schools, companies and universities across Britain. We were enthusiastic to make change (and gain economic stability): 'Once bodies of knowledge, or certain practices, become common currency in the professional domain is it not our responsibility, as educators, to give dance students access to them? How else do we move forward?' (Clarke 2003: 5). My concern is that British contemporary dance training resolved the postmodern challenge to disperse with a single fixed identity (Graham or Cunningham technique, for instance) by instigating movement languages that avoid extremes and sit in the middle between linearity and fluidity. Favouring the place of mind–body health, the dancing body does not get off the ground. It has no aggression in its physicality, but neither is it fragile – it is, instead, dynamically safe. Afraid of pain, looking in rather than out, the trend in contemporary dance in Britain has been a merging of forms to create a pleasant, bland homogeneity that is all hugs and no bite. The balletic hierarchical identity is certainly not the answer, but neither is the amalgamated mush. I helped prepare for this dilemma in the 1970s, preaching the importance of the subjective body, rejecting conventional training, developing a fusion of techniques into one class, giving more importance to conceptual than physical development. I see the resulting middle mush today as the negative flip side of the legacy, the residue of that important and necessary 1970s agenda.

If I sound as if I am standing on a soapbox, I am! I am saying what I think about training and you can shout me down.

We can teach ballet, contemporary and release, Bharatanatyam, African dance forms, contact improvisation, Cunningham and many other forms of training. But we can teach them for their *different* philosophies and embodied knowledges, not mixed together. Of course, ballet is now informed by body–mind knowledges, and must be slowly, carefully and repetitively taught, adapted for contemporary training. But the discipline of ballet is ballet. Release technique is release. Respect the upward lift and the downwards fall, but let's not hang about somewhere in the middle, caring more for students' conceptual development and health and safety than physical articulation. The students will take care of how these two extremes play together through their choreography and improvisation. We are no longer living in the 1960s and 1970s under the shadow of oppressive Enlightenment systems. Students have a voice; they say when enough is enough; they are quite capable of directing their own training. They find their own movement expressions once their bodies are rigorously skilled in the extremes of techniques. We can trust their intelligence and nurture their bodies through. We, as teachers, can give them this challenge, drive them, encourage them, make them sweat. They want it! The only time is now.

As dancers, we must train, every day. It doesn't have to be ballet technique but it does have to be a training that we can consume, absorb and be absorbed by; a technique to which we are subservient while learning; a technique in which we are always hungry for the continual repetition that will bring new knowledge and discipline to our bodies. And we can *think* while we are dancing; we can think physically into our bodies constantly and at every moment of the dance. We can be in the body of the dance right now and in each moment differently. We can think intelligently, imaginatively and spontaneously. Every movement has a dynamic, a quality; each is different to the next, just as each word is different when placed next to another. We can explore the differences, embody each gesture fully; shift and change. We can switch from linearity to fragmentation instantly and totally, and play between looking out and looking in. We can question the focus of each physical task. We can extend our legs with pointed feet, feel muscles taut and held, precise and sharp. We can learn how to jump and fall and how these two depend upon each other's oppositions. We can open and extend our bodies as if we are stretched and balanced on the edge of a precipice. We can feel that vulnerability, exposed to the air like a cold shower washing over us, then fold into a complexity of liquid joints. We live in 2006: the knowledges of the different extremes are out there. We can grab them and gulp them down like fresh water. We don't need to get stuck in that middle place of sleepy, comfy suffocation. Take a risk – go there, all the way.

British culture in 2006 is a consumerist, throwaway culture, where choice is all-important. This climate, with the student as client, has encouraged an education of tasters. Take a single bite and throw away the rest. Embodying a physical training rigorously, in depth and every day, is not fashionable. But look to see where contemporary choreographers such as William Forsyth, Wayne McGregor, Fin Walker, Lloyd Newson and Carol Brown find their dancers. For the most part, the dancers they select have embodied a rigorous training, often in ballet. Why? Because ballet, like yoga or aikido, is a technique that requires discipline, a knowledge of central weight and gravity, physical intelligence, a quick memory, the ability to change and to understand the conflict of opposites, contradiction, tension, rhythm and focus. Released from its dependence on transcendent expression, it embraces hard work and builds stamina. It is physically rigorous and articulate. Certainly, ballet choreography is, for the most part, two-dimensional, relentlessly repetitive, saturated by style and narratively dreary. And yes, performing ballet can become so habitual and repetitively patterned on the body that dancers find themselves wondering what to have for dinner while performing. But that is not the fault of a finely-tuned training; it is, rather, the lack of innovative choreographic process compared to that in the independent dance sector. That is why so many ballet dancers leave to work with contemporary choreographers. It is also because they are confidently ready for the next level of professional experience that requires 'letting go' of ballet's hierarchical choreographic structures and externally directed styles.

Letting go of fixed patterns of movement and expression is the deluxe element of dance training for contemporary performance. Letting go is the sophistication of knowledge, the deconstruction of classicism. Letting go comes with the maturity of continuous practice and with a generosity, acknowledgement and love for both tradition and innovation. That is why Derrida returned again and again to the classic literature as a place from which to re-figure language. That is why Pina Bausch's dancers return to the ballet barre day after day. Letting go into the experience of something new requires the lived knowledge and constant re-embodying of the thing that we wish to release. We need to live the extremes, not some halfway middle mush place in between.

I share this fear of middle mush because of its consequences for female bodies in particular. It opens up the paradox again between subjectivity and invisibility. Virtuosity and external expression have acted as a technique of disguise and displacement that work in contradiction to the internal focus and hold the real body secret. I have learnt that we need both body–mind wholeness and virtuosity to engage our audiences. We can enjoy the creative spark between the spectator's desire for polished product and the engagement with performance as process. Re-claiming, re-figuring and re-owning the dazzle as a play for performance must be our way forward, not giving up on it altogether.

Maybe . . .

Figure 10 Emilyn Claid in *Virginia Minx at Play* (1993). Publicity image.
Photographer: Chris Nash.

III Maybe . . .

Depth becomes surface and ambiguous points of play

30 PROCESS TO PRODUCT

Spanning the trajectory from collectively devised work to collaborative work that includes a directorial role are two performances: *Grace & Glitter* for Extemporary Dance Theatre (1987) and *Back to Front with Side Shows* for CandoCo Dance Company (1993). Moving between the two, I came to understand how a director can open the space for process, yet also draw that process into an articulate product.

X6 collective feminist experiments spawned *Grace & Glitter*, a piece for eight women performers. Issues of race and gender underlie a theme that explored relationships between British black Caribbean and white women.[1] Maggie Semple and I devised the piece in collaboration with the performers. With our black and white fists in the air, we were determined not to separate dance from politics. Here, the 1970s figures of feminism, androgyny and parody intermingled as we employed theatrical, political, narrative, autobiographical and cross-disciplinary strategies. Phallic muscular bodies, strident figures of defiance, fluid moving bodies, glamour bodies – stereotypes of tomboys, strippers, prostitutes, mothers, schoolgirls, ballet dancers and Amazons – all made their appearance. Through the women's relationships and stories, the spectators were 'invited to appreciate the sharing and co-operation between women but at the same time the struggle of survival' (Adair 1987).

The performance begins with an aerobic power dance. Dressed in black sportswear, tight vests, shorts and Reebok trainers, the women pound the stage with jumps, high kicks, rolls, running and lifting. There follows a scene with the women dressed in glamorous tight dresses and high heels, strutting, preening and tittering. Enter the tomboy figure, Lindsey Butcher, who is teased and bullied but finally comes into her own as she easily outruns Saorse Baron. Saorse performs a parody, running after the agile Lindsey while trapped in a tight dress and high heels. Dawn and Chantale Donaldson, sisters in real life, perform a loving duet to blues jazz – two black women wearing white tutus. Dawn, Chantale and Kaye Hunter dress each other's hair and discuss how histories of black women are passed down from mothers to daughters through the daily hair ritual. Enter Fin Walker, a white woman wearing an Afro wig and dancing to Bob Marley. The black women dismiss her, ripping the wig off her head. Another group dance follows, a fluid lyrical dance complete with baggy T-shirts and trousers. There are fight scenes between jealous couples and a rape scene. As the three black women parody the stereotypical images of West Indian grandmothers, the white women parody their 'upwardly mobile' working-class mothers. A pre-recorded text accompanies the performance, written by Tash Fairbanks and spoken by Maggie Semple's mother. With her West Indian dialect, Mrs Semple speaks of 'a tidal wave of women down the years' (Fairbanks 1987). A tutu strip takes place. Ballerina Lindsey Butcher finds herself caught in the spotlight, centre stage in a white tutu. The other four performers join her – as professional strippers – each in her own spotlit corner of the stage. Saorse teaches the ballerina to strip. However, Lindsey's final stripper pose changes to that of a female body builder. Prostitutes, in high heels and raincoats, streetwalk. They are hard and angry, glaring at the audience, breaking into a powerful jazz disco routine while little remote-controlled cars zoom back and forth across the stage, running riot around their feet. The final image portrays the two musicians, Sylvia Hallet and Lucy Wilson. They sit on a bench, exchanging hats slowly. They get up and walk towards the back of the stage while the six young women, dressed again in their aerobic gear, standing still, feet apart in a power stance, facing the audience, let out a long piercing war cry.

Grace & Glitter was about women's lives and loves, nurturing subjectivity and visibility for black and white women. The women were vibrant, angry and funny. They were identifiably present and expressive, committed to the experience of performing empowered liberated women. The piece was packed with ideas. But it focused on process rather than product.

Back to Front with Side Shows (Emilyn Claid 1993) was devised with CandoCo Dance Company, an integrated company of disabled and non-disabled performers.[2]

Five performers stand still in a tight group, upstage centre, facing straight ahead. They are dressed in black vests and trousers – the contours of each body defined. In the front of the group is David Toole.

As the lights come up, he walks five steps forward. He has no legs. He supports the weight of his torso on long, muscular arms with tactile elegant supple hands. His hands are slightly turned out, for balance. The rest of the group follows: Jon French in his wheelchair, Kuldip Singh-Barmi also in a wheelchair (but feigning disability) and the three women: Helen Baggett, Sue Smith and Charlotte Derbyshire in close proximity. This little procession makes its way downstage centre. David dismisses Kuldip with a nod. Kuldip leaves his own wheelchair stage right and makes a full circle of the outside of the space, bent double, mocking a disabled walk. He finds David's chair stage left, sits in it and wheels himself along with his feet. He travels back the way he came, around the outside of the space, and returns to David. Kuldip jumps, nosedives and lands on his hands with his feet on the chair behind him. Lowering his torso, he rests his elbows on the floor. He props up his head with his hand and looks at David. Using Kuldip's body as a slanting bridge, David climbs up to reach his wheelchair. And so the piece begins.

The initial meeting to discuss the choreography for CandoCo was held at the old Laban Centre at New Cross, London. We sat in the building's atrium and chatted. The performers shared memorable personal moments and fantasies in the café and in the pub. I listened while they talked among themselves. David was keen to dress up and subvert the figure of the circus freak. He wanted to wear high heels on his hands. David's initial catwalk from back to front, centre stage, represented a trace of the fantasy. Jon recalled his frustration of his experiences in hospital following the accident that left him disabled. Sue and Helen talked rebelliously of embodying fast, risk-taking movement material. Kuldip joked, teased and spilt his sparkling dynamic magic over the others.

In 1993, disability was just becoming visible in Western dance culture and there was a growing political awareness about inclusion. CandoCo Dance Company was at the forefront of integrated performance. But in the studio the performers let fly from political correctness. They were big-hearted, fearless, trusting, passionate and highly energized individuals ready to have fun, parody the 'softly softly' approach and be irritated and impatient with each other regardless of dis/ability. They were not afraid to install conventional attitudes in order to subvert the stereotypical treatment of disabled people. Their rebellious spirits were not interested in finding a lovely dance that would make everybody feel happy and safe. Each performer wanted to test the boundaries, take him/herself to an extreme.

After several days of improvising, personae began to emerge that became more defined through the interactions between one another. Each performer drew out different sides of her/himself, depending on who s/he was playing against. Kuldip was the trickster, the jester; David was the master of ceremonies, the magician, leading the way, controlling the action, remaining aloof and detached; Jon was the artist, the poet, dreaming in his own world; Sue, Helen and Victoria provided the core energy of the piece, carrying the dance movement and shaping the space. They were the catalysts; they set the mood changes, provoked dynamic shifts and drove the action. They worked together as a powerful force, physically strong, rebellious, direct and determined to take on the world, refusing an indecisive middle ground. Physical risk persistently surfaced during the process, so it became part of the performance.

Kuldip kicks, turns, falls, while David, twisting and jumping off his hands, slips deftly and silently under and between his legs and feet. Kuldip's high-kicking legs miss David's body by a fraction. David runs across the stage on his hands and is chased by Helen and Sue, who drag him back by his arms. David somersaults out of his wheelchair and lands in Jon's lap. David jumps into Kuldip's arms and Kuldip falls backwards, flat onto his back, splat on the floor. Jon's wheelchair is tipped off balance and Jon falls backwards with David on his lap, a fall broken only by Kuldip's prone body beneath the chair.

Kuldip pulls Jon from his wheelchair onto the floor. Kuldip and Jon engage in a boxing match. Kuldip supports Jon's torso while they punch at each other, boxing being an activity enjoyed by Jon before his disabling accident. Kuldip wrestles spontaneously, encouraging Jon in his desire to fight, matching blow for blow, while respecting Jon's vulnerability.

Jon, David and Kuldip sit in their wheelchairs. Sue, Helen and Charlotte attend to them. The women act as 'carers': patting, fretting, adjusting and pampering their 'patients' in an obsessive and excessive fashion. They chat and laugh with each other over their patients' heads as if these men are absent. Smothered and powerless, the patients begin to push the carers away but the carers return in a sequence that becomes more impassioned with each repetition. Independence is returned to the wheelchair users as they employ their virtuoso techniques for fast, furious wheelchair manoeuvres across the space.

The performers owned the material. The image described in the previous paragraph emerged from conversations about hospital care. Their discussion and improvisation revealed the power dynamics between wheelchair users and caregivers, and the dynamics between the disabled men and the non-disabled women. The scene became set when enough information had been gathered. Through the set structure, the performers re-conjured the emotional weight of the event through parody.

Not satisfied with only physical risk, we tested emotional and sexual boundaries. Just as disability itself has been considered to be 'other' – invisible in Western culture except to the medical profession and the circus – so the notion of disabled people having sex has been a taboo (Kuppers 2003).

Helen lies on her back; David lies beside her and strokes his hand intimately down the front of her body. He shifts his weight onto his hands and walks his hands onto her body to initiate a kiss. Charlotte sits on Jon's lap, straddled over the wheelchair, and engages in a long kissing session. Kuldip and Sue hurl each other to the floor passionately and competitively.

The performers were not there to realize my vision. I was there to realize theirs, to facilitate their stories. My role at the early stage of the devising process was to hold open the door, creating the space so that the performers, as people, could discover their own performance. The dynamic imagery of the different disabled and non-disabled physicalities, combined with the steely, mechanistic aesthetic of the wheelchairs, was already there. At the beginning, I provided not the content but the undercurrents, tasks and means through which the content would emerge. I looked through the relationships for the source of the work, the elements that would drive the piece into its own making. This involved me in a continual process of setting up and letting go of fixed pre-conceived ideas on a daily basis. I resisted choreographing at this stage – working backwards towards the threads that would weave themselves into new material.

As the performance deadline approached, my role switched. I no longer facilitated, making gaps for the performers to create material. Instead, I took a role in front of the action and began to shape the work, taking the process into product. They owned it; I shaped it. Recognizing when to switch from directing behind the action to in front of the action was an important learning process. Understanding how to open the space for the material to emerge and then shape that material so it can be accessible to the audience are, for me, two different but necessary stages of a collaboratively devised process.

Towards the end of the piece, David signals to Kuldip, who leaves the stage and returns with a black wooden box that he puts down in front of David. David opens the lid upwards and consequently disappears from audience view. He takes a hat out of the box, and passes it to Kuldip who passes it round the group until it reached its owner. The last two hats to emerge are wedding hats: a top hat and a bride's veil, both covered in cobwebs and lace. David hands the top hat to Kuldip and puts the veiled hat on his own head. He closes the lid and

Figure 11 David Toole and Sue Smith in *Back to Front with Side Shows* (Emilyn Claid 1993). CandoCo Dance Company.

Photographer: Anthony Crickmay.

climbs onto the box. He stands looking out. Kuldip and David turn their heads sideways to look to each other. They return their faces to the front. They deliberately take off their hats and exchange them. David now wears the top hat.

> Haunting, vaguely liturgical, punchy, cacophonous, and eventually incorporating Strangers In the Night. Dramatic lighting on six dancers in black. Singh-Barmi appears in one of the wheelchairs ('cheat!', you think – we know he does not need one) – then leaps out to become a devilish figure, tipping John French out of *his* chair for a punch-up on the floor (double shock). A sort of Hammer Horror ambience with sexy bits; David Toole's mesmerising, witty expressions; a climax with funny hats.
>
> (Dougill 1994)

Collaborative devising requires confidence for everyone involved as we face the fear of exposing personal emotional experiences and unknown pathways. Fear fixes the hierarchical roles of director and performers. The devising process requires letting go of fear, admitting to mistakes, allowing performers to speak. Letting go of the fixed hierarchical roles suggests that 'one is forced to advance beyond familiar territory, far from the certainties to which one is accustomed, towards an as yet uncharted land and unforeseeable conclusion' (Foucault 1969: 42). The devising process takes time and invites chaos as it disperses with the notion of a single text or universal narrative and opens itself to a multitude of potential directions.

Back to Front with Side Shows employed a process that respected performers in the creation of the material, allowing performers full ownership of the work. The performers' relationships rather than the outside eye directed the cues for action. The performers themselves knew how to make things happen, they owned the tools for change. Owning the material allowed spontaneous and interactive relationships to occur on stage. Performers discovered fresh impetus in the material as it was being performed, as they were always in a process of reaching a new level of self-discovery. The process was theirs. However, *Back to Front with Side Shows* was not just about process, but also about product. Devising shifted to directing, authorship to readership.

Unlike *Grace & Glitter*, the earlier collectively devised experiment, *Back to Front with Side Shows* was not about real-bodies-doing-real-things-in-real-time as performance. It was about drawing the real events and relations between performers into a surface shape and sharp focus for performance whereby the timing and structure of the performed images dislodged the indulgences of reality. Both *Grace & Glitter* and *Back to Front with Side Shows* were issue-based pieces dealing with concerns close to the hearts of the performers. *Grace & Glitter* emphasized process over product in an empowering experience for women dancers – sometimes knocking the nail on the head with a feminist hammer. *Back to Front with Side Shows* shifted the real into a tightly timed form, giving attention to the external choreographic shape. The piece was owned by performers, yet read by spectators via a collective process, but a directed product. The timing of *Grace & Glitter* often depended on the real time of embodying the emotional narratives. But real time is too revealing for dance theatre product where precise editing and articulation dominate. CandoCo performers owned the emotional depth of material while simultaneously trusting the structured surface shape. The work derived from the reality of the performers' lives, allowing them physically to own the material. Yet that reality was transformed through edited timing and directed space into a polished surface for performance.

Side step. David Toole has no legs. He stands on his hands looking out at the audience, then collapses down on his forearms to rest. He looks cool, detached, sultry, almost bored. He gives nothing away. He does not play or react to spectator's gaze. Our gaze hits his legless body and bounces right back to us. Lloyd Newson, who worked with David in *The Cost of Living* (DV8 2000), says:

> Because of David's physicality, it is easy to project your own feelings and imagined history onto him. But regardless of this and the immediacy of his body, David himself carries his history and identity when he performs, in his voice, his focus, his manner. What is fantastic about David is that there seems no barrier between who he is on stage and who he is in real life. This creates a power and presence that is very true, very direct and speaks straight to you.
>
> (Newson 2003)

Seductive relations between the real body and performed illusion take a twist when David performs. Walking, running on his hands, reaching out his arm, sliding gracefully in and out of his wheelchair are every-day pedestrian gestures for David. In performance, these gestures become dazzling, his movements appear as amazing feats, vast and spectacular. But it is when he rests on his elbows, small and still, looking directly out, real and present, that I most feel the absence of his legs. When David is motionless on stage, he becomes extraordinary to spectators, who are drawn to watch his ownership of vulnerability. Spectators are placed in the position of fascinated voyeurs. David, as a real non-performing body – a body without legs – becomes wondrous in the spectators' gaze. The spectacle is his absence. Because he has no legs, I, as spectator, remember what I cannot see. His presence is shadowed by what is not there. He does not need to construct an illusion. He only has to be himself.

31 FULL BODY EMPTY BODY

Performers find ways to shift process to product. This is a practice of full body becoming empty body, whereby meaningful authored movement passes into surface shape. I devise physical material from auto-biographical narratives, emotions and desires. Then I look for ways to take the material to a less literal place, in order not to give it all away. Emoting on stage, with the full dancing body, leaves little space for the audience to engage. At the same time the intention is not to become an abstract body, where the material no longer has connections to the emotional source.

In *Virginia Minx at Play* (1993), I inhabited different remembered personae of my history, drawing on their emotions and physicalizing their desires. The creative challenge, the juice of the work with emotions and memory, was to find the place on my body where fullness of memory and emptiness sparred with each other on a fine line of tension. I looked for the place where physical task and emotion met.

'Portrait' was the penultimate section of *Virginia Minx at Play*. Creating the material took me through a series of childhood and family memories. The structure followed the journey from young girl to old woman, passing through adolescence, tomboy, rebellious teenager; through sexual experience, eating disorders, motherhood, drunkenness, loss and ageing. My own experiences mingled with those of my family. Each embodiment was full of memory and emotion. I began work in the studio by writing family memories that would then be re-constructed on my body.

I re-worked the child's body language, gestures, energy level, muscle tension, posture: I rocked on the outside of my feet, smiling shyly, my head to one side, hands tucked under my armpits. I knew when I found the appropriate gesture because the emotional memory flooded back into my body. I relived the gestures and the rhythm of the breathing repeatedly, finding every detail, every turn of head and angle of chin, storing them as kinaesthetic memory, as gestures that felt connected to the experience. Having fully re-embodied the child's story, I extracted the emotional and experiential memory as the source of gesture. I trusted my body to re-construct the gestures as physical tasks. The challenge was to recreate the body language of the experience with every muscle, eye movement, angle of the head, and placement of fingers and toes as physical task. I emptied my body of emotion, leaving the empty shell. Embodying the gesture as a series of empty tasks brought the memory to the point of re-claiming and filling me with emotion. The re-construction of each gesture in performance allowed me to sense the moment when it would fill once more with emotion. I worked to find that fine line between content and form, balancing in the space between full body and empty.

In the final pose of 'Portrait', I am curved forwards from the waist, my torso twisted and tilted sideways towards the audience, shoulders slightly lifted, knees bent. My wrists cross over one other in front of my body, elbows resting back against my ribs, chest caved in. My hands are turned upwards, limp with palms open. My focus is to the space ahead, eyes and face empty. The emotional physical memory that conjured the physical image was that of the futility of my mother's death.

Re-embodying the pose as a physical task brought a sense of grief flooding back. I repeated the gesture again and again until I found that place, just before, just at the brink, while the gesture was still empty, before the tears, on the long wail of the breath. I hovered between the empty gesture and the full memory of emotion. The fullness slipped away leaving the empty illusion. But the empty gesture was not a gesture of no-thing. It became empty through a fullness of real body doing. It was a reversible process; repeatedly letting go of the real to re-construct an illusion in turn provoked the memory of the real. And the real itself became a constructed memory. Each experience was moulded and then extracted, leaving an empty cast that carried its depth as a surface.

32 THE CHAMELEON

Lloyd Newson was a wizard at the play of full body, empty body. For Lloyd, Extemporary was a platform from which to spring. This was a fragment of his life, before DV8 Physical Theatre, at a time when the lights were just coming up on his illustrious career. Extemporary's repertory company system may have had its problems but the presentation of several different choreographies in one evening promoted a seductive strategy of disguise and displacement for Lloyd (Phelan 1993). Like a chameleon, Lloyd disappeared to re-appear differently, in each and every piece. As a performer, he had to become empty in order to embody each persona. In this way, he was author (fully owning and inhabiting each persona) and ambiguous for the spectator (who observed the play between the different personae) simultaneously:

> It was interesting being asked to portray different personas, but I had to find a reason, a rationale . . . a journey for each piece or character. It didn't necessarily have to be narrative; but it needed, at the very least, to make emotional sense. If I couldn't find a route to do this then the piece was empty for me.
>
> (Newson 2003)

In 1983, I watch Lloyd perform five different personae in one programme.[1] *12XU* (Michael Clark 1983) is a duet for Lloyd and Yacov

Slivkin. Accompanied by loud punk music, the two men physically grind their bodies in a language of subverted ballet and Cunningham move-ments. Legs lift in sideways *arabesques*, hips swivel, backs twist against long leg lunges, shoulders flick and shrug, extended arms cross one another, and jumps land in off-balance poses. Yacov and Lloyd run backwards with limping steps, then contract their torsos and fall on the floor. They support each other in lifts, subverting the ballet *pas de deux*. Seemingly endless, exhaustive material drives on and on against the harsh punk rock sounds.

> I imitated and absorbed the subtleties of the movements Michael gave me – the qualities and dynamics; but you can't *be* Michael Clark. So you find your reasons for doing the piece; in my case, pushing my body to a physical extreme, connecting to the subversive violence in the music (The Fall's '12XU'), feeling the nihilism underlying Michael's work counted against a desire for technical elegance.
>
> (Newson 2003)

Giraffes, Jellyfish and Things (Sally Owen 1982) teases the theme of Darwin's theory of evolution. Within this one piece, Lloyd plays an amoeba, a sea creature, a jellyfish, a chameleon, a frog, a chicken, a monkey and a short-sighted beatnik at a cocktail party. Lloyd creates a parody of each character and in so doing parodies himself. As the chameleon, he appears upstage left. He is crawling on hands and knees with his back slightly arched, head strained upwards, chin tucked in, eyes looking down. His elbows are angled outwards and he balances his weight on his fingers. As one hand moves forward, the opposite leg lifts, knee high to the side, foot clawed. It comes down slightly in front of the other leg. The sequence begins again. Slowly he makes his way on to the stage with sharp, exact gestures. Edgar, as lizard, moves swiftly across the space. Lloyd's bald head nods excessively, his chest expands, excitement mani-fested through his upper torso and neck. The audience laughs at the chameleon's pathetic show of excitement. Lloyd sits back on his heels. The lights change colour. With jagged gestures combined with heavy ponderous movements, he takes off his T-shirt to reveal another that reflects the change of colour. The lights change again. Lloyd sheds another T-shirt. The sequence repeats five times. 'Lloyd Newson as a chameleon, an extraordinarily jointed, back-rippling reptile, whose slow stalking and alert basking finally breaks out into the hasty sloughing of one leotard after another' (Jordan 1983: 32).

In *Naples* (Fergus Early 1982), Lloyd plays an Italian chef cooking spaghetti – upstage, dressed in a green sports jacket and white trousers.

Figure 12 Lloyd Newson in *12XU* (Michael Clark 1983). Extemporary Dance
Theatre, Riverside Studios, London.

Photographer: Dee Conway. With thanks to Extemporary Dance Theatre Archives at the
National Resource Centre for Dance, University of Surrey.

Occasionally he leaves his cooking to perform a solo, duet or trio. He performs the complicated Bournonville ballet steps with serious panache. Camp but gullible, Lloyd's Italian persona is teased by Avigail Ben Ari, who plays the 'Countess of Leisure'. She stuffs marshmallows into his mouth to bursting point. This is Lloyd's sugar hit, repeated night after night over long weeks of touring.

It Happened at Club Bombay Cinema (Karole Armitage 1982) finds Lloyd dancing another fast, raging, punk piece.[2] The performers dance a subverted classical/Cunningham language, articulate with leg kicks and flung torsos. The piece describes the raw-edged violence of a street shooting outside a cinema. Lloyd wears fake leather trousers. His torso is bare. He jumps, landing on the balls of his feet. With legs bent, he throws his body forward with his arms flung overhead. He leaps, twisting his hips in the air. He turns, slides and circles one leg high in the air. He jumps, landing with his legs wide, hops with his body tilted forward. He runs across the stage, partnering and pulling other performers. His arms fling sharply against his legs as he skitters across the floor. There are Scottish dance steps, classical ballet steps, mock Bharatanatyam gestures and club dancing. The piece persistently drives onwards and onwards. There are fractions of time when Lloyd stops to glare coldly at other performers and the audience.

At the end of the evening, Lloyd performs in his own choreography, *Breaking Images* (1982), a piece that explores the stereotypes of beauty in Western culture. The piece begins with Lloyd making muscle poses among warehouse mannequins. He wears jeans and T-shirt, and a wig to cover his bald head. Corinne Bougaard appears dressed as the ballet dancer, white tutu against black skin. They dance a romantic duet, interrupted as they begin to argue. Lloyd asks for the music to be turned off and the working lights come up. He accuses Corinne of being unable to 'get it right'. Corinne hits him, he falls to the floor and she rips off his wig. Lloyd gets into his leather gear and meets Yacov, also dressed in leather, dancing to Grace Jones. Yacov pulls Lloyd's jeans down to reveal a pink nylon slip. Yacov and Corinne laugh, but it is Lloyd who laughs the longest. Yacov and Corinne enter a box and begin to dance, close together in bright light. Lloyd shuffles up with his trousers round his ankles. He hovers beside them. Yacov and Corinne exit, leaving Lloyd in the box with the door closed. Lloyd's taped voice is heard saying: 'Let me out, that's enough now, let me out' (Newson 1982).

Newson is a funny iconoclast . . . Nothing is sacred to him; strong men, gay leather-boys, black ballet dancers – all get their come-uppance. Newson ends up in the orchestra pit, stripped of his wig, most of his clothes and all of his dignity. It is not just knockabout farce, however; the transformations of images come as genuine theatrical shocks. It is hard to tell what Newson is like as a choreographer but he is an arresting dancer and, on the strength of this piece, a true man of the theatre.

(Parry 1982: 30)

Lloyd fully inhabited the different personae of these pieces. Each one served as a disguise encouraging, in a single evening, multiple identities regarding the flesh-and-blood body of Lloyd. Lloyd embodied each persona and each persona embodied Lloyd. The real Lloyd remained an enigma, an ever more intriguing secret. Yet he was fully present as performer in each image. Lloyd brought his body, experience and his particular construction of gender, language and expression to work. Inhabiting every moment, he dissolved into the images, leaving them to speak for him. Furthermore, Extemporary toured year after year to the same venues. Audiences returned year after year to see Lloyd, bringing with them their memories of previous performances by Lloyd. The many different personae he embodied became complex layers of ambiguous memories, diffusing any real identity of Lloyd. Yet he was there, committed and focused.

33 BOYS TRANSCENDING

Writing of Lloyd turns me to the seductive ambiguity of men dancing. As we women were busy stripping our bodies of glamorous spectacle, male performers stepped to the forefront of the performing stage as the players of objects of desire in performer–spectator relations. Men performing, dancing the same internally focused, fluid movement language as women, do not become invisible in performance as other-of-the-other. Quite the opposite: watching qualities of feminine on masculine bodies is intriguing. The seduction between real and illusion, which eludes female bodies in the Western post-modern attention to absence, comes into play at the site/sight of male dancers. The intrigue of presence that is evoked by male bodies dancing a language that signifies as feminine is an important aspect of their appeal at the turn of the century. This is the allure of the feminized phallus.

The seduction of men dancing is not a new phenomenon. Classical androgyny, of which I wrote earlier, continues to frame the attraction, and not just in ballet. The androgynous aesthetic pervades contemporary dance culture. The 'looking' of the male performer allows him to retain his subject position while performing as object of the gaze – an engaging contradiction. In addition, the male dancer's embodiment of pleasure, power and desire, as object to be looked upon, influences his presence on stage. All these elements, in different ways, disrupt safe categories of male identity, engaging spectators in an ambiguity of masculinity and femininity.

Visual artists throughout the centuries have appropriated the Western fascination with androgyny: 'The androgyne is equivocal, uncommitted – and that is where its appeal lies . . . It allows us . . . to remain in a timeless world in which everything is still possible' (Walters 1978: 117–18). Depicted in the sculptures of classical Greece, androgynous images appear again in fourteenth- and fifteenth-century Florence in works such as Donatello's *David* (*c.*1433), Botticelli's *Venus and Mars* (*c.*1485) and Caravaggio's *David with the Head of Goliath* (*c.*1610). Michelangelo concentrated on depicting beautiful young men who were both powerfully muscular, yet also restricted and bound. For example, the athletic bodies he painted in the Sistine Chapel (1509–12) are posed passively with their power confined.

In the nineteenth century, androgynous images were given a misogynistic twist. The artist, Edward Burne-Jones, was one the first to depict the fragile and feminine male helplessly pitted against an aggressive and sexual female in his paintings, such as *The Depths of the Sea* (1887) and *The Wheel of Fortune* (1883). The boy androgyne, signifying perfect beauty, was still represented but placed in contrast to the feminine image of womanhood. The concept of androgyny that artists of the Decadent movement depicted in the last decades of the nineteenth century was an image threatened by a looming Victorian era of repression and misogynistic sexual division, where the image of the androgyne had come to signify weakness and effeminacy within a heterosexual context: 'Incestuous, narcissistic, adolescent, it implies a rejection of all mature sexuality; in the end, it is an image with only one meaning – sterility and death' (Walters 1978: 245).

In the Victorian era, when sexuality was established as a legitimate discourse with the Christian heterosexual puritanical stamp of approval (Foucault 1979), the feminized male no longer signified perfect beauty of spirit. Masculine heterosexual images were reasserted, objectifying and owning cultural representations of the female body, and androgynous images went into the closet.

Homoerotic images of male androgyny as a transcendent ideal did not disappear, but provided escape for artists in the Industrial Age when 'transcendence became a psychological need' (Ritter 1989: 175). Spiritual ascent characterizes Romanticism. A performance context, which inspired writers and artists in the 1920s, was that of the circus and, in particular, aerial acrobatics. Ritter (1989) and Franko (1995) refer to Cocteau's obsession with the performance of aerialist 'Barbette', a Texan man (Vander Clyde) who performed a trapeze act in drag. Cocteau, for whom the theatre expresses the 'essential idea of art as illusion' (Ritter 1989: 182), idolized Barbette, who could transcend his flesh-and-blood body to a place of pure beauty: 'Calling Barbette Apollo-like, he clearly heroizes the ability of the artiste to shed, like a god, his given gender' (Ritter 1989: 181). Cocteau's subsequent involvement with Ballets Russes, his passion for the dancing of Nijinski and the ballets he consequently wrote, demonstrate his continued fascination with androgynous transcendence (Ries 1986); a fascination that turns this discussion of classical androgyny back to dance.[1]

Here and now, in contemporary dance, the fluid femininity of dance languages performed on male bodies perpetuates the theme.[2] 'The men dominate the stage, especially David Hughes. He moves with the loose-knit fluency of a big cat, but there's a ruthless power to his dancing' (Mackrell 1997: 6).

This review of *Bank* (Siobhan Davies 1997) suggests critic Judith Mackrell is intrigued by the feminine illusion of the feline together with the athletic masculinity on David Hughes' body. His androgynous presence, the play of masculine body and feminine language, is an engaging force.

I watch Russell Maliphant move smoothly with soft, lyrical, loose-limbed but centred movement. He is performing *Unspoken* (1996), a duet for two male bodies. Both men are bald-headed and tall, with bare, sculpted, muscular arms. They wear sleeveless T-shirts and baggy trousers. Russell's language shows influences of ballet technique, gestures balanced and geometric, muscular and articulate. The upward aesthetic of ballet merges with downward aesthetics of release-based movements, the fluid multiplicity of directions disrupts the ballet line with non-linear fractured phrasing; languid physical enjoyment of undulating gestures is matched by muscular strength. With his male partner, Russell performs cascading lifts that appear to fall downwards, and slow motion downward falls that appear to lift up. They dance without bravura, with sculpted athleticism, understatement of gesture and silent footfalls. I watch and interpret. First, I am engaged by the feminine, masculine textures on his body, where his identity as a 'man' becomes understated.

These textures evoke an illusion of androgynous presence. His image is also the trigger for androgyny's mythical signification – transcendence and spiritual beauty. As an androgynous image, he appeals to the Western aesthetic of beauty.

Throughout *Unspoken* there is little face-to-face acknowledgement between the performers. All the partnered lifts are initiated from back-to-back or side-by-side. There is no interaction as sexually identified bodies. The bodies pass each other as shapes in space. There is no play of desire between these performers and the audience; there is nothing that will disturb each body's androgynous union within itself. By the merging of masculine and feminine textures, I sense the audience is in-spired to rise above desire, to aspire to something else: 'Russell Maliphant ... the natural poet, moving dreamily – lyrical and a bit mysterious' (Hunt 1991: 13).

In performance, Maliphant's sexuality and identity as a man is held as secret, seductive as a shadow. The illusion of androgyny displaces and disguises conventional truth about masculinity. His white maleness remains unquestioned. However, dance is performed on the body so this illusion is continuously shadowed by the real-ness of his male flesh and blood. Watching Maliphant dancing, the realness of his mortal, muscular anatomical and sexual body, his physical presence as a white man, constantly nourishes the illusion of transcendence. Inseparable and dependent on each other for signification as mythical, his male body performing the feminine creates the illusion of a union between mascu-line and feminine qualities and desires. This desire-less union provokes transcendent aspirations.[3] Spectators are awed by the androgynous play of real and illusion, masculine and feminine on Russell's body.

34 HIS LOOK, HIS GAZE

Fergus Early, in describing his performance, *Dances for Small Spaces* (1977), states how specific looking is the element that allows this intimate solo piece to reach an audience across a vast theatre auditorium: 'When I am performing, I know exactly where I am putting my eyes, in terms of what I am looking at. I choreograph my eyes' (Early 2003).

Performing *Unspoken* (1996), Russell Maliphant looks out, through and beyond the audience. He is doing the looking. His eyes do not entice or encourage the spectator to watch him. His look counteracts the vulnerability of being exposed as object in performance. His look, recognized from the spectator's perspective, as the dominant male gaze, turns the audience into the object. But this is counteracted, becoming unstable, as his male body is also the object of the spectator's gaze. In Richard Dyer's critical study of media entertainment, he states:

> When the female pin-up returns the viewer's gaze, it is usually some kind of smile, inviting. The male pin-up, even at his most benign, still stares at the viewer . . . as if he wants to reach beyond and through and establish himself.
>
> (Dyer 1992: 109)

Within the conventions of performer–spectator relations, a man can submit his body to become the object of desire in performance as long as he retains the look of the dominant gaze when performing as object of the gaze. In this position, the male performer's look takes on different guises. It becomes a look that ignores the spectator, or it can be the staring look that asserts dominance. It can be a look off stage or up – 'off' suggesting his interest in something else or 'up' suggesting his mind is on higher matters while his body is available for the spectator to objectify. Whatever the look, 'this does violence to the codes of who looks and who is looked at' (Dyer 1992: 104). Clearly, the play of who is looking at whom becomes intriguing.

Mark Simpson compares the images of the model, Marky Mark, as he poses on his own and with Kate Moss. On his own with his muscles, Mark grins and flirts, acting as feminine object of desire, while with Moss he 'gazes manfully straight at the camera, eyes half-closed, lips fully closed, with his lower jaw jutting arrogantly forward' (Simpson 1994: 102). This suggests that when a male model poses alone, presumably for a male market, he constructs himself (in cahoots with the camera) to be looked at as feminine object of desire. But when placed beside a woman, presumably for a mixed gender market, he must prove how 'manly' he is. He must do the looking. Steven Drukman takes up the complexity for male performers in their constructed play between the look and the gaze in his writing about the gay gaze and the male images of pop idols on MTV (1995). 'Traditionally, men had to maintain a phallic hardness to combat the softness associated with being the gaze's object (read: woman) . . . As in much of televised sports, they offer up male spectacle for eroticization but disavow the gaze entirely' (Drukman 1995: 91). Drukman goes on to say how this play of gaze and look is far more complex and fluid, diffused by 'MTV artists who acknowledge but subvert the spectator's pleasures' (Drukman 1995: 91). He concludes by quoting Richard Dyer: 'like so much else about masculinity, images of men . . . are such a strain. Looked at but pretending not to be – there is seldom anything easy about such imagery' (Dyer 1992: 116, cited in Drukman 1995: 92). Again, this ambiguity of looks is intriguing, an element of male performers' seductive presence as a play between looking and being looked at.

Side step. Theatrical drag acts are an intriguing illustration of the play between performing looked-at-ness and the masculine gaze. Drag performances offer the appropriation of glamour 'a masquerade of femininity designed by men' while retaining the dominant look (Simpson 1994: 178). Within traditional theatre settings, the male performer who desires to exchange his sameness for otherness does so from his place as male in patriarchal culture, where 'other' is represented as feminine. In Franko's discussion (1995) of gay drag performance, he acknowledges that because the gay male is still biologically a man and therefore subject within a phallocentric matrix, he has had to *perform* his otherness: '[H]e is basically in a theatrical rather than a speculative rapport with his own nascent "identity" as other' (Franko 1995: 95). Within the binary system, this has meant performing as feminine: 'The gay male wishes to exchange sameness for otherness, but he must do so in the very terms of the same' (Franko 1995: 95). He does so by disguising himself with the fetishistic illusions of femininity.

> The point of which is not to become a woman (they wish to keep their penis) but to bind the fear and fascination of the feminine to the male body. This produces a dilemma for the gay man: how to reconcile his own fascination with his own fear.
>
> (Simpson 1994: 78)

This is a different discussion to that of the Harlem drag balls where black gay men are 'passing' as white and female. There, passing as female is more important than performing female. And passing as white is as strong a focus, if not more so, than passing as female. The performance of drag is acknowledged within the context of the black gay community but not externally, where success in passing requires an ability to be invisible. Passing as white requires a non-performing performance, merging into a so-called Western white 'normality' (hooks 1992). In contrast, the flamboyant excesses of femininity flaunted by female impersonators and drag queens in theatrical and media contexts is an externally directed act, aimed at being visible to, and evoking reaction from, heterosexual audiences. This is a focus on gender play rather than colour. Furthermore, straight, transgender and gay black and white men perform these theatrical drag acts. The idea is not to dissolve into femininity but to keep the contradictions between masculine and feminine at play, to emphasize the performativity of Western culture's construction of femininity and masculinity.

Drag, therefore, as theatrical performance (by straight or gay men) most often appeals to its audiences when the feminine characterization is contradicted by the masculine looking, taking command. Hence the popularity of the many 'bossy' pantomime dames that have spilled onto UK stages over the years, the entertainer Danny LaRue, media satirist Dame Edna Everage and theatre performer Betty Bourne. As a form of popular entertainment, watching the performance of an anatomically male body performing the excesses of feminine illusion while retaining a masculine gaze is humorous. The laughter encourages release from heterosexual confines and fears of gender displacement. The seduction of drag performance is the intrigue of its paradox – the theatrical and performative contradictions of both genders on the male body. 'Is it incitement to gender rebellion or misogynist turn? This is the perennial question and the answer is, of course, both and neither' (Simpson 1994: 78).

I watch Matthew Hawkins (*Matthew and Diana on Manoeuvres* 1993) perform an ironic parody of ballet movements. Matthew wears an ornately decorated tutu, a tightly fitted bodice and pointe shoes. He *pirouettes*, *bourrée*-s and *arabesques* his way around the stage with Diana Payne-Myers as his partner. His facility to perform what have been conventionally considered to be feminine ballet gestures, draws into focus, and displaces, the conventional construction of male and female roles in ballet. Cutting across this femininity is Hawkins' look. He is focused beyond the performing space and beyond the audience, as if concerned with something outside and away from the theatre and the performance. He looks through the audience, holding the gaze. Simultaneously, he is aware of being looked at from all angles, an awareness that qualifies his style. His body moves with self-consciousness ingrained into the muscularity. As he presents his back, front and side to the audience, he walks knowing that every micro detail of that walk is being looked at. The contradictions of looking out, as subject of the gaze, and enjoying the pleasure of his body being looked at (therefore each tiny fracture of it must be masked in performance tension), add to his engaging presence. Although his body is displayed as a feminine object complete with its ballet apparel, he is not performing as female. Because of his outward looking gaze, Hawkins himself is still firmly established as subject of his performance. Within this dual system of signification his presence becomes engaging for its contradictions in identity. His dominant look in the subject position conflicts with his posing as a feminine other body; his muscular physicality contradicts his position as desired object/model and his ability to hold a dominant gaze in performance contradicts his desire to be desired. The points of contradiction hold my attention.

Matthew is in the position of being objectified and scrutinized by the spectator, yet he is able to play that scrutiny right back at the audience for his own purposes. His performance allows the audience 'to concede to multiple meanings, to ambiguities of thought, feeling, categorisation, to refuse closure' (Ferris 1993: 8). His projection outward while desiring to be looked at destabilizes any truth about a fixed male position.

I watch the performance of South African dance artist, Vincent Sewati Mantsoe, whose movement is sourced from Western contemporary dance, Aboriginal, African and Asian dance forms. He is visiting from Johannesburg and performing at The Place Theatre as part of the Dance Umbrella Festival in 2001. His look is different to that of Matthew's, as he appears to be looking at us as if someone else is doing the seeing. He performs three short solo pieces: *Phokwane* (1998, which takes its title from his parents' original names, Phoko and Nkwane), *Barena* (2000, 'Chiefs') and *Motswa Hole* (2001, 'Person Far Away'). He appears on stage with shaved head and bare torso, a physically compact and muscular figure, walking slowly, bent forward from his hips, his back flat and parallel with the floor. His arms are fluidly unfolding outwards like wings. Vincent's movement language holds traces of the different dance forms togther with quirky idiosyncrasies and emotionally expressive gestures. He tells his stories in movement form. One moment his lower back is swaggering, arched back with hands on his hips, then he gestures frantically with his arms and hands. He jumps and runs, coming to sharp abrupt stops, arms held in tense posed gestures. In *Motswa Hole*, there is a bowl of water on the stage in which he splashes. With rhythmic floor tapping, jumping with legs folded under him and slapping the floor with his feet, he invites the audience to splash in the water.

Each solo has an arresting final image. In *Phokwane*, he slaps his chest with one hand, pauses and then takes a few steps forwards. This sequence repeats until he is off stage. In *Barena*, he crawls out on his knees. In *Motswa Hole*, he walks out holding long threads of cotton cloth (life threads) over his shoulders. Each exit is slow with a quality of grand purpose. Most of all, I notice his face. As he expresses pain, passion, laughter and a history of experiences through his eyes, he also looks through us fearlessly. His presence engages me for he seems simultaneously to inhabit his images and absent himself from them. I am intrigued to know how.

In the after-show discussion, Vincent told us how he goes into trance when performing to allow the spirits of each piece to enter his body. The spirits perform through his body. He talked of his parents who are healers and advise him on his dances. He said that 10 per cent of his focus is on the choreography he is performing, and 90 per cent is on being in a trance:

> Spirits and Ancestors have been an important part of my creative process, with the belief that if I have to create a work, I always have to 'borrow' with respect, appreciation and the understanding of the movement source. I perform a traditional ritual at least twice a year. The reason is twofold, one, this is where I remind myself of the important rules from the Ancestors, and two, it gives me the opportunity to ask for permission to 'borrow' some of the traditional movements, especially the ones which may not be performed in public.
>
> (Mantsoe 2001)

Vincent's movements were full of expression; the stories were there for us to see, at the surface. Yet he was absenting himself on the inside so that another force, the spiritual force, could enter his body: 'Africanist religions are geocentric (earth-centred). Deities make contact with humans when they are embodied by their followers in danced ceremonies. Thus, dance and the dancing body are manifestations of the mind–spirit' (Gottschild 1996: 9). Vincent drew the spirits inside of him and let them express themselves through his dances. When the spirits possessed him, his external expressive image was full and alive but he was not there. As another intriguing but different play of looking and being looked at, Vincent had absented himself from his own looking, allowing another spiritual presence to enter and look out through his eyes.

35 BODIES OF PLEASURE

The independent performance culture took hold alongside the gay liberation movement. In dance, men began to use performance as a medium to explore gay politics and masculine identities. In contrast to the performance images of classical androgyny in ballet, the performances by openly gay/queer self-identified performers such as Michael Clark, Javier de Frutos, Nigel Charnock and Lloyd Newson engage the audience through their play with the *conflict* between masculine and feminine desire. These artists consciously counteract notions of union or classical transcendence from desire. Male bodies experience the act of desiring to be desired as an expression of power. Over the past 20 years, male dancers have re-claimed and subverted, upheld and rejected, the 'little death' male/female partnership of Bataille-esque eroticism. They draw attention to sexuality, physical sensations of pain and pleasure. They do so by falling.

'Eurocrash' established itself as a dance genre in the late 1980s, formulated as the marketable trademark of physical theatre, helping define the work of LaLaLa Human Steps, Vim Vandekeybus, DV8 Physical Theatre and Pina Bausch. Bodies fly through the air, throw themselves hard onto the floor without recovery, slam their weight against other bodies, walls and floors. Eurocrash has been exploited for its ability to engage both performers and spectators in a postmodern subversion of transcendence. The fall to the floor without rebound is itself an erotic play with self-destruction: 'Underlying eroticism is the feeling of something bursting, of the violence accompanying an explosion' (Bataille 1987: 93). The crash to the floor had an emotional source, an expression of abandonment, anger and loss, a rejection of the romantic idyllic meeting between bodies.[1] Lloyd Newson, as director of DV8 Physical Theatre, persistently draws spectators' attention to the raw vulnerability of flesh-and-blood desires and the dance with death that such desire can provoke. Nigel Charnock, in *Dead Dreams of Monochrome Men* (DV8 1988), repeatedly climbs a ladder to increasing heights and throws himself down to the floor. Charnock exposes the erotic clash with death. His jumps convey that there is no partnership, no continuity and no promise of life after death. Eroticism and sexual desire cannot be hidden any longer behind transcendent doors – sexual relations can lead to death. While classical androgyny signifies a 'denial of original sin' (Walters 1978: 34), Charnock entitles his solo show *Original Sin* (1993). His performances positively burn with overt references to God, sex, death and pain. He lays them out on the table for all to see. Transcendence is exposed as a false hope. This is it – baseness, a downward fall and an appointment with death, with no saviour. Michael Clark, adored for his classical androgynous transcendent image in *Soda Lake* (Richard Alston 1981), deliberately brings transcendent images down to earth in his own work. His collaborations with Leigh Bowery, such as *No Fire Escape in Hell* (1986), throw sexuality and gender back into the performance arena.[2]

Other gay male artists, such as trapeze artist/dancer Jeremy Robins, *Slippery When Wet* (1996), and Brenton Surgenor, *Written With the Body* (1996), present images of gay male dancers as strong, muscular and athletic. They desire to play the pleasure of sexual object as a macho body, sexualized and not at all transcendent. These artists openly fracture and demystify the universal Western stereotype; they take charge of subverting the classical reputation, expose homophobia, spill closeted secrets, and reveal the diverse differences of queer desires. They openly admit to the sensual pleasure and pain of their bodies.

More extremely, body art performers expose the erotic masochistic practice of pain and pleasure as performance statement. The erotic alliance of ritual and sacrifice (Bataille 1987) is exposed by the body art practices of performance artists such as Franko B and Ron Athey. Franko B is alone in the performing space, *Mama I Can't Sing* (1996), ritualistically taking his own blood, slowly, using the length of the performance. Ron Athey has AIDS. In *Deliverance* (1996), he undergoes an enema ritual on stage: he is hooked through the skin of his thighs and wrists to ropes attached to scaffolding, is fucked up the arse with a dildo and allows his blood to be taken. No life after death here. 'Flesh is the born enemy of people haunted by Christian taboos, but if as I believe an indefinite and general taboo does exist, opposed to sexual liberty . . . the flesh signifies a return to this threatening freedom' (Bataille 1987: 92). As I watch Ron Athey's performance, a woman throws up, spattering vomit on my shoulder, but neither of us leaves.

Outside of dance, gay and queer performance contexts, the patriarchal concept of masculinity rarely focuses on the eroticism of being male. Heterosexual frameworks still demand that men perform in the world as subjects in positions of control. Here, masculine sensuality continues to be portrayed in the media through imagery such as 'trains going into tunnels, cigars raised from the lips, guns held close to the hips . . . hard, tough, dangerous, erect', together with the goal oriented imagery of 'swords, knives, fists and guns' (Dyer 1993: 112–13). The symbolism used to describe conventional heterosexual masculinity conjures a host of signifiers but rarely the term 'seductive'. For Baudrillard (1991), male heterosexual sexuality as a sign in itself has not been engaging, flirtatious, fluid, sensual or even movable, as these qualities disrupt the fragile erection of phallic significance, a delicate structure that 'must be defended by retrenchments, institutions, and artifice. The phallic fortress offers all the signs of a fortress, that is to say, of weakness' (Baudrillard 1991: 16).

In Western, phallocentric, media-driven culture, men don't get to enjoy openly performing the vulnerable – the desired one – the submissive object. Dance performance is one context that allows men to let go of that loaded historical baggage. Dancing, men have access to their bodies of pleasure and pain. But, from a patriarchal perspective, the expressivity that men allow themselves when dancing with each other signifies as femininity and, therefore, submission. Admitting and submitting to an expression of pleasure, as object of desire, is associated with passivity, which is associated with losing authority: 'To be penetrated is to abdicate power' (Bersani 1988: 212).

Within a sadomasochistic (S/M) context however, submission is not a place of weakness but one of power. The (gay and straight) practice of sadomasochism, in particular, provides a positive framework for reversing the notion of passivity as demeaning, displacing the notion of sexuality as (only) about genital pleasure (Foucault 1985; Bersani 1988).

> Foucault praised S/M practitioners as 'inventing new possibilities of pleasure with strange parts of their bodies'. He called S/M 'a creative enterprise, which has as one of its main features what I call the desexualisation of pleasure'.
>
> (Bersani 1995: 79)

More importantly, S/M, in its frequent reversing of roles, allocates agency to the submissive role. Receiving pleasure as object is given the leading role, therefore reversing the roles for men and women constructed by patriarchal culture. S/M allows bodies to submit to pleasure as a statement of power, without fear of its associations with the demeaned signification of 'female' weakness and passivity.

> S/M raises, however crudely, important questions about the relation between pleasure and the exercise of power, and invites . . . a psychoanalytic study of the defeat, or at least the modulation, of power by the very pleasure inherent in its exercise.
>
> (Bersani 1995: 83)

By referring to S/M, I am not suggesting that experience of the practice of S/M is necessary to appreciate the power of submission. Neither am I suggesting, by referring to the writers, Foucault and Bersani, that S/M is specific to homosexual culture. Rather, an appreciation of the sexual politics of S/M is relevant to the discussion of male dancers' performing presence. Performers such as Javier de Frutos, Nigel Charnock and Michael Clark take charge of submitting their bodies to the pleasures of moving and being watched. They turn submission into power; they use submission as a politically subversive tool on their bodies.

My point, once again, is that the play of pleasure on the male body is intriguing and seductive in its oscillation of what is real (male body) and what is illusion (feminine expression). Men dancing, by themselves or with other men, socially, culturally and politically, subvert the hegemonic order. This is part of their attraction in postmodern contemporary performance culture.

I watch Javier de Frutos' solo, *Transatlantic* (1996). Javier is performing naked. The piece is constructed in small sections. Each section is composed of a repetitive movement theme that is framed in by lighting a particular space – a circle on the floor, a doorway, a window.

In the first episode, the movement is gestural, verging on the grotesque, gender-less and monstrous. Javier walks with his arse stuck out, back arched, his body stiffly leaning forward, his legs moving like a newly born colt, wobbly yet stiff. In another episode, Javier moves across the back of the stage on his stomach, arching and pushing like a reptile. In another, he holds a small window frame in front of his torso and uses his left arm and hand to gesticulate amusingly within and without the frame: a playful irony, revealing a part of his naked body as the framed object of my gaze.

Transatlantic exposed Javier's body to the vulnerability of its position as naked object. Yet his specifically constructed images, his strong facial expressions and dominant eye-focus contradicted any notion of a passive beauty. He controlled our gaze on his body. His technical skill, muscular body and athleticism confirmed that his masculinity would not be threatened by his nudity.

Interestingly, Javier's naked body, with its bald head, hairless chest and dangling penis, became his costume, almost a uniform. Speaking at a post-performance, Javier (de Frutos 1996) explains that performing naked is not about sexual seduction. He says he wants to work with raw nerve, to choreograph the organs and work with the effect of light on naked skin. Javier reveals that he is more concerned to explore his body's awkwardness than its harmonious beauty. The material for *Transatlantic* emerged from his experiences and feelings in America at a particular time, especially those connected to his mother. Through its repetition in performance, his nakedness became part of a performance style. As he 'dressed up' in nakedness for *Transatlantic*, I wondered, as a spectator, who was the real Javier. His constructed performance image was his real naked body, begging the question as to who Javier might be when he was clothed and not performing.

Usually, nakedness is not in itself seductive. The body revealed neutralizes seductive elements. For the stripper, the secret is no longer secret once the clothes are off (Barthes 1973). Male stripping only enchants a spectator because: 'The phallus can never be shown – instead we are palmed off with the paltry penis . . . As with 'Pass the Parcel', the enjoyment of stripping is, of course, in the unwrapping not the revelation' (Simpson 1994: 187).

The stripper must reveal 'nothing (castration) as everything (fetishistic glamour)' (Simpson 1994: 187). Yet Javier in performance, through his repeated nakedness, became, in a sense, fully clothed. He retained his real self as secret. Javier managed to reveal nothing as everything by a process of stripping in reverse. His manipulation of movement and gesture, traces of stories, gimmicks, images, the physical realization of his pleasure, seemed gradually to dress his body. As his performance continued, his naked body became ever more clothed and the presence of his 'real' body ever more secret. Javier's naked body became a surface appearance of illusion rather than the anatomical real.

Mark Morris' *L'Allegro, il Penseroso ed il Moderato* (1988) has a triumphant reception at the London Coliseum in 1997. This is a joyous, exuberant, passionate series of dances set to Handel's music together with the poems of John Milton and using 25 dancers. This piece illustrates the seductive engagement of the men and the simultaneous invisibility of the women.

I watch running, skipping, light-footed figures, skimming and circling, mimicking birds, flowers and gambolling ponies, embodying pastoral images of melancholic and happy days. *L'Allegro* offers choreographic shapes that curve and arch through a massive expanse of space. Witty, parodic comments, closely worked to the meaning of the text and the music, are splattered between pure dance extravaganzas. The piece is serious and playful, respectful and teasing, playing at the edge between utter kitsch and high art. Classical, formal shapes mix with folk dance patterns, outrageously flamboyant gestures with simple, slow walking, weaving lines. Most of all, *L'Allegro* expresses the pleasure of dancing to music for the spectator's gaze.

The male bodies are dressed in shiny lycra tights and soft Grecian-style shirts, reminiscent of classical ballet, in bright pastoral hues of pinks and greens. They trip and skip lightly across the stage, one moment performing as a flock of birds in flight, the next hugging each other and holding hands in childlike bliss, expressing an obvious androgynous delight, enjoying themselves (and each other). Morris' personal signature – the eccentric, detailed, wafting, flicking arm and hand gestures, simultaneously flamboyant and effeminate – acts ironically and subversively on the male bodies, flaunting and teasing the conventions of masculinity.

It is a work to make one laugh and cry . . . the cheeky number (so cleverly timed on the music) in which the men alternately fight, kiss and slap each other's bottoms, the wonderful passage conjuring up a flight of birds, with Kraig Patterson incarnating the trilling lark.

(Dougill 1997: 19)

I watch the women and their presence reads somewhat differently to that of the men. The female dancers in *L'Allegro* are dressed in long, flowing dresses in pinks, greens and browns, and many of them have long, flowing hair. The choreography and movement material is light and lyrical, similar to that of the men, with Morris' eccentric, affected style. But Morris' movement language, the joyous sense of wit and parody, is lost on female bodies, returning them to the status of 'mother nature' with references to rituals of life and death, circles, weaving shapes, and rounded, grounded gestures of giving birth. This symbolism, ever present in *L'Allegro*, appears on the male bodies as outrageous, amusing or kitsch, while on the female it reads as wholesome and respectfully feminine: the movement merging with the female as an essential statement of womanhood. When the male mimics the actions of birds; it is witty, clever, surprising. When the women mimic the gesture of birds or gather in a circle signifying some life-giving ritual, the body and gesture read as unifying, whole, real, feminine on feminine. On the male dancers, these gestures of pleasure fascinate and amuse, displacing heterosexual constructs of stable male authority and power. On the female dancers, the feminine gestures appear as an element of respectful idolization of the concept of womanhood. Morris' wit rides the male with confidence and ironic subversion. The female is left to be feminine, simply 'lovely'; there are no traces of irony to suggest that femininity could be just as much a performed play of pleasure for the women as it is for the men. There are no traces of masculinity that might offset the feminine flow and create an engaging ambiguity.

On exiting the stage, the male bodies I speak about here, even against their desires, resume places as subjects in patriarchal culture. In the new millennium, the heterosexual–homosexual boundaries are radically shifting, opening up the controversies of essentialism and performativity. Gay men have consistently performed as straight men, now straight men perform as gay. Heterosexual and gay men become 'mothers' and child carers. Transvestism is a practice of heterosexual men in family life while transgendered bodies 'pass' as straight women. This fluidity provokes Phelan to remark, 'if the ascendant term in the binary hetero-homo is beginning to shift . . . perhaps too the binary visibility-invisibility will also shift' (Phelan 1993: 97). However, phallocentricism still prevails.

The binary may have become subverted and dysfunctional in a queer post-structuralist new millennium, but the male body off stage is *not* object; he resumes subjectivity in a culture that still encourages binary representations. This crucial undeniable factor, in conflict with the image of his dancing body, precisely feeds the necessary clash of real and illusion and evokes seductive relations in performance.

The performer–spectator relations of engagement that are sparked when watching men, reveal clues for women. When a male body dances, he displaces feminine qualities of pleasure from any natural affiliation to either anatomical body. Simultaneously, as male dancers displace qualities of (heterosexually defined) masculinity, power also becomes a constructed play without natural affiliation to either anatomical body. If masculine power and feminine pleasure are constructed performance qualities for male dancers, they can also be play for the female dancers. Women, too, can embrace both extremes as performance play. The interweaving, interlocking, overlapping, gender-free practices of power and pleasure, masculinity and femininity provide a focus for rekindling seductive performer–spectator relations in the post-feminist world of dance performance. I am treading a queer path.

36 LETTING GO OF FEAR

Nigel Charnock is a body of desire let loose. He throws himself further than the others, seeming to lose himself entirely to the task at hand. I have watched Nigel spanning across an electrified spectrum of performance personae. I have seen him as the snivelling desperate loner at the cocktail party (*Strange Fish*, Lloyd Newson, DV8 1992), I have seen him as the drag queen in cabaret while at Extemporary Dance Theatre, and I have watched him climbing up walls and falling to the floor (*Dead Dreams of Monochrome Men*, Lloyd Newson, DV8 1988). He has commanded my attention through his brilliant manipulation of language: a fast, witty, sharp, coarse tirade of words about love, sexual acts, loss, loneliness, murder, bisexuality and God (*Original Sin*, Nigel Charnock 1993). I have seen him vulnerably exposed, sitting nervously in a chair, wearing white boxer shorts; watched him switch from aggressive violence, to small, crouched timidity. He has conversed with a life-sized skeleton, carried a cross on his back, thrown babies across the stage and held court from a bed (*Human Being*, Nigel Charnock 1997).

Figure 13 Nigel Charnock in *Human Being* (1997). Publicity image.
Photographer: Hugo Glendinning.

In 2002, I watch Nigel Charnock as he improvises with other participants at the Performing Arts Labs' Dance Lab. There are 20 people,
positioned around the outside of the space. Anyone can enter and exit
at any time. Nigel hovers at the side of the space, watching other
performers intently. Hunched and hard, his body acts as a leash,
enclosing his passion for a few moments, then lets him fly. Moving swiftly,
Nigel grabs a long-handled broom from the side of the space, moves
directly to the centre of the space, spins wildly, extending the broom
violently, holding its handle, barely missing other performers. Nigel
climbs the doorframe, folding his body over the top of the door, and
stretches his legs in extended lines and arches his back, balanced on
the painfully narrow ledge. Falling without fear, he runs and skips,
minces, flicks his body, embodies a feminine preening drama queen,
turns in his legs, pins his knees together, hunches his shoulders, and twists
his torso. He grabs another body, clings on obsessively, holds the other
suffocatingly close. In the next moment, he is in the corner shivering, a
grotesque body. He sings opera with physical gusto, plays the piano and
harmonica and links arms with another performer for a promenade
around the space.

He dances with extreme energy, flinging his weight, caught between
the limitations of his human body and his unlimited imagination.
He performs contorted, anguished movements on the floor. His body is
painfully thin, a bruised shell. Nigel's body holds him in the present
moment even as he reaches to further and further extremes of his
different desires. Reviewing Nigel in *Strange Fish*, Keith Watson remarks:
'Using his whippet-like frame as a conduit for a succession of punishing
autobiographical (we assume) exposés, both physical and emotional, this
was a man who took no prisoners on stage' (Watson 2003: 7).

Nigel improvises across characters, moods and qualities without hesi-
tation, without self-conscious barriers, with abandoned passion. Yet Nigel
is within each moment, knows exactly where and how he is wielding
his body (and his broom). He embodies every contrasting move, thinking about spatial relations, group dynamics, physical potential and exact
timing, while ensconced in extreme and different risk-taking actions.
He arrives at each point by the most direct route, without blocking or
excuses. He is absorbed, dissolved into the action, yet his action is entirely
present.

Nigel's presence never fixes; he welcomes the monstrous chaos lurking
behind safe definitions of identity. He crosses between anger, laughter,
the sublime, pathos and serious intent. He is a clown, hostess, drag queen,
lizard, conductor, sacrificial victim, boy, mother; he is wrenched between
grotesque and beauty, and thrives on the contradictions. He is the queer

hybrid body spanning the spaces between the extremes of gender. As Fuchs (1996: 139) writes about the pop idol, Prince, Nigel is 'so allusive and complex, simultaneously reaffirming and refuting familiar boundaries and identities'.

Swinging across from one full body to another, Nigel metamorphoses in an intimate act of performing extremes, without respite, where pain is no barrier. His imagination is boundless, his desire moves beyond his own flesh, even as he inhabits his flesh. He drives his body in storm torrents.

But I am not writing about Nigel over there performing while my body is here as the static observer. I am not just watching, passive and objective. I feel rebellious, sharp, on the edge. I am running with him. His presence meets mine. It's as if a wire on fire connects us, where subjects and objects are incinerated. His body and my body are pulled into a diffused alive-ness. When I watch Nigel, there is only the immediacy of this moment now. Nigel gives everything, spills it all into the laps of those around him and is replenished by our active witnessing; I am limited only by my own capacity to keep up.

Can I let go of my fear as he lets go of his? Can I allow that direct moment when bodies and eyes burn? This work is dangerous; it demands you go with him.

> It's Charnock's very versatility, and his wilful refusal to fit the stereotypical bill as choreographer, comedian, dancer, director or writer . . . that has made him one of the most original and entertaining talents to hit British dance in the past twenty years. Yet he remains scandalously undervalued and blatantly misunderstood by the dance press.
>
> (Watson 2003: 6–7)

This is the space where performers and spectators dissolve in a vibrant moment of present time and not everybody wants to let go of their seats. This is not minimalism, this is not cool; this is not an attention to absence. His own words demonstrate his positioning in the British dance scene:

> When I see abstract painting and when I see abstract dance I can't see the source, I can't see where it has come from. Maybe I am not supposed to. Maybe the artists don't have the responsibility to tell me where it comes from. But I can walk past a painting; I can't walk past dance. I have to sit in a seat with a lot of other people and watch it. I appreciate it but questions in my mind occur all the time. Where has this come from, what is it for? Why I am here? The

performers seem to leave their hearts and souls and minds in the dressing rooms. And I am thinking, 'You are not here, you are vacant, you are absent from this'. This is dance for the middle class white intelligentsia.

(Charnock 2003)

Nigel clearly rejects that post-modern minimalist new dance aesthetic. Throw yourself in or get left behind. Nigel demands that we be fully engaged, as he is.

37 RE-FIGURING ANDROGYNY

After Extemporary, I return to a way of life where performing and living are intertwined, one becoming the other. As an independent dance artist I make my own work for my own body. My re-embodied understanding of the seduction of real and illusion in performance begins with expressions of desire, as a lesbian – or rather as a queer androgyne. It begins with the recognition that even something so deeply embodied and experienced as sexual feeling is a performative choice. I flirt with her, turn her on, objectify her and satisfy her. I find myself turned on in return, at the core of me, consumed by an act that has been considered as masculine desire. Where is the truth of gender and sexuality as we switch and flip between giving and taking? Our performance becomes the truth. I look at her looking at me. We take our time, between playing hunter and hunted, in a place where anything is possible. I express this newfound freedom somewhat over-enthusiastically in a life that becomes performance.

My first performance expression of lesbian desire is the solo *Witch One* (1992). I stand still in a closely defined spotlight, in a strong stance, feet slightly apart. My head is shaved. I wear tightly fitted black trousers, black boots and a black denim jacket studded with glitter. I look out; I watch the audience. I present my right hand to the audience, palm upwards, wrist slightly lifted, fingers open. I drop my weight into my left hip, taking my torso slightly forward, letting my right knee relax. My left arm, elbow opening out, reaches towards the right palm. With the first two fingers of my left hand I stroke the palm of my right palm. I watch the audience. Releasing the look, I turn my head to the side and smile.

Lying parallel to the ground, just off the floor, my weight is supported on my left forearm and toes, torso tilted to face the audience. My right hand is held against my pubic bone. Looking down, as if hovering over another body, I move my hips and hand forward and back in a constant sexual motion. I lower my head towards the imaginary partner and, in one fast flip, I am on my back, unfolding and opening my arms and legs. I return to the first position and balance on my left forearm. The sequence repeats three times, flipping from on top to below, after which I squat back on my heels, then throw my head back and laugh.

Witch One explored the performative gestures of masculine and feminine role-play, switching between a desire to objectify, dominate and initiate, and the desire to be desired, to submit and to take pleasure. The masculine role was asserted through an active, precise gaze, stylized language, direct gestures and upward lines of stretched and extended legs. The feminine role was asserted as an active desire to be desired, looking down or away, with circular hip movements and delicate hand gestures.

Lesbian practice and theory contests the meaning and normality of *being*. As a lesbian, I reject the notion of a natural or original being. Loving women as a lesbian has contested any essential truth or normality about masculine and feminine desire, so living all aspects of my life appears as a constant appropriation of masquerades and performances. I fully inhabit all the different identities of my self. The acts become real.

Homosexuality in Western culture has become a necessary and much-discussed abnormal from which the so-called normal defines itself (Foucault 1979). If the so-called normal is constructed over the abnormal, there is no original heterosexual normality, only a constructed normal revealing 'the original to be nothing other than parody of the *idea* of the natural and the original . . . thus, gay is to straight not as copy is to original, but, rather, as copy is to copy' (Butler 1990: 31).

Sue-Ellen Case describes the performance work of *Split Britches* and the performers, Lois Weaver and Peggy Shaw – cult figures of lesbian theatre.[1] 'The point is not to conflict reality with another reality, but to abandon the notion of reality through roles ... A strategy of appearances replaces the claim to truth' (Case 1988/9: 70).

Performing life as a lesbian, I pay my respects to the historical legacy of butch and femme, the ironic role-play and performative masquerade of male and female in lesbian culture. As theatrical figures in performance, the 'butch/femme couple inhabit the subject position together' (Case 1988/9: 56). The play of butch and femme roles are recognized in relation to each other, the two positions create each other and are dependent on each other. The terms 'butch' and 'femme' have provided liberating, ironic and playful devices with which to emphasize the fictional non-essentialism of gender identity:

> They do not identify these butch-femme roles with 'real' people or literal images of gender, but with fictionalised ones, thus underscoring the masquerade. The history of their desire, or their search for a sexual partner becomes a series of masks, or identities that stand for sexual attraction in the culture.
>
> (Case 1988/9: 68)

However, the figures of butch and femme can install, as much as subvert heterosexual identities. The imagery is confined to identifiable flip sides of lesbian sex, rejecting but also mimicking a heterosexual binary (Hart 1993). The identifiable performing presence of butch and femme as separate subjects marks performers as lesbian. The butch/femme dynamic plays within its own closed system of lesbian desire. Lesbian becomes a safe category of gender *within* heterosexual/homosexual signification. While recognizing the disruptive masquerade, the spectator simultaneously reads a binary relationship of gender. Defined by butch and femme, bodies are fixed in identity as lesbian.

Making *Witch One*, I was seeking a different performance of gender and desire. I was exploring androgyny, not through the identities of butch and femme as separate bodies, but through the acknowledgement of masculine and feminine desiring on one (my) body.[2] Re-figuring androgyny, I am not assuming a classical androgyny, a transcendental union of masculine and feminine, a manifestation that excludes difference. Neither am I referring to the feminist negation of androgyny that grounds masculine and feminine in the essential reality of anatomical bodies. Nor am I suggesting a middle or third place, or the creation of an abstract, empty body that negates identifiable figures. As I sat back on my heels in *Witch One* and laughed, I was laughing at the discovery of different spaces conceived between extremes: 'We do not laugh because of what makes sense or because of what does not. We laugh because of possible meaning, because of the *attitude* that causes us to enunciate signification as it brings us jouissance' (Kristeva 1980: 181–2).

Performing as an androgyne in *Witch One* was less like a two-way imagining on one body, a double act in one, but more of a waking up to multiple imaginings on my body, embodied but fictional, real and illusion. As a verb, to androgynize, the body in action temporally spans between identities that emerge in the gaps between things. As androgynizing bodies, we no longer have fixed identities – we become performing hybrids, and hybrid bodies span across the divide between things.

I am re-figuring androgyny as an embodied *play between* gender characteristics, spanning across, knowing the extremes – playing the many combinations in between – in one body. Recognizing gender attributes as performative acts, I construct plays, separating my body and its expressive desires from any essential belonging to either gender, yet acknowledging the extremes of both – playing rather than being specific identities.

Playing exercises the imagination as a physical dynamic, a network of connections. To play is to improvise. Play describes non-linear sequences of creative narratives, logic itself becoming the play. Play suggests parody and self-reference, an ability to step aside from rationality and subjectivity, an opportunity to approach life as a game of chance. Play provides a vital element in the performance of gender. The practice of play allows for spontaneity. Play suggests a game, which has its own seductive element – you never know at the outset who will win or lose. A game implies rules that can be made and broken, and playing a game offers more creativity than the end goal of winning or losing. Play allows for love, humour, joy and anger. Play is the un-thought, outside of being.

Being an identifiable sensible identity does not evoke such ambiguous possibilities of meaning as does *playing* identity. *Being* only comes to exist through doing and playing and it is only through the repeated performance of doing/playing that identity comes to be (Butler 1990). In other words, playing is the prerequisite of identity. Play precedes being, playing creates the possibility of being.

> Play is always a play of absence and presence, but if it is to be thought radically, play must be conceived of before the alternative of presence and absence. Being must be conceived as presence or absence on the basis of the possibility of play, not the other way around.
>
> (Derrida 1978: 292)

38 QUEER LIVING

I relish the notion that a performing body can be between identities, that the dynamic pulse of living is the movement between things, becoming things. This is a queer perspective. Inhabiting the places between identifiable objects finds an academic parallel in the hopefulness of queering.

Queer theory takes off from where lesbian and gay theories of performativity settle. However, queer living in this context has nothing to do with somebody's sexual orientation or the anatomical identity of someone who is desired. Eve Sedgwick refers to queer as: 'The open mesh of possibilities, gaps, overlaps, dissonances and resonances, lapses and excesses of meaning when the constituent elements of anyone's gender, of anyone's sexuality aren't made (or can't be made) to signify monolithically' (Sedgwick 1993: 8).

Living queerly sets desire free. Where desire comes from is exchanged for where it is going, removing the emphasis from the impossible-to-possess lost object. The importance of queer is in 'freeing desire from its location' to 'render queer *the relations* between images and bodies' (Probyn 1995: 9; emphasis mine). The act of queering evokes bodies in a process of transmuting, making, doing, trans-crossing, always on a journey with no final destination but with junctions of creative change. Queer is a slippery term that blows freely over the coagulated conventional systems of binary definitions of desire.

The history of psychoanalysis has signified desire as a linear narrative that presents a subject who lacks, and as such is forever reaching to find the lost object. Lack and loss, as both subject and object, become the motivating life force rather than reaching beyond this search to become desirous in the *now* and the now's future. Of course, desire can be about lack and loss, particularly of the lost mother, but desire is also a drive that enables us to move forward into new experiences: to create relationships, feed imagination and ambition, evoke an exchange of knowledge and allow us to feel different things. Queering desire climbs out of psychoanalysis in order to see a breadth of landscape, substituting routes for roots, how for why, playing for searching. The notion of an always-lost moment is acknowledged, then deconstructed, changing desire from a search for the *one-and-only* meaning into desire as a *play* for meaning. The seduction of reading queer dancing bodies in performance is the desire/pleasure to play with identity and meaning at the body site. In theory and practice, the activity of searching and desiring is the seductive element, not the meaning itself.

> There will be no unique name, nor even the name of Being. It must
> be conceived without *nostalgia*; that is, it must be conceived outside
> the myth of the purely maternal or paternal language belonging
> to the lost fatherland of thought. On the contrary we must *affirm* it
> ... with a certain laughter and with a certain dance.
>
> (Derrida 1973: 159)

As long as the focus remains on loss and lack, desire is never experienced
for what it could be – a living, physical drive through life. Desiring is
physical; it is an embodied act: I do it, you do it, we are always desiring.
The act of desiring is an erotic, productive, inventive force; it is thought
of in terms of intensities and energies, movements and connections
between surfaces, 'a pleasure/unpleasure always of and for themselves'
(Grosz 1995: 182) rather than (only) a fixed binary of vertical depth.
As a way of looking and doing, queer living blows open moments of the
linear narrative of desire, fills space, expands moments of time, displaces
subjects and objects – creates networks of interweaving elements that
hold open the moment of desiring. 'Does the erotic rely on clear definitions between male and female? Or is the blurring of these distinctions
its very source?' (Ferris 1993: 9). Eroticism becomes the act of desiring
in practice. 'The fantasy I've been calling performative queerness is ...
about the unexplored spaces between expressions, the possibilities of
movement, the non-names not yet imagined' (Fuchs 1996: 150).

For me, *Witch One* was a beginning. What followed was a series of
theatrical performances that addressed androgynous queer desire head
on: *Laid Out Lovely* (1994), *Fifi Le Flesh* (1995) and *Did I Speak?* (1997).
These works offered audiences overt and perhaps overly enthusiastic
images of queer sexualities. Reviewing *Fifi Le Flesh*, Jan Parry (1995: 12)
writes: 'Emilyn Claid, whose narcissistic, near-pornographic solo got
Dance Umbrella off to a bad start ...' *Fifi Le Flesh* includes slide images
of different queerly imagined sexual figures between identities. There are
five stereotypical portraits: a Lana Turner-style femme, a Valentino-style
butch, an angel, a leather-clad S/M dyke and a Gothic romantic
vampire. The images are camp and ironic, initially recognizable as
stereotypes; then, as the piece progresses, these stereotypes begin to fragment. Valentino appears wearing a bra, the S/M leather dyke wears
Lana Turner's long blonde wig, the angel wears a leather harness, Lana
Turner holds two black dildos in her upturned palms. Interspersed with
these images are ones of my naked back, appearing androgynous.

I watch for the look of the wild in your eyes rise up from the sweet
and tear me apart. You watch like a wolf till I submit to your

power, bite till I bleed, dive into the wet, climb on my back, draw blood from my flesh and drink from my womb . . . Watch out for the look of the wild in my eyes rise up from the sweet when I thrust into you.

(Claid 1995)

Queering is an expression of optimism, yes, but its slippery surface can have negative connotations. For some, the term 'queer' suggests a unifying dumping ground for lesbian, gay and transgender sexuality – in fact for all perversities that can be identified against the norm. Sedgwick (1993) claims that the notion of a dumping ground can be contradicted by the

> [e]xperimental, linguistic, epistemological, representational, political adventures attaching to the very many of us who may at times be moved to describe ourselves as (among other possibilities) pushy femmes, radical faeries, fantasists . . . drags, clones, leatherfolk, ladies in tuxedos, feminist women or feminist men, masturbators, bulldaggers, divas, Snap! queens, butch bottoms, storytellers, trans-sexuals, aunties, wannabes, lesbian-identified men or lesbians who sleep with men.
>
> (Sedgwick 1993: 8)

The term remains a discursive site, 'the point of departure for a set of historical reflections and future imaginings' and as such should not be 'fully owned' (Butler 1993: 228). The expansiveness of the term 'queer' is also its limitation. The historical reflections place queer as a deroga-tory and degrading 'slur' for identifiable, gay sexual behaviour (Butler 1993: 223) yet it is now used to formulate positive future directions. Lesbians and gay men have rejected the term because of its expansive-ness, because it has been uprooted from a fixed sexual orientation and has no essential roots. This is a danger implicit within queer's subversive potential where 'the singularity of queer theory can only reside in the way in which it puts desire to work' (Probyn 1995: 7). Butler (1993: 228) criticizes queer theory/practice as being a 'predominantly white move-ment'. But Sedgewick contradicts this: 'artists of colour whose sexual definition includes "queer" . . . are using the leverage of "queer" to do a new kind of justice to the fractal intricacies of language, skin, migra-tion, state' and in this way, 'the gravity . . . of the term "queer" itself deepens and shifts' (Sedgwick 1993: 9). The future imaginings of queer access a way of living in the world that is different to the normal, allowing for imaginative creations where one thing dissolves to become another. Simultaneously, queer's history roots these relations in the flesh-and-blood reality of sexed bodies. Positive and negative, queer's paradoxical nature gives agency to performing bodies.

In queering androgyny, I am not performing a third gender or a neutral transcendent place of perfection, nor an ideal centre, essence or middle point. Instead, I am performing the possibility of many articulated identities spanning across a vast arc between two extremes. This is a movement of imagination that pushes the boundaries, traverses the lines between, a movement that suggests, crosses, copies and provokes chaos, weirdness, a boundless sexing arising from the ashes of gender.

39 RE-DRESSING THE GIRLS

Of what relevance is my personal story of queer androgyny at this point? To illustrate how desires, sexuality and emotions of flesh-and-blood bodies influence performing, watching and writing. Remembering this full body, we can transfer and translate the actions of desire into movement language, into the play between points – looking and being looked at, linearity and fragmentation, directed time and fluid space, power and pleasure – as seductive ambiguity. There is a direct correlation between feeling and action where one gives meaning and image to the other. This is not to say we must be queer to appreciate dance. I am asking us to remember that we have bodies of desire that influence our watching and dancing. Without the narrative of desire, as a memory, as a connection to my body, the moment of watching becomes dispassionate, abstract, removed, without connection or meaning. We need to acknowledge our real-ness while observing our performance – as spectators and as performers – even if and, more importantly, because we cannot possibly identify what is performed and what is real.

So I look again at women dancing but from a queer perspective, observing how queer androgynous desire translates into dance languages and performance. I see women embrace the vertical aesthetic as a powerful language tool together with the somatic movement intelligence of a horizontal aesthetic. I look for dancing where the horizontal takes risks with vertical ascendancy, internal becomes external, and body equals mind. I watch as women fully inhabit the task of moving as an external means of expression. They claim real-ness and illusion, internal listening and articulate language. They play many spaces between, rather than identify as one or the other. Improvisation plays equally with repeated lines, somatic sensation with choreographed form. It is all performed. Just because the fluid and internal somatics of dancing emerged simultaneously with a feminist quest for subjectivity does not naturalize them as a true expression that somehow belongs to the essential female body – even though the movement may *feel* as if it arises from some internal, imaginary place. Instead, both fluidity and linearity become non-hierarchical performed points that make and dissolve each other and through which play is possible. We are in a liminal space. We are polymorphous bodies. Emerging in the performance play between the extremes are different performers' figurations of presence.

Liz Aggiss is a performer, choreographer, filmmaker, writer and professor of visual performance at Brighton University. I watch Liz in her famous solo, *Grotesque Dancer* (1986).[1] Inspired by the German expressionist dancer, Valeska Gert, this solo has become a cult dance piece, with a risk-taking, breathtaking, no-compromise embodiment of determined, persistent precise physicality, visual imagery and humour. In 1986, at Dartington College of Arts, I remember seeing Liz pinned aggressively to a spotlight, hunched forward, shoulders and upper back curved, arms held in running position, fists clenched, elbows out, her body in profile but her face looking directly out to the audience. Her grimace changes to a grin. I remember her performing rhythmically repetitious gymnastic knee bends, her knobbly knees and muscular calves proudly but vulnerably exposed as a statement against conventional beauty. No pretty steps here.

I remember Liz dancing and singing to ironic pastiches of German lieder (songs). She begins the piece wearing a black wig, white T-shirt, black 1920s bloomers, white socks and black gym shoes. She ends the piece bald-headed, in a black evening dress and heels.

Liz veered away from the British post-modern new dance aesthetic of the 1980s:

> *Grotesque Dancer* was never singularly about dance steps but responded to contemporary dance circa 1980. It challenged, championed and resisted the dominant visual aesthetic, mostly sweatpanted pedestrian workwear. It disobeyed the current vogue of breathy-gentle-touchy-feely-considerate tactile dance language that was infusing the contemporary dance world.
>
> (Aggiss 2006)

Feisty, androgynous Liz, with her strong, muscular, powerful body and ironic femininity. She turns and twists masculinity and femininity into the performance of extreme macabre. As a rejection of the soft fluid formlessness of *jouissance* improvisation, Liz creates a grotesque illusion of beauty on her flesh-and-blood body. Here, vulnerability and arrogance are intermingled, creating a vital presence of real and illusion.

Carol Brown is a performer, choreographer and academic whose research explores relations between architecture and dance, combining virtual forms and live bodies in performance. I watch her perform *Ocean Skin* (1998). She runs continuously in circles, with long leaps and strides, round and round and round. One arm, linear and defined, trails behind her. She stops. She removes her smart silk jacket to reveal a blue see-through sleeveless tunic over white loose trousers. Her body outline is sharply delineated through the tunic. She begins to move on the diagonal. Stepping in parallel, in Greek frieze lines, her torso twists against her legs. Her back arches forwards, her hip juts to the side, her elbows, rising above her head, are angular – broken wings. She performs fast and exact articulate movements with her legs extended and feet pointed. Her strong back twists and arches as she flings herself sharply downwards and sideways. Her leg and arm gestures distort, are hyperextended: beauty and the grotesque in disharmony. Dynamics are sharp. She flings herself to the ground and supports her weight on her forearms, her shoulders and her elbows. She throws her body, parallel to the ground, in soft long curves; softness hits against muscular extension and strength. This is erotic. she turns to move in a straight line towards the audience, looking out. She talks to the audience. She is in control.

Carol describes for me the act of performing:

> It is something that pierces the present moment, that pulls me up, captures me, gives a sense of fullness, saturating attention so that everything within and without is brought into a field of forces. In this communication with the audience, I can sense this state, a quality of listening and sounding simultaneously through the body. It is like a spell in a sense, mesmerizing. There is something in the language; I don't know what it is until I perform it. In that state of performative becoming, I understand something about my physical language that I didn't understand in the studio. It manifests itself; it speaks back to me. I carry a legacy of information, all these other bodies co-present with me, in my sense of being a performer. There is an accumulation of lineage and genealogy, performing a history of lived being.

> (Brown 2003)

I am drawn to her arrogant definition of the space around her, her direct objectifying look, her precise controlled actions, her body intelligence and physical discipline. Simultaneously, I notice how she self-consciously enjoys her body's movements and how her physical actions are observed. She is aware of her back; she moves from the centre of her body; there is a soft sensual quality in certain gestures and in the turn of her head. I notice that it is not one or other of these qualities that engages me but the ability to play between them, to be in her body while articulating a spoken language. She performs glamour and vulnerability; she looks and desires to be looked at. These contradictions smack against and slot into each other, energized points of friction in a positive/negative embrace.

Wendy Houstoun, former DV8 diva, now makes her own work as performer–choreographer, crossing the boundaries between theatre and dance. I watch Wendy perform *Haunted, Daunted and Flaunted* (1997). The stage is empty except for an upstage microphone and a jacket hanging over a chair. Over the speakers, a voice makes an announcement about an assault on a young woman. The disembodied male voice informs me that this performance will be a re-construction.

Wendy appears, simultaneously speaking and dancing. She describes the events leading up to the attack, the journey the woman took and how she was watched. Wendy's text interweaves the description of the event with comments on her own movements. 'She carried on, on the diagonal, everything seemed to have returned to normal. As she reached behind her, she suddenly had a feeling she was invisible. As she rolled away it could be awhile before she went out again' (Houstoun 1997).

In the next scene, Wendy sits in the chair talking into the microphone. She now takes the role of the woman herself post-assault: 'Sometimes I try saying hello. Sometimes I just make weird faces. Sometimes I cross the road at a shallow diagonal' (Houstoun 1997). The text is rhythmical, giving it a dream-like quality. She puts on the jacket. 'Sometimes I just change my name. Sometimes I try to be invisible' (Houstoun 1997). She picks up the gun. Wendy's poetic, hypnotic, inwardly focused text abruptly changes. She faces the audience. She walks, zigzagging sideways towards the audience, then stands looking out. 'My name's Veronica.' She begins to panic. 'What are you looking at, what are you looking at, sod off you fucking creep, just piss off' (Houstoun 1997). A loud crashing sound interrupts – rock music begins. Wendy dances. Her legs, thrown from the hips, sharply kick, stab and circle. Her leg movements dominate the language; they are her weapons, warding people away. She holds the gun in her right hand. She rolls on the ground, tosses her body, performs tiny steps on the spot and hesitates in stillness. She lifts her right leg; the gun is aimed along the line of her leg. Her leg and arm open and circle round behind her. Wherever her foot points so does the gun. 'She is a spanner in the works . . . Twisting and lunging back and forth, she randomly fires off the gun, until suddenly she finds it poised by her head. The image is unsettling' (Dodds 1998: 13).

The mood changes: Wendy steps into the role of storyteller. She becomes lyrical; her arms and back become liquid. The mood changes again as Wendy, now smoking, drinking and joking, talks about herself. She goes back over her past memories, provoking images from different years. She says, 'I remember in 1989 I did this a lot' (Houstoun 1997), flinging her right arm from her chest outward to the side. She traces back to being a baby. The text and movement work together in present time to describe the past. This is comic entertainment. She switches to minimal action and a more sinister mood. Towards the end, the words and actions drift into abstraction, hypnotic once more. 'I stole away, I hid, I hid away, I hid away from hurt, I dragged, I dragged up, I dragged up the dirt . . .' (Houstoun 1997). Wendy holds the gun close to her body, points it towards herself, twisting and writhing on the floor.

Embodying different perspectives of the story, blowing the narrative apart, Wendy brings the audience into an active play for meaning: who, she asks, is watching whom and from what perspective? Wendy shifts her personae between the objective and subjective, from observing the scene to being the tragic victim, playing many figures of herself in the narrative. Dangerous and exciting, Wendy is haunted by her own life.

Wendy embodied both movement and text, physical and spoken languages. Each was rich in content, articulate and complex in its humanity. The movement and text were not creating a unity. The text ironically commented on the action and vice versa. Sometimes the words gave identity to the gestures but when gestures were repeated with different words, the meaning was displaced. Often, quite arbitrary movements were juxtaposed with text, displacing the emotional drama of the words, words and movement working out of rhythm with each other. There were different styles of text: argumentative, autobiographical, documentary and fictional. Painful personal memories were displaced by poetic verse, different tenses, first person, third person and sometimes by addressing the audience as 'you'. Wendy's presence was sometimes in front and sometimes behind the text, alternating between playing directly to the audience and focusing inward, letting the words dominate. Movement and text merged with one other as harmonized poetry in motion only towards the end. Sometimes the movement slipped off

Figure 14 Wendy Houstoun in *Haunted, Daunted and Flaunted* (1997). Publicity image.

Photographer: Chris Nash.

Wendy's body with ease, sometimes with tension and contradiction. Nothing was comfortable. The movement languages shifted between balletic articulations, fluid-released gesture, and parodies of jazz and English stage-school dance styles. With her articulate technique, Wendy performed a love/hate relationship with her dance history, always human, often dismissive. Teetering on the edge of the suicidal and the self-reflective, acting as victim and aggressor, she inhabited and commented on the text and the movement. Wendy parodied the tragedy with her ironic use of text and movement, without pretension, without hierarchy – with wit and a small black gun. She hovered at the place where irony becomes self-destructive. Wendy's presence slipped into the gaps between her performed identities. She was a comic, angry, abstract, theatrical and pedestrian figure. She was tragic and mocking. She was all and none of these things, an intriguing figure between fully lived and performed surfaces.

I watch Jenny Tattershall and Lee Clayden perform Fin Walker's *The Self* (2002). Jenny stands in front of Lee. She falls backwards; he catches her under her arms. Her legs are straight, feet pointed. He throws her back on to her feet, grabs her shoulders and turns her sideways so they are both facing the same direction. Jenny leans sideways onto Lee, their hips touching, Jenny bends her back and lunges, her left leg forward; Lee drops his weight over her back. Jenny ducks down under his arm, comes up sideways to face him. She grabs Lee's arm, pulls him towards her, his head drops to her torso. She shoves her hip forward. Lee bends forward, lifting Jenny onto his back. Lee puts her down and they turn towards each other, still holding arms, a point of tension. Lee bends down, grabs Jenny's left leg and takes it forward; Jenny lifts her other leg off the floor to meet it. Her torso tips backwards, legs and torso making a boat shape. They are still entwined. Jenny wraps Lee's arm in her own. Jenny gets to her feet and turns to face Lee upstage. She jumps, crashing into Lee, who wraps his other arm around her waist, pulls her up further. Jenny's legs are stretched, feet pointed. Returning to the floor, Jenny pulls Lee by the arm, his shoulder twisting forward. She pulls him back upright. She turns in towards him, he grabs her and tilts her backward to the floor, brings her up. She leans out away from him; he pulls her back in towards him. They make a complete turn together, first one way then the other, pulling on each other's arms to make the turns. . . . This sequence lasts 20 seconds. It is intensely taut, bodies closely entwined throughout.

The Self continues for 20 minutes, during which the dancers rarely break out of contact. Each gesture initiates the next, discordant and contradictory, alive with physical attack. The tense bodies have the quality of a fight but with precise knowledge of the other's timing, her/his weight and the next move. The energy is sharp and dangerous, exact and precise. Using the skills of contact improvisation to drive the part-nering work, *The Self* brings contact duet work into a sharp polished performance dynamic. There cannot be a moment of forgetfulness in this piece as the dancers throw each other from one fast swerving tilt to another.

Fin Walker is a performer–choreographer. She initially trained through a somatic body–mind approach to dance, focusing primarily on Alexander technique with release-based contemporary dance and ballet:

> I didn't think I had the facility in the hips to be a dancer, so there was something else I went looking for, a sense of self and identity as a mover. But the training didn't allow for a great openness of the body, we didn't work the body for flexibility and strength. So then I started to work to open my body, to exploit my body's facility and at the same time try and extend what that facility was. These two elements fascinate me – the sense of self and the facility of the physical body. What you can create in the studio with those two elements has a wealth of possibilities.
>
> (Walker 2003)

Fin's experiential dance history began with an internal focus and then moved outwards to extend her vocabulary and embrace the articulated linearity of performance techniques. Jenny Tattershall approaches Fin's movement language from the other extreme after nine years of external projection as a ballerina with The Royal Ballet:

> Fin said to me, look and see things. She said, free up your head, if you see something then really see it, see the wall, and be within that moment. In ballet I was always looking out, always ahead of myself, thinking of something other than the moment now. It is interesting to realize you don't have to be out there, you can be contained and within yourself, and it will create just as strong a presence as if you are trying to project.
>
> (Tattershall 2003)

To dance Fin's work, such as *The Self* (2002) or *Essence* (2005) per-formers require an exact awareness of internal and external focus in each moment. The dancers work in such close proximity and at such dangerous speed that, without a total focus in the moment, injury is more than likely. The dancing:

resonates in the memory because of the superb quality of the complex movement which is essentially abstract, yet hints at personal histories and dangerous relationships. The emotional focus shifts constantly and the audience are taken on a breathless ride full of thrills.

(Dixon 2005: 51)

Interesting in Jenny's dancing is the engagement of vertical and horizontal aesthetics on her body. Falling, catching, leaning out parallel to the floor, fragmented arm gestures and contact skills are characteristic of the horizontal aesthetic. The external projection of articulate, precise balletic legs and long lines are recognizable as the vertical aesthetic. At the interface, dancers experience a range of risk-taking, passionate, challenging movement dynamics. 'For me it's about embracing your body, sexuality, femininity, also your strength and power, being able to work with men's bodies, male energy. I love seeing women being powerful in that way' (Walker 2003).

Combining the skills of horizontal and vertical techniques, Jenny feels her weight on the floor while simultaneously experiencing an upward lift; breathes down in her belly instead of her chest during strenuous movement; initiates movement from the central weight of her body instead of from her chin. She combines strong upwardly moving lines with fluid falls to the floor, lifts another body by working with, rather than against, gravity, conjuring the dynamic frictions of a Möbius strip: 'The inverted three-dimensional figure eight. The Möbius strip has the advantage of showing the inflection of mind into body and body into mind, the ways in which, through a kind of twisting or inversion, one side becomes the other' (Grosz 1994: xii).

There is no hierarchy here between vertical and horizontal. Poststructuralist philosophies consider the horizontal as a 'thought of difference, not identity' (Lechte 1994: 217), where the vertical does not exist in opposition but as a form for the horizontal. The vertical is incorporated into the horizontal as a difference. The horizontal elements of dancing give rise to the vertical, not as a separate and opposing entity, but as an *articulation* of the horizontal. The vertical line is not something to be gained, but is an active play, an evolving movement, emerging out of and returning to the horizontal plane. Power 'is an energy, an activity, a series of directions' (Grosz 1994: 147). The vertical operates through and returns to the horizontal axis like the iris flower to its rhizome.

I watch Stine Nielson standing still in *a life altered* (2000) created by Angela Woodhouse.[2] Angela makes work for extraordinary and intimate sites. I am informed before entering the studio where *a life altered* will take

Figure 15 Jenny Tattershall and Lee Clayden in *Essence* (Fin Walker 2005). Publicity image.

Photographer: Ravi Deprees.

place that only one spectator at a time will observe the performance. In a corner of the studio is a small room enclosed by tall makeshift screens. These screens are painted a grey-blue colour. There is a single electric light bulb shining into the interior of the space. The rest of the studio is dark and empty accept for three chairs placed in a line facing away from the constructed room. I am led, with one other spectator, to the row of chairs and told to sit and wait. The spectator next to me is led to the room. She returns five minutes later. Angela leads me inside the room, which is approximately six feet square. There is one performer, Stine Nielson, and one chair, on which I am asked to sit. Stine stands still, tall, calm yet poised. She begins to move slowly, tiny gestures, sometimes just fingers, a simple step, a change of level, a turn of her head. She reaches her arm out sideways; it almost touches my body, intimately close. Her slow minimal gestures are 'not about filling time with move-ment but about filling movement with time' (Woodhouse 2000). I am drawn to the intimacy and detail of her movements. Rather than observe Stine as a whole person in time and space, I find myself focusing on the sound of her breath, the peachy skin colour of her hand, her fingernails, the soft downy hairs on her arm, the micro rather the macro closeness of her body.

After a few minutes, I am led back to my waiting-room chair and the other spectator is led away once again. The process repeats three times. Each time I enter the room, the chair and Stine's body are in a different relationship. Each time she moves slowly and intimately close. At one point, Stine lies on the floor at my feet. She moves her torso slightly. As I watch, she opens her eyes and catches my look. I am thrown into a relationship with Stine where I cannot separate myself from her performance. She sees me and I see her without the usual boundaries of theatrical light and spatial perspective. I become aware of my physical body. We watch each other and perform for each other. Angela describes her own work:

> There is a sense in which each of the two bodies circulates each other with their gaze. There is a kind of searching, mapping, reaching with the gaze where the two are gradually wrapped up and subsumed in the mass of the other. As the viewer takes advantage of the opportunity to scrutinise, they gradually recognise that they are themselves under scrutiny.
>
> (Woodhouse 2000)

Dissolving the perspective of space also dissolves the separation between performer and spectator, the space of objective reasoning. When a performance is no longer fronted to a single direction, we, as spectators, are jolted into an awareness of our own bodies in the space and the various directions of looking. Watching becomes an embodied active movement, more so than when sitting in the dark at a distance. When spectators physically participate in the performance, move from place to place with the performers, subjects and objects scrunch and grind into each other.

To let go of the need for secure identities, living with and enjoying the ensuing chaos of meanings requires effort – physical work – risk-taking and a plentiful imagination. When spectators enter the performer's space they are subsumed into the act of performance and confront their own presence as authors of the work. 'The potential for a responding eye, like the hunger for a responsive voice, informs the desire to see the self through the image of the other' (Phelan 1993: 16). As I attempt to analyse Stine's presence in *a life altered*, I am self-conscious. I am faced with my own presence in the space as I describe hers. Her sensuality is also mine, her eroticism is reflected in my eyes; her miniscule movements are also my movements; our roles of subject watching object have become each other. The *mise en scène* surrounds me and includes me in the moment of interaction, body for body and eye for eye. As formal perspectives of space dissolve, so do fixed relations of desire (Briginshaw 2001). The desire to know, to understand, folds back on itself; I can only know Stine through knowing myself, and I can only know myself through Stine, a perpetual un-knowing as a physical act of desiring to know.

Disrupting performer–spectator relations in *a life altered* lets presence loose from its fixed relationship to subject/object binaries. These fixed positions are observed with a sideways glance, no longer controlling the action. The spectator's act of looking becomes a passionate physical and erotic practice. Bodies looking and being looked at slip and slide and fold around each other when the space between performers and spec-tators dissolves. Looking at you looking at me looking away, looking up, looking in, or not looking, or catching a glance, a glimpse, becoming you becoming me. To interpret one is to interpret the other, immersed and interconnected as an experience of absent/present queering desire where spectators are within and around the work and the performers perform to multiple, intimate fronts. *a life altered* is not something that spectators watch and performers do, but something that is shared as embodied action, where who is engaging whom is no longer definable. There is no right or wrong position from which to observe and inter-pret; there are only choices. The formality of conventional perspective is no longer a tool with which aesthetically to qualify the performance. Good, bad, success and failure are no longer attributable when here and there, who looks at who are up for grabs. To be honest to this experience, I admit to an inability to make judgements. I allow myself to enjoy the perpetually unfinished task of becoming absent.

Liz Aggiss, Carol Brown, Wendy Houstoun, Jenny Tattershall, Fin Walker and Stine Nielson, as female performers, return to engaging performer–spectator relations but on their own terms. These artists understand how object–subject relations can be played as performative tools. Authors of their performances, they appreciate the necessity for external articulation in language to allow personal statements to be represented in performance. With a post-feminist outlook on life and love, these women re-inhabit, after the feminist negation, the role of object of desire – but differently. This time they choose to be there as subjects of their own work. These women take back the power of looking out an articulated finesse, and interweave it with the *jouissance* of a somatic imaginary. They express their desires through movement and words, as qualities, aesthetics and expressions of their work. As spectator, I return the gift.

Jouissance is the life force of language; it may exist without language but is acknowledged as an expression through language. *Jouissance* is invisible as formless other-ness but it finds an expression through language. The somatic body, then, recognizes language as an expression of itself. Nothing is fixed about language if it is diffused by *jouissance*; it becomes a momentary construction that dissolves back to a chaotic body, re-versing itself to emerge again differently. One force becomes another, an endless folding one into the other without homogeneity as Deleuze's poetic narrative of Leibniz and baroque describes: 'Movement, then, cannot be stopped. Two really distinct things can be inseparable, two inseparable things can be really distinct, and belong to two levels, the localisation of the one in the other amounting to a projection upon a point' (Deleuze 1993: 12).

A point, like standing still, is the gap within all this movement. If the narrative of a body performing could begin as 'Once upon a time', then stillness blows open the 'O' of once, zooming in on the micro moment where a scene is about to be introduced, where the past action is completed and the next has yet to begin: neutral. The *Concise Oxford Dictionary* (1995: 916) defines neutral as 'not helping or supporting two opposing sides . . . not strong or positive . . . neither positive nor negative . . . sexually undeveloped, asexual'. This is not, however, how I use the word because it implies a translation onto the dancer's body that is dull, stilled and non-energized. Rather, the neutrality here finds its parallel once again in Derrida's concept of *différance* referring to a place of departure: 'an absolutely neutral receptacle, that suppresses nothing,

releasing the innumerable, the unforeseeable, the invention of the other'
(Caputo 1997: 105). As a neutral moment, stillness is full of past, present
and future action; a practice of body intelligence that is as busily worded
internally as it is silently visual in appearance.

Stine, standing still, integrates three different directions of attention.
She focuses inwards to the kinaesthetic somatic sensations of the body.
She connects outwards, owning the moment in time, as the one who
looks and is looked at. Third, she is aware of the place of her body in
three-dimensional space. A series of physical thoughts are set up without
hierarchy and without stasis, active in all directions, working along every
muscle and fibre. Her skin is transformed into a million eyes. Standing
still, Stine draws attention to an acute physical awareness of each
moment of every action to achieve any particular point. The goal may
be an image of stillness but she is constantly waylaid by the activity of
getting there.

Like the pixelated image, each movement towards and away from any
point is enlivened by thousands of minute and complex contra flows
working on a micro level internal to the body, which require constant
mind-full attention in their ever-changing evolving motions within every
action. This use of energy creates sparks that fly off the performer,
bringing her/his body to the attention of the spectator. In this way
stillness is a point that penetrates the space before language and after
language, a fused charge of inside and outside.

In stillness, our bodies never stay in one place; they are forever
running away, in excess, doing too much, too little, overemphasizing,
over-compensating. We are constantly pulling them back to an apparently still place. This is the friction that keeps performing presence alive.
In the search for the easy route to a place of rest, our bodies require
constant reminding and contradicting, tugging towards and away from
this live place called stillness.

Conclusion

40 EYE FLIGHT

Seduction re-turns as a liberated practice. Seductiveness in performance becomes an interactive, interchangeable, pleasurable play of multiple meanings and identities between performers and spectators – a physical action of desiring. Identifying subjects and objects, who is seducing and what is seduced is secondary to the act of playing itself.

The audiences for British independent dance culture enjoy a multiplicity of meanings at the site of the performer dancing. Strategies for engagement depend on a reading of ambiguity on a performer's body, enticing the spectator to search for meanings and interpretations. Performance has become the spectator's art.

> A text is made of multiple writings, drawn from many cultures, and entering into mutual relations of dialogue, parody, contestation, but there is one place where this multiplicity is focused and that place is the reader, not, as was hitherto said, the author.
>
> (Barthes 1977: 148)

But that does not mean that performers have ceased to be authors. For performers, it is about being very much the author, in each moment, with body–mind intelligence and focused physical work. Whether driven by somatic internal intelligence, cross-disciplinary partnerships, emotions, person-as-political agendas, narratives or articulate codified dance skills, most artists have something they desire to say. Furthermore, our statements owe allegiance to frameworks of culture, racial difference, physical dis/ability, feminism, postmodernism, hetero- and homosexuality, each with its own historical quest for subjectivity and identity.

What matters when dancing is our embodied understanding of the two-way play between points, opening to the frictions of non-hierarchical directions as they rub up against each other, inhabiting the conflict of energies in and on our bodies. Here is the physical work that spans the bridge between extremes of inside and outside, giving and taking, looking and being looked at, desiring and being desired, masculinity and femininity, vertical and horizontal, linearity and fluidity, moving fast and standing still – not as a happy medium or a union, or a hierarchy of opposites but as a clashing intelligent physicality between points of difference. An articulate language in the world is informed by somatic intelligence; an engagement with internal physicality energizes an external expression. One dynamic infiltrates another, becomes another, inside becomes outside and back again. And if we fully embody each point of difference we don't perform them simultaneously. We are always moving towards and away from the points. This is what keeps performance alive, the contradictions, the spanning across, and the disjunction that cannot settle in and on the performer's body. Theatre is born of conflicting desires, not harmonious unity. To ignore the extremes of embodied experiences and cultural constructs would be to contract the length and breadth of the spaces between. 'You don't reach the BwO and its plane of consistency by wildly destratifying' (Deleuze and Guattari 1988: 160).

As performers we commit ourselves to the work by fully inhabiting each and every physical task. In this immediate attendance to the task, our pedestrian identifiable authored bodies disappear, becoming something else. Full body becomes empty body. On one hand, our actions are real. On the other – as we move across tasks, switch and let go and re-inhabit – these actions become a surface of images for spectators. Watching ambiguity in Beckett plays, Phillip Zarrilli (1997: 106) writes: 'Actors, of course, cannot "act" ambiguity, but they can locate, define, embody, and enact a precise set of physical actions for which there is no conclusive, single referent.' Through inhabiting the task, we disappear, leaving traces, surface images. The practice is one of pouring sand, from one vessel to another, empty to full, full to empty, as we negotiate the real and illusion of inhabited physicality on our bodies. This is how ambiguity surfaces on a performer's body – for the spectator. This is how performers are perpetually becoming something else.

First, we embody a practice of contradictions between internal focus and external expression. Second, we are so fully engaged in each task that our real bodies become an empty surface for ambiguity to play. This is the performer's work.

The spectator's work is different. Watching independent dance performance, we desire to be intellectually, emotionally and physically engaged by different performers dancing. We enjoy the interactive play for identity and meaning on the performer's body. We are engaged when performers' bodies and images parallel each other, switch, acknowledge and dissolve through each another, where what is real and what is illusion are spectators' multiple choices. We are no longer satisfied with sitting in a plush velvet seat watching a play of real and illusion whereby illusive, transcendent beauty subsumes flesh-and-blood earthly reality, and our desire and perception is identifiably fixed and short-lived (though we might be dazzled by the dancers' technical skill and extremes of linearity). We are not content to sit back and be entertained by narratives that have happy endings. (Yet we might be tempted by the possibilities of narratives as we remember and connect to the familiar longings and patterns of our past.) We are no longer only engaged by the minimalist body of new dance that rejected transcendent illusion and encouraged invisibility as a tool for subjectivity. This was an elitist position, an outcome of (white) artists' political rejection of Enlightenment. (Yet we might continue to support a post-modern minimalist approach to visual performance.) We desire to watch performers who are passionately dynamic and vitally energized. (But we don't want them to give it all away.) We are not complacent or easily pleased. We love fantasy and illusion but not at the expense of the reality of the live action. We want both and neither and the many possibilities in between.

As spectators we are enticed back into the oscillating act of watching the performer's real body become surface illusion as an ambiguity between one and another. But the illusion is not out there, created by the performer. Creating the illusion is our *work*, as spectators. We desire the images on a performer's body to change and dissolve and re-emerge differently. Achieving this is our practice, our responsibility. The practice of seductive ambiguity, as relations of engagement, is our physical activity. The performers are doing something different in order to allow us to practice our art.

Here and now, in British independent dance, spectators watch, and we span the arc between the extremes of knowing and becoming – a place of 'gayness, diversity and plenty' (Kristeva 2003) between performers and spectators. Kristeva uses this phrase as an alternative to the term 'love' with its banal misuse within the frame of fixed subject–object relations. The phrase provides an apt parallel for performer–spectator relations in British independent dance. This is a performance context of multiple yet specific differences, individual expressions and movements in collaboration, unique points on a shared platform – on each body and between bodies.

Our work as spectators is to remember the conventions and codes but not to be fixed by them. We know we can engage in a play of not knowing but desiring to know. We let go of the desire for fixed meanings but search for meanings all the same. We acknowledge the roots and histories of things but receive knowledges as a network of things. Our watching practice becomes physically contradictory, similar to the performer's practice. To see is a verb, an action state, eyes are engaged in the *movement* of seeing. Seeing is a movement of travel, a trajectory through the space between my eyes and the object. Aware of the act of looking, I am engaged in eye flight. Looking is an act of intrinsic anticipation, direction, projection, travelling, motion, map reading, awareness of moments before and after. What happens when my trajectory of looking meets that of the performer, who has eyes all over her/his body? Often, my looking machine meets no resistance, its feelers, probes, lasers, cameras and computers fly a straight course, landing on the performing body. Or our eye flights meet smoothly mid space, flying one over the other, giving way, passing parallel, missing each other. But sometimes our eyes meet in an embrace, grasping each other, wrangling and tangling for permission to fly on, locked in a tension of desires, where we must choose who moves first – a clash of energizing particles in open space. Here, in the meeting of flight paths, presence is sparked. Watching is physical. I become an active audience.

I asked independent artists how they approach a practice of presence in performance.

Fin Walker, performer, choreographer and director of Walker Dance, Park Music:

> Being in the moment, connecting with the moment whatever that might be, even fear – not locking the moment – accepting and being with the fear. Secondly, it's about non-attachment, moving through it, not fixing. It's about existing in the body. In solo work, I like connecting with the audience. I am using them as an improvisation tool. I look for my inspiration from the audience. I connect visually.
>
> (Walker 2003)

David Waring, performer, choreographer and director of Transitions Dance Company:

> Arrogance, an unwavering self belief, an innate sense of theatricality, an ability to immerse yourself into the work, a desire to be contentious, to be different, to be fully there in the moment with no apology. More than anything performing is a desire to interact and make human connection. Certain performers are frenetic. Their interface with the material is a battle, a conflict in the body. Some performers are simultaneously needing and not needing to perform, a love/hate relationship with dancing, like an addiction. That's engaging.
>
> (Waring 2003)

Wendy Houstoun, performer, director, filmmaker:

> Danger – for the spectator. I like performance when I am brought to a place of 'not knowing' – when I can't be sure what's happening. I am fascinated by small gestures, when you know something else is going on, but you can't see it. I like to see a performer who is lonely. I like a performer who takes responsibility for being alone. Someone who doesn't need confirmation from me, someone who is willing to accept not being liked. I like faces that don't try to please. It's like having a secret. It's more about what you hold back than what you give. Allowing people to witness. I like to think of it as a hiding-in-front-of-things . . .
>   I focus on breath. A breath pattern can hold people's attention.
>
> (Houstoun 2003)

Jenny Tattershall refers to her years with The Royal Ballet:

> In ballet you are performing from such an early age, you learn the tricks of the trade as you going along, without realizing it. By the time you get to the Opera House it has become part of you.
>
> (Tattershall 2003)

Kirstie Simson, contact improvisation teacher and performer:

> It's about honesty. The work is in opening to what is genuine. I try to create an open space that lets people in. The big challenge is in letting myself be who I am. It is very scary to go out there, to

physically go out there, letting go of everything that fixes. So that is my work, to create an atmosphere of open-ness, so the audience and I can trust the moment of play that is happening. I cannot let the fear block me at that point or the process will stop. This dynamic attack is attractive but dangerous.

(Simson 2003)

Lloyd Newson, director of DV8 Physical Theatre:

When we do an audition, we are looking for ownership of move-ment material, discovering if the performer understands the origin of the movement, physically and emotionally. The performer's execution and engagement with the material will tell me about the performer, and how this translates to their presence on stage. It's about whether they're inside or outside of the material. What makes a really great performer is when someone can mix the two qualities – the conscious with the unconscious. But the baseline is you need to be the character, totally present in the moment.

Some performers inhabit personas very deeply – like Daniel Day Lewis. However when he played Hamlet in London he lost the balance, he lost the outside eye. The people, who are capable of losing it, have the potential to be great, but if they don't want to self-destruct and want longevity they also need to understand how to contain themselves.

(Newson 2003)

Carol Brown speaks about the early stages of her research into mixed reality performance and her collaboration with Mette Ramsgaardtamsen:

Spawn[1] is a mixed reality environment, part real and part virtual. There is an avatar – we call it our virtual other – that exists in an ontology and a morphology of its own. It has its own laws of physics in non-perspectival non-Euclidean space based on spline geometries and nurbs. It doesn't have any gravity, no front, back, left, right. The avatar is morphing and changing, being kinetically modelled through our movements. It is a gorgeous perfect thing a divine space, breathtaking, slippery, beautifully coloured. The extreme otherness of Spawn makes me think of Sigourney Weaver in *Alien* and the effort to incorporate the alien, the other, something foreign to us. So far we have got it to respond to us, now we want to respond to it. The reciprocity will be very interesting.

Presence is affected deeply by this challenge. The dancers felt robbed in the first instance; they felt depleted and they felt they were fumbling around being asked to do very banal things, demoralized and lacking in agency. The virtual other is a beautiful perfect thing. It looks gorgeous, it is a divine space, slippery, morphing, densely coloured, and you want to engage with its weightlessness. Its presence can seem to overwhelm the presence of the dancers and our work is in finding a conversation with it, so it can affect the dramaturgy of what we are doing. Its virtuality and impossible geometries (it would never stand up) suggests a kind of infinity. In this way, the metaphysics of presence are challenged and contested by the virtual.

(Brown 2003)

Eva Karczag:

Playing lightly, with complete absorption, utter conviction and intense pleasure, I enter and inhabit emergent worlds of the imagination and abandon myself to the physical delight of moving. Moving is grounded in an intelligent and articulate body, comfortable in itself and finely tuned to openness and receptivity. Movement is deeply sourced so has a uniquely personal quality, is curious so demands re-awakening from moment to moment, and has a simplicity and directness that invites and draws the viewer into a fluid and expanded viewing space. Open focus and clear intention, sensuality and passion, an inner excitement and liveliness, fuel the encounter. Attention to process is as crucial within performance as it is within daily practice and the development of the piece. Being right there, riding the ups and the downs, recognizing and catching the crests, inwardly and outwardly aware, I experience immense generosity.

(Karczag 2005)

Mary Prestidge:

I like to see people as real as possible. If I can get hooked into somebody's journey that's great. I get attracted to performers who are engaged with what they are doing, I like seeing people struggling with things and not being embarrassed about struggling. Of course virtuoso can be delicious – the sublimely fluid is the new dazzle! I like genuine, raw, repetitive things, I remember seeing a running race as a performance, that went on for 20 minutes. They were really going through it. It was real. I liked that.

(Prestidge 2003)

Jacky Lansley:

I use a variety of techniques to enable that sense of being fully present, and part of that process is exploring the boundaries of emotionality and feelings. When I am working with performers, both dancers and actors, I try and create safe structures to explore areas of personal experience. It has become very clear to me that in order for a performer to give a profound performance and fully inhabit the movement language they need to develop awareness about themselves. Actors know about this, dancers sometimes don't; and so in my teaching and choreographic work with dancers I am exploring ways of working; this is part of presence. During the process of inhabiting space the body is dilated and expands to fill the moment. It is this inhabiting of the performance material that creates presence. Presence is a process, not just a concept, a recognition within the performance context that there is a layered meaning to presence involving, for example, emotional presence, physiological presence – which involves a sense of simultaneous technical practice – where it might be possible to dip in and out of the choreographic image/ character to check the line of the head, a neck and sense of volume – and textual presence, involving the embodying of the narrative, meaning or character of the choreographic text. The notion of presence is probably far richer, deeper and more complex than we yet know, and is unavoidably dependent on the performer's visceral reality and subjective experience for its happening.

(Lansley 2003)

Dr Vena Ramphal, filmmaker and choreographer:

In repertoire, Bharatanatyam presence is linked up with ideas of Beauty. There is this idea that beauty is itself auspicious. Physical beauty has a metaphysical significance. Beauty in itself is considered to be beneficial and good. So the idea is that the body animates this idea of beauty. If I am to perform a piece but my mind is somewhere else and my eyes are glazed over, even though my arms and legs might be technically perfect, it would not be considered beautiful. The image of beauty would not be considered correct because my being in the body didn't enliven it.

(Ramphal 2002)

Fergus Early:

> The majority of our [Green Candle's] work happens in non
> theatrical spaces with audiences who are not dance or art audiences
> specifically: we perform to children, old people, people in hospitals
> and people with learning disabilities. What is really crucial, is that
> performers think about that: who the children are, who the old
> people are. They have to have empathy. Their audience is not an
> abstract group that just arrives and sits in seats; our performances
> are planned for that specific audience.
>
> (Early 2003)

Maedée Duprès:

> It's that complete connection of the person–performer or relation-
> ship to themselves. Firstly, in how they are able to bring about their
> mind, body and all their senses to whatever is the choreographic
> choice. Then, secondly, being able to give one's all, which is a
> learnt channelling of energy (plus talent of course), to project that
> choreographic meaning out to an audience. A wonderful melange
> of introvert and extravert at once! The mind can be a big trouble-
> maker, therefore what I think at each moment is crucial to me, as
> clarity resonates through being open and connected in space. The
> role of the eyes provides a vehicle for that clarity of intention.
>
> (Duprès 2004)

The thread that connects these artists' voices is the attention they give
to being physically there, the necessity to inhabit each moment of the
performance in order to not be there, to create the illusive or ambiguous
surface that engages spectators. These artists draw attention to the
contrary frictions of embodiment, how the act of inhabiting requires a
performer to pay attention to events and conditions inside and outside
the body. When the internal and external trajectories rebound off each
other, when depth plays surface, is the moment of fusion that sparks the
piercing point of presence in performance.

Performing, watching, writing – I have switched back and forth giving
attention to deep-rooted embodied physical practice and ambiguous
surface images. Dance performance is seductive and engaging when
we pay attention to ontological histories of being – in order to let them
go. We might choose to let them go, and play between them, but
these histories do not leave our bodies. Every performer has a history
of practices; every spectator has a bank of memories and a vocabulary

existence of perceptions. We bring that with us to performance, an ontology that can be unpacked to consider its complexity, patterns, non-hierarchical relations and connections to other stories and other bodies. Acknowledging performing and watching in this way allows us to re-claim figurations from the past as memories of equal richness and difference with which to play. Histories are recognized as they re-emerge in movement languages and expressions on bodies and between bodies. We can remember and identify the narrative of each gesture as it appears in the world and gives way to the next. With many memories, our bodies become hybrids of themselves, liminal and nomadic. We re-claim the different moments, not as fixed illusions or essential truths, but as qualities, moods, dynamics and languages with which to create: 'Everything is there, but *floating*' (Barthes 1977: 215). Dancing becomes a complex map, exuberant traces of images in change, before fixing can take place.

Writing, performing, watching, the performance figures identified in this book become free-floating memories, layers, shadows, markers and referents. Like the rules of a game that are spontaneously abandoned but not forgotten, the markers remind us of embodied practices while no longer subscribing to the fixed identities. The more referents the better, for the relations between them become more intricate in memory. As shadows of ontology, the memories become a network of platforms, existing side by side, structures on which to climb, up, down, sideways. As a writer, I can move between each imagined platform, jumping, crossing, climbing, catching, spinning, sliding, falling and grabbing hold. Here, an interpretation of presence teases, suggests, comes close but is already becoming another, surfacing within a frame of identities no longer relevant except as signposts at a crossroads, directions that lead nowhere and everywhere, within which the movement of falling in the gaps, swinging between the bars, becomes the dynamic of imagination.

Stop. Pull myself back to my body. Letting go might be an alluring force. But there is still a real body doing, a body with a cultural background, identifiable history and a wealth of embodied experiences from which defined practices emerge. My performing practice has a depth and interior, experienced in real living time and space. Before considering how to write between figures, I respect the figures as depths of their own experiences in practice. Drawing attention to these experiences has been a strategy: the insertion of moments of pause, identifying in order to move on and through. Because practices have been *lived*, I recognize how they can withstand being dismantled into horizontal surfaces in performance.

Performing, watching and writing fold into one another. As we inhabit that liminal risk-taking space, identities become relations between things, things become other things, place becomes space, abstractions become narratives. We can laugh and be still. We release queer from fear. Use androgyny, seduction and ambiguity as verbs. The empty gaps are a full body of work. Competition, glamour and polish run rampant. Catch them before they catch you. Bring out the low art and pulverize the high. Rebel and feel passion. Transcend and fall and run round in circles. What we choose to take with us is mapped on our bodies. We re-find things we thought we had lost. We re-visit places but the memory is stronger. Faces and smells conjure shadows of the past. Meetings in the present evoke other times. We are haunted by what we choose to forget. Each gesture carries its own history. Performing, we unwrap time from our bodies. Forget but remember that old thing called gender; forget but remember his body sees her body; remember to forget all fixed figures of masculinity and femininity. Stretch your skin out on the table; mould it into different shapes. Declare to know things but make up the answers. Take moments from the story and spread them apart; construct extensive imaginations on fragments, phrases and fleeting images. Knowledge is relative. There is no original. Follow leads, gather threads, hoard bits and discard the rest. As creatures in camouflage, adapt, change, shift through the gaps, re-invent, re-style, hold ten directions, weave several lives, do five jobs at once. In several dimensions, move sideways, backwards and co-ordinate forces. Hunt and be hunted. Pull and be pulled. Dive into the current, then swim aside to the calm. Pause. Then dive again, catching another ride with the change of the tide. These are survival tactics. Life's pattern is complex. Neutral is active; stillness moves fast. Let go of Saturday night routines, likes and dislikes, solemn intellectual engagement, middle-of-the-road safe aspirations. Uncover the naked hybrid in movement, image and expression. Be raw; make mistakes. Turn from the micro to the macro, from the minute detail to the landscape; see how one fragment of knowledge connects to another, to another, to another. Let go but remember.

My mother sews. Beside her are plastic bags, filled with scraps of fabric, years and years of leftover bits. There are leftovers from my costumes and everybody else's costumes, from dressmaking her own skirts and blouses, garments from the Women's Institute, and children's clothes. All those years of memories, scraps in plastic bags, heaped

around her feet. Nothing is wasted, like leftovers
in the larder, waiting for the weekend kedgeree.
Another bag contains cardboard shapes of
different sizes, cut in hexagons, diamonds and
triangles. Cardboard from cereal packets, grocery
boxes, Christmas boxes, recycled birthday cards.

She takes a scrap of fabric and wraps it round
a cardboard shape, stitches until it is firmly held.
A memory of 1964 prize-winning medieval princess
bodice wraps a piece of a cornflakes box. Mexican
national dance skirt wraps PG tips tea carton.
The violet on her evening blouse hugs the cornflour
packet. Hundreds of flat parcels are stacked in
piles, according to shape and size. She picks up
two little parcels, different historical moments, and
stitches them together. Thimble on her index finger,
the needle goes in and out drawing the thread
through, with neat symmetrical stitches. She is
careful not to sew through the bits of card.
She will use them again.

As she stitches, the fragments dissolve into
one flat, smooth surface. She places fragments of
memory that never matched in real life side by side:
contradictory colours, shapes and textures, all
conflicting, all together, bringing them to order,
in a new imagined pattern. She re-invents her life.
She brings the shattered shards, the separate
amorphous shapes and the explosion of scattered
spaces and times into apparent symmetry, with a
border, a centre and a curious choreography.

Coventry University Library

Notes

1 Setting the scene

1   Literary critic William Empson (1961) pre-empts Derrida by introducing seven types of ambiguity at work in English literature, suggesting that the author and the reader share in the creation of ambiguous interpretation.

> First-type ambiguities arise when a detail is effective in several ways at once . . . In second-type ambiguities two or more alternative meanings are fully resolved into one . . . The condition for third-type ambiguity is that two apparently unconnected meanings are given simultaneously . . . In fourth type the alternative meanings combine to make clear a complicated state of mind in the author . . . The fifth type is a fortunate confusion, as when the author is discovering his idea in an act of writing . . . In the sixth type what is said is contradictory or irrelevant and the reader is forced to invent interpretations . . . The seventh type is that of full contradictions, marking a division in the authors mind.
>
> (Empson 1961: 5–6)

3 The upward line

1   Jenny performed with The Royal Ballet company between 1993 and 2002 before leaving to work with independent choreographers including Fin Walker and Siobhan Davies.

2   There was a good and a bad side to this practice. Good, because why spend years and years of training when there was no possibility of making this transformation? And bad because the selection process focused on body rather than desire, ending many a young child's natural desire to dance.

4 Watching ballet: illusion becoming real

1   For Jean Baudrillard (1991) everything operates through the seduction of the empty sign whereby, due to the advances of technologies, the space between real and illusion has been closed. For the most part Baudrillard's project focuses on image reproduction technologies in a capitalist hyper-reality where 'the origin of things is not an original thing, or being, but formulae, coded signals and numbers' (Lechte 1994: 235).

5 Performing ballet: real becoming illusion

1 The notion of front is incorporated into ballet training, the language and aesthetic style becoming inseparable. The training emphasizes the space in front, between the performer and the mirror image, and tends to ignore the space behind. The performer's back is always in shadow, and performers concentrate on perfecting the front view. Movements are stylized to accommodate perspective, tricked to look better when watched from out front. A ballerina learns to angle her foot and hip in an outward and upward direction while executing an *arabesque* so that her leg looks higher and aesthetically pleasing from the spectator's perspective. The same position seen from the back can look unsymmetrical and ungainly – from the classical perspective.

6 Classical androgyny

1 Franko (1994) draws attention to the (much earlier) androgynous qualities of Louis XIV's performance as the rising sun in *Ballet de la nuit* (1653).
2 Kabalistic literature, astrology, Jungian psychology, philosophy, ancient Greek history, Gnosticism and Taoism all provide routes back with which to investigate the concept of androgyny (Singer 1989).

8 The Oedipal narrative

1 Mulvey's (outdated) manifesto explores the dominance of the male spectator's gaze as an element of erotic pleasure in film. Drawing on psychoanalytical and feminist narratives, she attends to the scopophilic instinct, the pleasure in looking at another person as object, 'subjecting them to a controlling and curious gaze' (Mulvey 1975: 8).
2 The narrative ballets, *Giselle, Swan Lake, Sleeping Beauty*, to name but a few, through various alternations, follow the narrative of 'male' desire, in which pleasure/desire is derived through manipulation of the role of female object. For instance, in *Swan Lake* (Marius Petipa/Lev Ivanov 1895) where Siegfried holds the centre of attention, we follow his quest for knowledge/love/ mother/perfection. This search is threatened and manipulated by Odile, the femme fatale, and the sexual woman, interrupting his homoerotic quest for himself/other. Odile manipulates the role of object, desires the prince and usurps his power. He succumbs to her presence as the phallic, sexual femme fatale. He accomplishes his quest to achieve a spiritual love by transcending the bodily reality of the female body. He meets the impossible to obtain the object of his desire, Odette, but only in death. Transcendence through death resolves the earthly reality of sex evoked by female flesh. This is a homoerotic fable. From this feminist perspective, *Swan Lake* is a story of his lack, his loss and his desire.
3 In appearance, ballet dancers, who are *required* to remain pre-pubescent, gender-less and sex-less, often mirror the so-called psychological disturbances by which eating disordered people are labelled. The origins, however, lie in a different place from non-dancer eating disorders precisely because it is a *requirement*. There is a reason to become bulimic or anorexic or both; just as it is reasonable for a Sumo wrestler to be incredibly fat, to be a ballet dancer one must be thin, *by whatever means it takes*. Tragically, as the requirement to be thin persists, eating disorders become habitual, sometimes turning

into a fully blown psychological dysfunction of anorexia, sometimes with fatal results (Harrison 2002).
4 Feminist readings focus on the phallic signification of the ballerina's body. Foster (1996: 13) describes the signification of the ballerina's technique, style and pliable body image that 'belie the phallic identity of the ballerina. They signal her situatedness just in between penis and fetish.'

10 Dying to please

1 *Virginia Minx at Play* (1993) was choreographed by Emilyn Claid. Music composed by Sylvia Hallet and performed by singer–saxophonist Heather Joyce. Design by Jacqui Gunn.
2 See Frieda Kahlo's painting, *The Broken Column* (1944).

11 Expressions from the lifeworld

1 The notion of the lifeworld is taken from Habermas' theories of communicative action (Habermas 1989). Lifeworld represents the values and understanding shared by a community or social group. They are inherently understood by that community. They exist before the organization of the systems that then legitimatize the lifeworlds. It is on the basis of these shared understandings that systems become legitimate (Szczelkun 2002).
2 The Radical Summer School was held at X6 between 12 July and 7 August 1976. It was the first of our public workshop events. In the morning were 'exploratory' dance classes and in the afternoon workshops in gymnastics. There were lecture demonstrations and a conference to 'discuss specific issues related to Experimental Dance today' (as promoted in a publicity poster now in the X6 archives).
3 Jacky Lansley now works as an independent performer, choreographer, director and writer of dance and theatre, based at her dance research studio in East London. Her most recent work is *Holding Space* (2004). See Lansley (2001) and Ricoux (2004). Fergus Early is director of Green Candle Dance Company, based in Bethnal Green, East London. Green Candle works in community and educational contexts, devising and performing education projects. The company has pioneered groundbreaking performance work for young people, older people, and deaf children and young people. Its annual Deaf Dance Summer School, run for the past seven years in conjunction with Sadler's Wells Theatre, is unique to this country. Fergus has choreographed and directed 19 full-length touring productions for the company, as well as several large-scale community shows. Maedée Duprès lives in Denver and runs the Living Arts Centre where she teaches Alexander technique. Mary Prestidge lectures at the Liverpool Institute for Performing Arts and performs in the improvising group, Liverpool Improvisation Collective. (Sarah Green, feminist activist and photographer, joined the collective at a later date (Jordan 1992).)
4 ADMA 'ran two large-scale festivals of new work in 1977 and 1988 and successfully pressed for an independent panel for dance and mime at the Arts Council, as well as for increased funding for the area' (New Dance 20 1981: 20–2). In 1981, ADMA organized the first National Conference of Dance and Mime Artists, held at The Place in London.

12 Figures of parody

1 The term 'figure' refers to Barthes (1979), who applies the term to physicalize 'fragments of discourse' (1979: 3) pertaining to acts of love. For Barthes, figures are the actions, emotions and discourses that the lover performatively experiences that are not defined as such, but rather as 'the body's gesture caught in action' (Barthes 1979: 4).

2 This quote is taken from the performance programme pamphlet *Mounting* (1977) issued at the time of the performance.

3 Kristeva's notion of semiotic is described in more detail in 'Figures of *jouissance*'.

4 Embryonic at X6, the tutu strip materialized at Chisenhale Dance Space and The Place Theatre in 1984 as *Raw Hide*. Lindsey Butcher performed a version in *Grace & Glitter* for Extempory Dance Theatre in 1989. It metamorphosed again for *Virginia Minx at Play* in 1993, when the ballet figure shifted to an opera diva enacting her consumptive dying act before the stripper music interrupts.

5 The complete version of this little ditty (with its 1970s feminist appropriation of the term 'fairy') sits on the back cover of *New Dance*, Issue 5, New Year, 1978. Subverting the ballet image continued to instigate parodic satire: Jacky Lansley and Fergus Early's *I Giselle* (1980), Early's *Naples* (1979) for X6 and, later, Extempory Dance Theatre (1982).

6 *Laid Out Lovely* was co-directed by Nigel Charnock and myself. Bronfen (1992), Franko (1995), Benshoff (1997) provided research readings on the subject of beauty and death.

7 Parody: 'a humorous exaggerated imitation of an author'; but also 'feeble imitation, travesty' (*Concise Oxford Dictionary* 1995: 994).

13 Subverting tragedy

1 *Beauty, Art and the Kitchen Sink* was first created for a workshop residency at the Laban Centre in South East London in 1984. It then became a piece of Extempory's repertory programme.

14 Feminist battles with androgyny

1 *Splendid Dance* (1978), devised by Sue MacLennan, Emily Barnes and Kirstie Simson.

2 *Flag* is described in Adair (1992): 219–22.

15 Within the frame of new dance

1 Szczelkun's Ph.D. research (2002) examines culture and democracy through the collective work of the Exploding Cinema (1991–9). Stefan was involved with the Scratch Orchestra (1968), Earth Workshop (an eco-commune 1972), *New Dance* magazine (1976) and then, later, Brixton Artists Collective (1983), Bigos (Artists of Polish Origin 1986) and Working Press, a writers collective publishing books by and about working-class artists.

2 In what is now a new dance manifesto, Fergus Early says:

> New Dance is not: baggy trousers, rolling about, Chinese shoes, contact improvisation, ballet to rock music, release work, image work, outside

performances, post modern dance, martial arts, self-indulgence, stillness, American, non-narrative ... New Dance does not exclude: formal choreography, tap, ballet class, baggy trousers, rolling about, Chinese shoes, jazz shoes, no shoes, army boots, self indulgence, contact improvisation, rock music, virtuosity, stillness, narrative.

(Early 1987)

16 Letting go of the mirror

1 Susan Foster (2002) offers a vibrant expose of improvised performance in New York in the 1970s. Artists such as Steve Paxton, Katie Duck and Lisa Nelson are interviewed about their improvisation work in *Nouvelles de Danse* (Paxton 1997; Duck *et al.* 1997; Nelson 1997).

17 Figures of *jouissance*

1 Quote used as a programme note for *Red of the Sweet* (Emilyn Claid 1992), a choreography for the female students at the Northern School of Contemporary Dance, Leeds.
2 Running-Johnson (1989: 177) suggests Cixous' theory of writing provides a strategy whereby women can write the feminine as a 'cultivation of their "difference" – of inherent libidinal drives which originate in the unconscious'. Running-Johnson's article focuses on Cixous' writing and its appropriation into theatre performance practice. 'The human physical element in theatre ... may be seen as an inherently subversive element, just as feminine writing can be characterised as potentially disruptive of the traditional masculine order' (1989: 180). Even though Running-Johnson does not mention dance, there are parallels between Cixous' writing about theatre and the figure of *jouissance* in dance: 'its insistence upon movement, profusion, free exchange and transformation, and the importance that it places upon the corporal' (Running-Johnson 1989: 179).

18 K/no/w body of illusion: seduction in reverse

1 *Trio A* took a year to make. It forms Part 1 of *The Mind is a Muscle*, originally a trio for David Gordon, Steve Paxton and Yvonne Rainer.
2 Eva teaches and performs internationally and is a certified teacher of Alexander technique.

19 Derrida's presents

1 For Derrida, dance becomes a metaphor for language. He suggests similarities between writing and dance, their appearance being also their disappearance. 'We would have to choose then, between writing and dance' (Derrida 1978: 29). This has become a point of contention for dance writers who, on the one hand, deconstruct the metaphysical fixed binaries and hierarchies of dance, but who do not want to lose the real embodiment of the dancer, on the other (Franko 1995).
2 Deleuze and Guattari refer to the secret as an analogy for becoming. The contents of the secret are always bigger than its form. What draws us to

desire its revelation is that 'something must ooze from the box, something will be perceived through the box or in the half-opened box' (Deleuze and Guattari 1988: 287).

20 Parallel emergences

1   Music: Charles Mingus. Dancers: Margaret Foyer, Natalie-Mai Pickup, Angela Warren and Greta Mendez.

21 Different visibilities

1   The debate concerning identities for British African and African–Caribbean dance forms is continued in Muraldo (2003). The HIP festival at the Place Theatre in London (2003 and 2004) celebrated the diversity of black dance identities. As a two-week festival held each year, HIP offered a wonderful opportunity to see a wide range of work by black British artists but also perpetuated a separatist 'exotic' experience to London dance audiences.

2   These performances were part of the Many Ways of Seeing Festival in 1978. Also performing were Fergus Early and Julian Hough in *Manley Struggles* (1978).

3   Performing Arts Labs (PAL), established in 1989 by Susan Benn, is a crucible for cross-disciplinary collaborations. PAL runs labs in film, theatre, opera, interactive media, dance and architecture. The Dance Lab offers an opportunity for professional performers, choreographers and collaborators to come together and engage in new collaborations for performance. This practice takes place every day without the pressures to produce a final product and without external judgements. The lab is performer-led.

4   Shobana Jeyasingh Dance Company. Dancers: Kats Fukasawa, Sowmya Gopalan, Radhimalar Govindarajoo, Mavin Khoo, Jiva Parthipan, Shane Shambhu. Music: Jocelyn Pook.

5   *Black like Beckham* is already an subversive twist on another film, *Bend it like Beckham* (Gurinda Chadha 2002), that explores the story of a South Asian UK girl growing up to be a football star.

23 The other of the other

1   See *Dancing without Steps* (Crickmay 1977), a film describing the work of Miranda Tufnell and Dennis Greenwood.

2   Kline (1998) compares the disguising tactics of surrealist artist Claude Cahun and Cindy Sherman. Cahun's disguise is constructed through an attention to absence, a stripping down of excess while Sherman works through an attention to an excess of presence.

24 Kristeva's crunch

1   The White Oak Project, directed by Mikhail Baryshnikov, performed at Sadler's Wells Theatre in October 2002. This is one of several revivals of *Trio A*. It is performed to the music of the Chambers Brothers. In 1970, a version was performed by a group that included David Gordon, Barbara Dilly and Yvonne Rainer at an anti-war rally in New York City. The performers were naked accept for US flags tied around their necks and

hanging down the front of their bodies. The audience wandered about in close proximity as the performers nonchalantly and mechanically went through their *Trio A* gestures.

25 Collective strategies

1 Musicians were Martyn Hill, Jon Keliehor and Nigel Osborne. For a discussion of the piece, see Early (1987: 12).
2 Tom Jobe performed and choreographed with London Contemporary Dance Theatre before becoming a freelance choreographer.
3 Anna Furse is talking about *Dirt* (1983), a collaboratively devised piece exploring pornography and prostitution, taking the (then radical) notion of women 'acting' sex as a starting point for a postmodern ironic view of the sex industry.
4 Mike Pearson (artistic director of Brith Gof 1987–97) writes of hypotaxis, indicating theatre performances that reject the dramatic text in favour of devised methodologies of collaboration.

26 The X6 legacy

1 Negative criticisms of *New Dance* magazine, X6 performances and collective processes are documented in Stephanie Jordan's book, *Striding Out* (1992).

27 Drawn to the mainstream

1 Designed by Craig Givens. *Naples* is a re-working of *Napoli* (Auguste Bournonville 1842).

28 Repertory versus project

1 Artists such as Lea Anderson, Laurie Booth and Yolande Snaith were emerging in the 1980s as independent artists.
2 Choreographer-led companies such as Siobhan Davies Dance Company, DV8 and Random Dance Company are now established clients of Arts Council England. However, this has only come after many years of working as independent project-based companies.

30 Process to product

1 Lindsey Butcher, Fin Walker, Saorse Baron, Dawn and Chantale Donaldson, and Kaye Hunter performed in *Grace & Glitter*. Music composed and performed by Sylvia Hallet and Lucy Wilson. Designed by Jaqui Gunn.
2 David Toole, Jon French, Kuldip Singh-Barmi, Sue Smith, Charlotte Derbyshire and Helen Baggett performed in *Back to Front with Side Shows*. Music composed by Andrew Deakin. See Benjamin (2002) for an in-depth discussion of working with disabled and non-disabled dancers.

32 The chameleon

1 Company members of Extemporary at the time were: Edgar Newman, Annelies Stoffel, Corinne Bougaard, Avigail Ben Ari, Yacov Slivkin and Lloyd Newson.

2   Music by Policeband, James White and the Savages, Ned Sublette and the Westerners, Quibani Films (sound track). *It Happened at Club Bombay Cinema* was performed by the whole company.

33 Boys transcending

1   There is not the space here to discuss the androgynous figures of media, pop culture and fashion. For instance, the flower-power hippies of the 1960s, the New Romantic pop stars such as Adam Ant, Spandau Ballet, David Bowie and Boy George, and the fashions of Vivienne Westwood, all of which draw attention once again to androgynous play on male bodies.
2   Germaine Greer (2003) chooses androgynous images of boys in a book that emphases a feminist reversal of the gaze, encouraging women to enjoy looking at boys bodies to counteract the conventions of men looking at girls. Why looking at images of androgyny and why androgyny is a seductive force that fascinates men and women in Western culture is not explored in this book.
3   Five years later, Russell performs *Sheer* (2002), a duet with Anna Williams (formerly with Ricochet Dance Company). As they partner each other in liquid falls and lifts, this union of fluidity and transcendence is complete, polished, honed to finesse, sublimely skilled. The language becomes virtuosity, dazzling; it parallels the aesthetic of ballet in its classical perfection of form.

35 Bodies of pleasure

1   In the 1970s, falling without rebounding upwards was taught as a body skill without emotional narrative in contact improvisation and Aikido workshops. Contact improvisation techniques gave performers the skills to fall without injury and signified a move towards a downward aesthetic of beauty.
2   Leigh Bowery created costumes for Michael Clark between 1984 and 1986. Works include *Our Caca Phoney H* (1985) and *No Fire Escape in Hell* (1986). He performed with Michael Clark in *Because We Must* (1987) and *Heterospective* (1989). Bowery 'offers us an image that manifests and simulates the characteristics of both male and female physique and attitude – showing us codes of seduction and communication through the body and its clothing, and producing novel concepts of glamour and beauty' (Mariuccia Casaadio, cited in Greer and Bowery 2002: 7).

37 Re-figuring androgyny

1   The work of *Split Britches* is discussed in Case (1988/9 and 1996), Dolan (1993), De Lauretis (1990), Hart (1993), Rapi (1994) and Schneider (1997).
2   Still and Worton (1993) refer to Foucault's re-appropriation of conventional concepts:

> It is crucial for him to employ/redeploy . . . By re-inserting into contemporary discourses on homosexuality the terms and concepts of the past, he challenges us to scrutinise all terms that we might use, re-appropriate or invent to describe ourselves or other.
>
> (Still and Worton 1993: 54)

39 Re-dressing the girls

1 Music by Billie Cowie. Re-constructed in 1999. For a discussion of work by Liz Aggiss, Billie Cowie and Divas, including *Grotesque Dancer*, see Aggiss and Cowie with Bramley (2006).
2 Stine Nielson is a freelance performer now working with CandoCo Dance Company.

40 Eye flight

1 *Spawn* (2003) is a collaboration between Carol Brown and virtual architect Meta Ramsgaardtamsen, with dancers Catherine Bennett and Catherine Gardner.

Bibliography

Adair, C. (1987) *Grace & Glitter* programme notes, London: Extemporary Dance Theatre.

Adair, C. (1992) *Women and Dance*, London: Macmillan Press.

Aggiss, L. (2006) 'Reconstruction: Or why you can never step in the same river twice', in L. Aggiss and B. Cowie with I. Bramley (eds) *Anarchic Dance*, London: Routledge.

Aggiss, L. and Cowie, B. with Bramley, I. (eds) (2006) *Anarchic Dance*, London: Routledge.

Badejo, Peter (1993, 8 March) 'What is black dance?'. Position paper presented at Black Dance Conference, Nottingham Playhouse.

Banes, S. (1977) *Terpsichore in Sneakers*, Middletown, CT: Wesleyan University Press.

Barthes, R. (1973) *Mythologies*, London: Palladin.

Barthes, R. (1977) 'The death of the author', in *Image, Music, Text*, London: Fontana Press.

Barthes, R. (1979) *A Lover's Discourse*, London: Penguin Books.

Bataille, G. (1987) *Eroticism*, London: Marion Boyars Publishers Ltd.

Baudrillard, J. (1991) *Seduction* (translated by B. Singer), New York: St Martin's Press.

Bazin, N.T. and Freeman, A. (1974) 'The androgynous vision', in C. Secor (ed.) *The Androgyny Papers, Women's Studies*, 2(2): 185–215.

Beardsley, M.C. (1975) *Aesthetics from Classical Greece to the Present*, Tuscaloosa: University of Alabama Press.

Benjamin, A. (2002) *Making an Entrance: Theory and practice for disabled and non-disabled dancers*, London: Routledge.

Benjamin, J. (1988) *Bonds of Love: Psychoanalysis, feminism and the problem of domination*, New York: Pantheon Books.

Benshoff, H.M. (1997) *Monsters in the Closet*, Manchester: Manchester University Press.

Bersani, L. (1988) 'Is the rectum a grave?', in D. Crimp (ed.) *AIDS*, Cambridge, MA: MIT Press.

Bersani, L. (1995) *Homos*, Cambridge, MA: Harvard University Press.

Boal, A. (2000) *The Theatre of the Oppressed* (translated from Spanish by C.A. and M.-O.L. McBride and E. Fryer), London: Pluto Press.

Briginshaw, V. (2001) *Dance, Space and Subjectivity*, London: Palgrave.

Bristow, J. (1997) *Sexuality*, London: Routledge.

Bronfen, E. (1992) *Over Her Dead Body*, Manchester: Manchester University Press.

Brown, C. (2003) Interview with author, London.

Burt, R. and Huxley, M. (1985) 'La Nouvelle danse: comment ne pas jouer le jeu de l'establishment', in M. Febvre (ed.) (1987) *La Danse au défi*, Montreal: Parachute.

Butler, J. (1990) *Gender Trouble*, London: Routledge.

Butler, J. (1993) *Bodies that Matter*, London: Routledge.

Caputo, J.D. (ed.) (1997) *Deconstruction in a Nutshell: A conversation with Jacques Derrida*, New York: Fordham University Press.

Carter, A. (1999) 'Dying swans or sitting ducks?', *Performance Research*, 4(3): 91–8

Case, S.-E. (1988/9) 'Towards a butch femme aesthetic', *Discourse: Journal for Theatrical Studies in Media and Culture*, 11(1): 55–73.

Case, S.-E. (ed.) (1996) *Split Britches: Lesbian practice/feminist performance*, New York: Routledge.

Charnock, N. (2003) Interview with the author, Performing Arts Labs Dance Lab, Bore Place, Kent.

Chauchard-Stuart, S. (1996, 8 May) 'Suits you, madam: interview with Diane Torr', *Independent*: 6.

Chicago, J. (1979) *The Dinner Party*, New York: Anchor Press.

Cixous, H. (1981) 'The laugh of the Medusa', in E. Marks and I. de Coutrivron (eds) *New French Feminisms*, Hemel Hempstead: Harvester Wheatsheaf.

Claid, E. (1977, Summer) 'Fergus Early and Craig Givens, Dance of the Hours from the Ballet of the Night. ADMA Festival of Dance and Mime', *New Dance*, 3: 13.

Claid, E. (1995) *Fifi Le Flesh* performance text, London.

Claid, E. (1998) 'Yes? No! Maybe . . .', unpublished Ph.D. thesis, University of Surrey.

Claid, E. (2002a) 'Playing seduction in dance theatre performance', *Discourses in Dance*, 1(1): 29–46.

Claid, E. (2002b) 'Standing still . . . Looking at you', *Research in Dance Education*, 3(1): 7–19.

Clarke, G. (2003, Winter) 'Towards a rigour of the imagination', *Animated*: 4–7.

Concise Oxford Dictionary (1995) 9th edition, Oxford: Clarendon Press.

Copeland, R. and Cohen, M. (1983) *What Is Dance?*, New York: Oxford University Press.

Coupe, L. (1997) *Myth*, London: Routledge.

Crickmay, C. (1977) *Dancing without Steps*. Presented as part of Art and the Environment for the Open University. Broadcast on BBC2.

Crickmay, C. (1982, March) 'The apparently invisible dances of Miranda Tufnell and Dennis Greenwood', *New Dance*, 21: 7–8.

Crickmay, C. (1986, Spring) 'Rosemary Butcher: A decade of her work', *New Dance*, 36: 10–15.

Crisp, C. (1983, 2 November) 'Extemporary Dance/Riverside', *Financial Times*.

Dale, R. (1995, March) *Sex Acts*. Presented as part of the QED series. Broadcast on BBC2.

De Frutos, J. (1996, 21 October) *Transatlantic* post-show discussion, Purcell Room, London.

DeLauretis, T. (1984) *Alice Doesn't: Feminism, semiotic cinema*, London: Macmillan Press Ltd.

DeLauretis, T. (1990) 'Sexual indifference and lesbian representation', in S.-E. Case (ed.) *Performing Feminisms*, Baltimore: John Hopkins University Press.

Deleuze, G. (1993) *The Fold: Leibniz and the baroque*, Minneapolis: University of Minnesota Press.

Deleuze, G. and Guattari, F. (1988) *A Thousand Plateaus*, London: Athlone Press.

De Marigny, C. (1993, Spring/Summer) 'Life and art on the cutting edge', *Dance Theatre Journal*, 10(3): 4–11.

Derrida, J. (1973) *Speech and Phenomena and other Essays in Husserl's Theory of Signs* (translated by D.B. Allison), Evanston, IL: Northwestern University Press.

Derrida, J. (1978) *Writing and Difference*, Chicago: University of Chicago Press.

Derrida, J. (1981) *Dissemination* (translated by B. Johnson), London: Athlone Press.

Derrida, J. (1995a) 'Khora', in T. Dutoit (ed.) *On The Name*, Stanford, CA: Stanford University Press.

Derrida, J. (1995b) 'Passions', in T. Dutoit (ed.) *On The Name*, Stanford, CA: Stanford University Press.

Dixon, M. (2005) 'Fin Walker: Speaking to the heart', *Dance Theatre Journal*, 20(4): 49–51.

Dodds, S. (1998) 'A spanner in the works', *Dance Theatre Journal*, 14(1): 12–14.

Dolan, J. (1993) 'Desire cloaked in a trenchcoat', in L. Hart and P. Phelan (eds) *Acting Out: Feminist Performance*, Ann Arbor: University of Michigan Press.

Dougill, D. (1981, 15 November) 'Miranda Tufnell and Dennis Greenwood', *Sunday Times*.

Dougill, D. (1994, 30 January) 'Very able bodies', *Sunday Times*.

Dougill, D. (1997, 15 June) 'Brightest and the best', *Sunday Times*: 19.

Drukman S. (1995) 'The gay gaze, or why I want my MTV', in P. Burston and C. Richardson (eds) *A Queer Romance*, London: Routledge.

Duck, K., Vetcher, M. and List, G. (1997, Autumn) 'Round table discussion' (transcribed by H. Carrie, translated by M. Bom), in *On the Edge: Dialogues in dance: Improvisation in performance: Nouvelles de Danse*, 32/3, Brussels: ContraDanse Publications.

Duprès, M. (2004, 16 February) 'Performing presence', email Denver/London.

Dyer, R. (1992) *Only Entertainment*, London: Routledge.

Dyer, R. (1993) *The Matter of Images*, London: Routledge.

Dyer, R. (1997) *White*, London: Routledge.

Early, F. (1987, April) 'Liberation notes etc.', *New Dance*, 40: 10–12.

Early, F. (2003) Interview with author, London.

Empson, W. (1961) *Seven Types of Ambiguity*, Harmondsworth: Penguin Books.

English, R. (1980, Summer) 'Alas alack the representation of the ballerina', *New Dance*, 15: 18–19.

Fairbanks, T. (1987) *Grace & Glitter* performance text, London: Extemporary Dance Theatre.

Fawkes, I. and Mann, J. (1981, Autumn) 'ADMA Conference '81' *New Dance*, 20: 20–2.

Ferris, L. (1993) 'Introduction: Current crossings', in L. Ferris (ed.) *Crossing the Stage*, London: Routledge.

Foster, S.L. (1996) 'The phallic pointe', in S.L. Foster (ed.) *Corporealities*, New York: Routledge.

Foster, S.L. (2002) *Dances that Describe Themselves: The improvised choreography of Richard Bull*, Middletown, CT: Wesleyan University Press.

Foucault, M. (1969) *The Archaeology of Knowledge* (translated by M.S. Smith), London: Routledge.

Foucault, M. (1977) *Discipline and Punish: The birth of prison*, London: Penguin Books.

Foucault, M. (1979) *The History of Sexuality*, Volume 1 (translated by R. Hurley), London: Penguin Books.

Foucault, M. (1985) *The Use of Pleasure*, London: Penguin Books.

Fraleigh, S.H. (1987) *Dance and the Lived Body*, Pittsburgh, PA: University of Pittsburgh Press.

Franko, M. (1994, Winter) 'Double bodies. Androgyny and power in the performances of Louis XIV', *Drama Review*, 38(4): 71–80.

Franko, M. (1995) *Dancing Modernism/Performing Politics*, Bloomington: Indiana University Press.

Freud, S. (1905; Standard Edition 1960) *Jokes and their Relation to the Unconscious*, Volume 8 in the Standard Edition, London: Hogarth Press. Reprinted in S. Freud (1991) *Jokes and their Relation to the Unconscious*, Volume 6, London: Penguin Books.

Freud, S. (1933; Standard Edition 1964) 'Femininity', in S. Freud (1964) *New Introductory Lectures on Psycho-analysis*, Volume 22 in the Standard Edition of the Complete Psychological Works, London: Hogarth Press.

Freud, S. (1920; Standard Edition 1955) 'Beyond the Pleasure Principal', in S. Freud (1955) *On Metapsychology*, Volume 11 in the Standard Edition, London: Hogarth Press. Reprinted in S. Freud (1991) *On Metapsychology*, Volume 11, London: Penguin Books.

Fuchs, C.J. (1996) '"I wanna be your fantasy". Sex, death, and The Artist Formerly Known as Prince', *Women & Performance: A Journal of Feminist Theory* 8:2(16): 137–51.

Furse, A. (2000) 'Bleeding, sweating, crying and jumping', *Performance Research* (5)10: 16–31.

Gelpi, B.C. (1974) 'The politics of androgyny', in C. Secor (ed.) *The Androgyny Papers, Women's Studies*, 2(2): 151–60.

Glassman, B. (2003) Interview with the author, London.

Gottschild, B.D. (1996) *Digging the Africanist Presence in American Performance*, Westport CT: Greenwood Press.

Green, S. (1977, Summer) 'Emilyn Claid', *New Dance*, 3: 10.

Green, S. (1979, Spring) 'Reviews: Spring shows through at X6 Dance Space: Events on April Fool's Day and Passion Sunday', *New Dance*, 10: 12–14.

Greer, F. and Bowery, L. (2002) *Looks*, London: Violette Editions.

Greer, G. (2003) *The Boy*, London: Thames & Hudson.

Grosz, E. (1989) *Sexual Subversions. Three French feminists*, Sydney: Allen & Unwin.

Grosz, E. (1994) *Volatile Bodies*, Bloomington, IN: Indiana University Press.

Grosz, E. (1995) *Space, Time and Perversion*, London: Routledge.

Habermas, J. (1989) *The Theory of Communicative Action, Vol. 2, Lifeworld and system: A critique of functionalist reason* (translated by T. McCarthy), Cambridge: Polity Paperback.

Halprin, D. (1990) *One Hundred Years of Homosexuality*, New York: Routledge.

Harrison, L. (2002) Email communication with author, Vancouver/London.

Hart, L. (1993) 'Identity and seduction: Lesbians in the mainstream', in L. Hart and P. Phelan (eds) *Acting Out: Feminist Performance*, Ann Arbor: University of Michigan Press.

Hayes, C. (1978, Spring) 'Many ways of seeing – Dance at Riverside Studios', *New Dance*, 6: 5–6.

Heilbrun, C.G. (1973) *Towards a Recognition of Androgyny*, New York: Alfred A. Knopf.

Heilbrun, C.G. (1974) 'Further notes', in C. Secor (ed.) *The Androgyny Papers, Women's Studies*, 2(2): 143–9.

Heilbrun, C.G. (1980) 'Androgyny and the psychology of sex differences', in H. Eisenstein and A. Jardine (eds) *The Future of Difference*, Boston: Barnard College Women's Centre.

Hofstadter, A. and Kuhns, R. (eds) (1964) *Philosophies of Art and Beauty*, Chicago: University of Chicago Press.

hooks, b. (1992) *Black Looks: Race and representation*, Boston: South End Press.

Horwitz, D.L. (1996) 'The New York Negro Ballet in Great Britain', in T. deFrantz (ed.) *Dancing Many Drums*, Hanover: University Press of New England.

Houstoun, W. (1997) *Haunted, Daunted and Flaunted* performance text, London.

Houstoun, W. (2003) Interview with the author, London.

Hunt, M. (1991, Spring) '. . . and quiet flows the Thames', *Dance Theatre Journal*, 8(4): 13–15.

Hutcheon, L. (1989) *The Politics of Postmodernism*, New York: Routledge.

Irigaray, L. (1985) *This Sex Which Is Not One* (translated by C.P. Cornell), Ithaca, NY: Cornell University Press.

Jeffreys, S. (1997) 'The queer disappearance of lesbians', in B. Mintz and E.D. Rothblum (eds) *Lesbians in Academia*, London: Routledge.

Jordan, S. (1983, 25 February) 'Odds on', *New Statesman*: 32.

Jordan, S. (1992) *Striding Out: Aspects of contemporary and new dance in Britain*, London: Dance Books.

Juno, A. and Vale, V. (eds) (1991) *Angry Women, Re/Search No. 13*, San Francisco: Re/Search Publications.

Kaplan, E.A. (1983) *Women and Film*, London: Routledge.

Karczag, E. (2005) In conversation with the author, Dartington.

Kearney, R. (1994) *Modern Movements in European Philosophy*, Manchester: Manchester University Press.

Kline, K. (1998) 'In or out of the picture: Claude Cahun and Cindy Sherman', in W. Chadwick (ed.) *Mirror Images Women: Surrealism and self-representation*, Cambridge MA: The MIT Press.

Kristeva, J. (1980) *Desire in Language* (translated by L.S. Roudiez), Oxford: Basil Blackwell.

Kristeva, J. (1981) 'Women can never be defined', in E. Marks and I. Courtivron (eds) *New French Feminisms: An anthology*, Brighton: Harvester.

Kristeva, J. (1984) *The Revolution in Poetic Language* (translated by M. Waller), New York: University of Columbia Press.

Kristeva, J. (2003, 23 November) 'On Genie Feminine and Art (The work of Hannah Arendt, Melanie Klein and Colette)'. Seminar presentation, Tate Britain, London.

Kuppers, P. (2003) *Disability and Contemporary Performance: Bodies on the edge*, London: Routledge.

Lacan, J. (1979) *The Four Fundamental Concepts of Psycho-analysis*, London: Penguin Books.

Lansley, J. (1977, New Year) 'Writing', *New Dance*, 1: 3.

Lansley, J. (1978, Spring) 'Women Dancing', *New Dance*, 6: 10–11.

Lansley, J. (2001) 'A fierce silence', in *The Open Page: The Annual Journal of Magdalena Project*, Holstebro, Denmark: Odin Theatrets Forlag.

Lansley, J. (2003) Interview with author, London.

Lechte, J. (1994) *50 Key Contemporary Thinkers*, London: Routledge.

Lévi-Strauss, C. (1963) *The Structural Study of Myth*, Suffolk: Basic Books.

Lorde, A. (1984) 'Uses of the erotic', in A. Lorde, *Sister Outsider*, Freedom, CA: The Crossing Press.

Macaulay, A. (1983) 'Not actually extemporising', *Dance Theatre Journal*, 1(2): 28–32.

McKenzie, P. (2003, 25 April) *Black like Beckham*. Broadcast on Channel 4.

Mackrell, J. (1997, 17 May) 'Arts: Return to tender: The thrill: Judith Mackrell revels in the erotic tenderness of Siobhan Davies' *Bank*, and salutes one of the great survivors of modern dance', *Guardian*: 6.

Macleod, K.S. (1997, 19 October) Fashion feature, *Style File* in *Sunday Times*: 17.

McRitchie, L. (1977, Summer) 'Mounting', *New Dance*, 3: 20–3.

Mantsoe, V.S. (2001) 'What is the inspiration for my work?'. Available at www.sekwaman.co.za (accessed 4 October 2003).

Meehan V. (1977, Summer) 'Timothy Lamford and Julyen Hamilton', *New Dance*, 3: 12.

Meisner, Nadine (1979, Summer) 'Jacky Lansley and Rose English at the X6 Dance Space', *New Dance*, 11: 20.

Mendez, G. (1978, 14–20 July) 'Not just darker dancers', *Time Out*: 15.

Mendez, G. (2003) Telephone interview with the author, London.

Mendez, G. (2005) Telephone interview with the author, London.

Mulvey, L. (1975, Autumn) 'Visual pleasure and narrative cinema', *Screen*, 16(3): 6–18.

Muraldo, C. (2003) 'Terminological inexactitude', *Dance Theatre Journal*, 19(1): 32–7.

Nelson, L. (1997, Autumn) 'Conversation with Lisa Nelson' (interview/transcription by Agnès Benoit), in *On the Edge: Dialogues in dance: Improvisation in performance: Nouvelles de Danse*, 32/3, Brussels: ContraDanse Publications.

Newson, L. (1982) *Breaking Images* performance text, London: Extemporary Dance Theatre.

Newson, L. (2003) Interview with the author, London.

Nietzsche, F.W. (1969) *On the Genealogy of Morals/Ecce Homo* (translated by W. Kaufmann), New York: Vintage Books.

Norris, C. (1987) *Derrida*, London: Fontana Paperbacks.

Novack, C.J. (1990) *Sharing the Dance*, Madision: University of Wisconsin Press.

Parry, J. (1982, July) 'Extemporary Dance Theatre', *Dance and Dancers*: 29–30.

Parry, J. (1995, 12 November) 'Ur indoors', *Observer*: 12.

Paxton, S. (1978) Letter to X6 Dance Collective. London: X6 Archives, Chisenhale Dance Space.

Paxton, S. (1997, Autumn) 'Conversation with Steve Paxton' (interview/transcription by Agnès Benoit), in *On the Edge: Dialogues in dance: Improvisation in performance: Nouvelles de Danse*, 32/3, Brussels: ContraDanse Publications.

Paxton, S. (2001) 'Improvisation is a word for something that can't keep a name', in A. Dils and A.C. Albright (eds) *Moving History/Dancing Cultures*, Middletown, CT: Wesleyan University Press.

Pearson M. and Shanks, M. (2001) *Theatre/Archaeology*, London: Routledge.

Phelan, P. (1993) *Unmarked: The politics of performance*, New York: Routledge.

Plato (1994) *Symposium* (translated by R. Waterfield), Oxford: Oxford University Press.

Prestidge, M. (1979, New Year) 'The Zena Mountain Show', *New Dance*, 9: 10.

Prestidge, M. (1999, Winter/Spring) 'Short guide to the handstand', in *Contact Quarterly*, 24(1): 67–70.

Prestidge, M. (2003) Interview with the author, Liverpool.

Probyn, E. (1995) 'Queer belongings', in E. Grosz and E. Probyn (eds) *Sexy Bodies*, London: Routledge.

Rainer, Y. (1965, Winter) 'Some retrospective notes on a dance for 10 people and 12 mattresses called "Parts of some Sextets"', *Tulane Drama Review*, 10: 168–78.

Rainer, Y. (1968) 'A quasi survey of some "minimalist" tendencies in the quantitively minimal dance activity midst the plethora, or an analysis of *Trio A*', in G.E. Battock (ed.) *Minimal Art*, New York: Dutton; reprinted in R. Copeland and M. Cohen (eds) (1983) *What Is Dance?*, Oxford: Oxford University Press.

Rainer, Y. (2003, 26 July) 'Out of a corner of the sixties', colloquium at Greenwich Dance Agency, London.

Ramphal, V. (2002) Interview with the author, London.

Rapi, N. (1994) 'That's why you are so queer', in L. Gibbs (ed.) *Daring to Dissent: Lesbian culture from margin to mainstream*, London: Cassell.

Ricoux, E. (2004) 'Work in progress: Interview with Jacky Lansley', *Dance Theatre Journal*, 20(1): 7–10.

Ries, F.W.D. (1986) *The Dance Theatre of Jean Cocteau*, Ann Arbor, MI: UMI Research Press.

Ritter, N. (1989) 'Art and androgyny: The aerialist', *Studies in Twentieth Century Literature*, 13(2): 173–93.

Running-Johnson, C. (1989) 'Feminine writing and its theatrical "other"', in J. Redmond (ed.) *Women in Theatre, Themes in Drama II*, Cambridge: Cambridge University Press.

Scarry, E. (1985) *The Body in Pain: The Making and Unmaking of the World*, New York: Oxford University Press.

Schneider, R. (1997) *The Explicit Body in Performance*, London: Routledge.

Secor, C. (ed.) (1974a) *The Androgyny Papers, Women's Studies*, 2(2).

Secor, C. (1974b) 'Androgyny: An early reappraisal', in C. Secor (ed.) *The Androgyny Papers, Women's Studies*, 2(2): 161–9.

Sedgwick, E.K. (1993) *Tendencies*, Durham: Duke University Press.

Showalter, E. (1977) *A Literature of their Own*, Princeton, NJ: Princeton University Press.

Simpson, M. (1994) *Male Impersonators*, London: Cassell.

Simpson, M. (1996) *It's a Queer World*, London: Vintage.

Simson, K. (2003) Interview with the author, London.

Singer, J. (1989) *Androgyny: The opposites within*, Boston: Sigo Press.

Snow, T. (2003) 'Black like Beckham' in 'Black and Asian History Map'. Online. Available at www.channel4.com/history/microsites/B/blackhistorymap/articles_02 (accessed 9 August 2005).

Solomon, A. (1993) 'It's never too late to switch', in L. Ferris (ed.) *Crossing the Stage*, London: Routledge.

Still J. and Worton M. (eds) (1993) *Textuality and Sexuality: Reading theories and practices*, Manchester: Manchester University Press.

Studlar, G. (1990) 'Masochism, masquerade, and the erotic metamorphoses of Marlene Dietrich', in J. Gaines and C. Herzog (eds) *Fabrications*, New York: Routledge.

Szczelkun, S. (1977, Spring) 'Going back', *New Dance*, 2: 14–15.

Tattershall, J. (2003) Interview with the author, London.

Thorpe, E. (1989) *Black Dance*, Woodstock, NY: The Overlook Press.

Tong, R. (1989) *Feminist Thought – A Comprehensive Introduction*, London: Unwin Hyman.

Volinsky, A.K. (1925) 'The Book of Exultation', cited in R. Copeland and M. Cohen (eds) (1983) *What Is Dance?*, New York: Oxford University Press.

Walker, F. (2003) Interview with the author, London.

Walters, M. (1978) *The Nude Male*, Harmondsworth: Penguin Books.

Waring, D. (2003) Interview with the author, London.

Waterfield, R. (1994) 'Introduction', in Plato *Symposium* (translated by R. Waterfield), Oxford: Oxford University Press.

Watson, K. (2003) 'The heart of the chatter', *Dance Theatre Journal*, 19(2): 6–9.

Weil, K. (1992) *Androgyny and the Denial of Difference*, Charlottesville and New York: University Press of Virginia.

Whitford, M. (1991) *Luce Irigaray: Philosophy in the feminine*, New York: Routledge.

Woodhouse, A. (2000) 'The dance deferred. The dance embodied', unpublished MA dissertation, University of Surrey.

Zarrilli, P.B. (1997) 'Acting "at the nerve ends": Beckett, Blau and the necessary', *Theatre Topics*, 7(2): 103–16.

Zurbrugg, N. (ed.) (1998) *Jean Baudrillard: Art and artefact*, London: Sage Publications.

Index

(Numbers in italics indicate illustrations; numbers followed by 'n' indicate notes.)

Related titles from Routledge

Anarchic Dance

By Liz Aggiss & Billy Cowie

Available in one package for the first time, *Anarchic Dance*, comprising a book and DVD-Rom, is a visual and textual record of the work of Divas Dance Theatre. The DVD-Rom features extracts from Aggiss and Cowie's work, including the highly-acclaimed dance film *Motion Control* (first premiered on BBC2 in 2002), rare video footage of their punk-comic live performances as *The Wild Wigglers* and reconstructions of Aggiss' solo performance in *Grotesque Dancer*.

These films are cross-referenced in the book, allowing readers to match performance and commentary as Aggiss and Cowie invite a broad range of writers to examine their live performance and dance screen practice through analysis, theory, discussion and personal response. As much as their practice is hybrid, maverick and hard to define, the various theories presented are equally challenging, lively and fresh.

Extensively illustrated with black and white, and colour photographs, this beautiful multi-media package is a celebration of Divas' boundary-shattering performance work. *Anarchic Dance* provides a comprehensive investigation into Cowie and Aggiss' collaborative partnership and demonstrates a range of exciting approaches through which dance performance can be engaged critically.

Hb: 0–415–36516–3
Pb: 0–415–36517–1

Available at all good bookshops
For ordering and further information please visit:
www.routledge.com